Professor Ross Donaldson is on the medical staff at UCLA and works in one of Los Angeles' main trauma centres, specializing in emergency medicine and global health. Extensive travels have taken him via tugboats and tuk-tuks through distant revolutions, landmined fields and warring countries. He has been a humanitarian in some of the world's most dangerous places, a NASA expedition doctor to one of the planet's highest lakes, and a care-giver to some of humanity's poorest people. Professor Donaldson's most recent humanitarian work involves frequent trips to Iraq, where he is helping to build an emergency medical system for the country's traumatized civilians. When in the States, he resides in Venice Beach, California.

www.rbooks.co.uk

THE LASSA WARD

ROSS DONALDSON

BLACK SWAN

TRANSWORLD PUBLISHERS
61–63 Uxbridge Road, London W5 5SA
A Random House Group Company
www.rbooks.co.uk

**THE LASSA WARD
A BLACK SWAN BOOK: 9780552775663**

First published in the United States of America
in 2009 by St Martin's Press LLC

First published in Great Britain
in 2009 by Bantam Press
an imprint of Transworld Publishers
Black Swan edition published 2010

A CIP catalogue record for this book
is available from the British Library.

Addresses for Random House Group Ltd companies outside the UK
can be found at: www.randomhouse.co.uk
The Random House Group Ltd Reg. No. 954009

The Random House Group Limited supports The Forest Stewardship Council
(FSC), the leading international forest certification organisation. All our titles that
are printed on Greenpeace approved FSC certified paper carry the FSC logo. Our
paper procurement policy can be found at
www.rbooks.co.uk/environment

Typeset in 11/16pt Bembo by
Falcon Oast Graphic Art Ltd.
Printed in the UK by CPI Cox & Wyman, Reading, RG1 8EX.

2 4 6 8 10 9 7 5 3 1

Mixed Sources
Product group from well-managed
forests and other controlled sources
www.fsc.org   Cert no. TT-COC-2139
© 1996 Forest Stewardship Council
FSC

Dedicated to Dr Aniru Conteh
Physician, Mentor, Friend

CONTENTS

PART V: LAST RITES

The song done, only the words remain.

—KRIO PROVERB

THE

LASSA WARD

JOURNAL ENTRY

July 29, 2003

Dear Mom,

I won't be sending you this letter. Some things, you see, are too difficult to share. And you worry enough already, I know.

I watch them die every day and feel helpless to stop it. Those around me are partially to blame. Yet how can I fault them? The men, women, and children are lost because of them, it's true, but also because of me.

I'm over my head – it's as simple as that. I thought I was prepared, but not for this. How could I have been? It's just too much and I feel so alone. There is danger around every corner.

'What am I doing here?' I can only ask myself. There is so much suffering and I make so little difference. What should we do amidst so much pain? Give up? Give in? Go home?

I grieve for them and for the loss of innocence. These

15

people deserve more than what the world gives. If I succumb, please judge me by my intentions and pardon me for my failures – those that I myself cannot forgive.

The heart, they say here, is made not of bone. I do so wish that mine was fashioned otherwise.

PROLOGUE

April 11, 2004

Reflected sunlight swims along the wall above the bed, as if borne on some hidden current. Masses of plastic tubing, which fill the room like tufts of floating seaweed, slowly drip their infusions into an outstretched arm. In the background I hear the heart monitor tapping a fading SOS.

I can sense, more than see, movement outside the room, barely visible through a window in the door. But inside, it feels surprisingly tranquil. The thermostat is set to a soothing seventy-five degrees. Comforting pastel hues cover the cabinets and walls.

High above hang six IV bags, and I watch the dispensing bubble of the nearest one. A stray beam of light highlights its dispensing chamber. Inside the half-filled reservoir, I can see a shimmering bead clinging to an inner silver thread.

Silently, I urge the drop to hold on and arrest the slippage of time, as if freezing this moment will somehow change reality. Yet I know it cannot be so – some things that are lost can never be regained.

Even in one of America's most luxurious and high-tech hospitals, some infirmities defy cure. Medicine, no matter where you are, invariably has its limits. In my heart, I know it truly is the end.

It seems as if I have led a series of starkly different lives, the last having started with that sudden change in health that so completely sapped my strength. I was almost another person then, when I took off my white doctor's coat, folding it neatly and placing it on the nearby stand, before collapsing onto the waiting gurney.

A nurse efficiently dressed me in a gown and asked me to take off my shoes. But I pretended not to hear her – it took three times before the point was made. I didn't want to remove them. I would be leaving soon enough, I thought. That was one of my first attempts, of many, at trying to control the situation.

ER personnel, most of whom I recognized, quickly placed monitors over my bared body. As bad as I felt, I helped strap on the blood pressure cuff and stick half the electrodes onto my own chest. It was mostly habit – I had done the same thing to others thousands of times before. Then I watched the screen as the machines began to register.

With oddly detached interest, I noted that my heart raced at more than twice its usual rate and that there was an abnormal beat after each normal one. In a matter of minutes various people swiftly inserted an IV, drew a blood sample, and took a chest X-ray. Medical students and doctors walked past as I waited behind a half-drawn curtain. I heard a friend, a fellow classmate, unknowingly take a medical history from the patient next door.

It was several days before my mom got to California. I know I kept the news from her, and others, for too long. But it took some time before I began to understand what was going on, and I hesitated at having to explain that I didn't know what ailed me. I was, after all, supposed to almost be a doctor.

Word got out eventually, however, after I failed to make my own return party. It was fairly uncharacteristic of me to miss such an event, especially since it was thrown in my honor, and my friends soon began to suspect the seriousness of my sudden infirmity. It's hard for me to say for sure, since I wasn't there, but I've heard it was pretty fun.

By the time my mother's plane touched down in LA, I had already interacted with countless doctors, many of whom had been former acquaintances and professors of mine. Despite having held numerous medical jobs and having gone through much of the long schooling, being a patient was a side of medicine with which I had little experience. Everything was the reverse of what I was used to. Now I was at the other end of the stethoscope, wearing the chilly gown that was impossible to tie in the back. Now it was my turn to accept what I had already begun to suspect: I was really in control of very little.

One of the nurses relayed the message to me that my mother was on her way, and from the hospital bed I pictured her anxious journey to see me. In my mind's eye, my mom wore a look of concern that I had never before seen on her familiar face. But it was an expression that I recognized only too well from distant lands – by then I had seen similar ones, worn by worried parents, more times than I would have wished.

I wondered what my mom would be thinking as she fought her way through traffic. Despite being a grown man, I am not ashamed of what a relief it was to know that she was near. I had never before suffered from more than the common cold, except for a bout of mononucleosis in college that was cured by ice cream and the hand of time. This, most obviously, was very different.

My mom would rightly want to know what had happened, I thought as I lay there staring off into the ceiling tiles. I recognized then how much I had kept from her, from the rest of my family, and from my friends. How much I had hidden away – to protect them, I had told myself, but to safeguard me as well, I now realized. But the past can never be changed. I only hoped that I would have enough time, and enough courage, to tell her.

I

SWEPT AWAY

1

SWEPT AWAY

June 30, 2003

Unrestrained cargo lurched precariously behind my head, but I did my best to ignore it. Instead, I clutched at the frayed seat belt in my lap and focused my eyes out the helicopter window, past streaks of frenzied raindrops, toward a growing brightness in the distance. There's no point in looking back, I told myself – the only option is forward.

The cabin, filled with the whine of the antique turbines, shuddered violently when we flew over dry land. The lumbering transport bucked in stubborn protest as a lone light drew us down into flickering shadows. As the aircraft finally struck the ground with a jarring thud, we tilted dangerously to one side for a few nerve-racking seconds before settling.

After quickly gathering my few belongings, I filed out the cramped doorway to sway briefly under the downdraft of the chopper and the weight of my backpack. For a moment I searched for a familiar face in the surrounding undergrowth, but I knew there was none to find.

Out of the dim jungle a bear of a man steadily plodded toward me. 'Merlin?' he yelled over the slowing chopper blades, naming the nongovernmental organization (NGO) that was providing my logistics.

I nodded my head in what I hoped was confident affirmation. 'Ross,' I shouted back as I shook his meaty hand.

'Mikhail,' the big man answered in a gruff Eastern European accent. He paused to fan his sweat-soaked T-shirt. 'Hope you're ready for the heat,' he added.

The two of us abandoned the small refuge of light to step into darkness. Our driver, a man with midnight skin, materialized out of the shadows to assist me with my backpack. Then my two escorts ushered me down a dirt path to a beat-up Range Rover.

Stickers of AK-47 machine guns, crossed out by big red Xs, covered the car. Bold letters underneath proclaimed NO ARMS. I slid into the passenger seat, trying not to second-guess my own intelligence: why had I voluntarily entered a place where vehicles needed to declare their lack of an arsenal?

Mikhail, clearly an assertive man, insisted on getting behind the wheel. Our chauffeur, rendered obsolete, climbed into the backseat and sulked there silently. 'You don't mind, do you?' Mikhail asked me. 'Just got here last week and I'm still getting my bearings,' he explained. As we lurched forward, I shrugged to myself, content for the moment simply to be on the ground.

A hot breeze engulfed us as we headed into the heart of the city. Freetown, the capital of Sierra Leone, was pitch-dark at night. My two guides and I drove without conversation, listening only to the steady hum of the engine as enigmatic buildings passed by the window. I tried to reassure myself that I could handle whatever my new home might contain, but didn't feel all that convinced. Nothing seemed even vaguely familiar to me. Nothing looked like home.

Headlights suddenly materialized out of the darkness, followed by the frantic honking of an oncoming truck. For a few fearful seconds, I found myself pressing down hard at an imaginary brake pedal beneath my feet, my adrenaline surging as the oncoming vehicle swerved by, barely missing us. 'Why did he do that?' Mikhail complained to our driver, after the road had again returned to the comfort of shadows. But while I tried to relax my legs, the backseat offered only indignant silence as an answer.

As we entered the sleeping city center, our car passed a sole lit sign, a plaque identifying the adjacent building as the Sierra Leone Reconciliation Court. The country had been at war since 1992, with the government in Freetown fighting the Rebel United Front (RUF). These two main combatants had raped, maimed, and murdered wantonly before finally signing a United Nation-brokered peace accord. The mandate of the court was to prosecute the worst of the prolonged conflict's many war criminals.

I watched the building pass, barely able to imagine the drama that had recently occurred within its walls. Just a week prior, judges there had issued an arrest warrant for Charles Taylor, the neighboring Liberian president. The magistrates accused the dictator of crimes against humanity, for creating the RUF and subsequently supporting the rebels by providing a conduit for the group's illegally mined diamonds to the international market. But no one knew what would come of the indictment. Charles Taylor was ensconced in nearby Liberia, safely out of the reach of international justice.

As the sign for the Reconciliation Court faded away in my side-view mirror, I recalled the many crimes with which Taylor was charged. More than two hundred thousand people had been killed and one million forced from their homes in a lengthy war punctuated by some of the worst human rights abuses known to the modern world. The atrocities were so extreme that they seemed almost unbelievable: arbitrary killings of civilians, widespread torture, systematic rape, deliberate amputation of limbs, and the forced recruitment of countless child soldiers, among others.

As I tried to come to terms with what it meant to have suddenly entered such a trauma-ridden land, Mikhail interrupted my uneasy thoughts. 'Up for a drink before we hit the guesthouse?' he asked casually.

I wanted nothing more than to find a safe room in which to huddle, but I didn't want to seem overwhelmed. 'Sure,' I cautiously agreed.

We soon pulled off the road and parked next to a small porch, where an anemic light guarded a few empty tables. As we sat down, our driver greeted the waitress. 'How dee body?' he said in a singsong timbre.

'Dee body fine,' the woman replied with a welcoming

smile. I tried to follow the pair's conversation in Krio, Sierra Leone's official language, but could identify only a few words of the English-based dialect that freed slaves had brought back to Africa.

Mikhail quickly ordered us a round of beers. When the waitress returned, she efficiently flipped off their caps, rubbed the open bottle tops with a used rag, and handed them to us. My large escort eyed his change in leones, unabashedly confirming the absence of fake bills before holding his beer up to the driver and me. 'To peace and health,' he said. The waitress encouraged us with a big pearl-white grin as we all three took a swig.

The driver continued to chat up the waitress, leaving Mikhail and me to ourselves. The burly Macedonian turned to stare openly at me for a few moments. 'So,' he finally blurted out, '*you're* the Lassa guy?' I was clearly a lot younger than he had expected.

I paused for a few seconds before answering. 'Yeah,' I finally grunted, doing my best to imitate my guide's gruff demeanor. Although it was hard to feign comfort with my brand-new title, I didn't want Mikhail to know how lacking I was in field experience. I had finished three years of medical school and a year of public heath, in addition to studying extensively before leaving. That would be enough, I silently hoped, to handle whatever challenges lay ahead.

'A doctor died of that here last year,' Mikhail continued with a knowing shake of his head, as if to say he was new to the country but was aware of that much already.

I was also well acquainted with the story of the fated

Freetown physician. He had died from Lassa fever, a viral hemorrhagic fever (VHF) limited to West Africa. His horrific demise was just one of the many details I had conveniently failed to mention to those close to me before I left for my trip. My dad and brother had told me I was crazy, while my mom had sighed deeply – her heart torn between needing to protect me and not wanting to stand between me and something I was passionate about. With worry already clearly evident in their voices, I had held my tongue. There was no need to burden my loved ones any more than I had already.

From the moment I had first heard about the dreaded Lassa virus, during my second year of medical school in a sterile California classroom that now felt very far away, I had been drawn to the illness. The disease is one of four famed VHFs (including Ebola, Marburg, and Crimean-Congo hemorrhagic fever) that share a terrifying tendency to spread from person to person, as well as a gruesome clinical picture of massive bleeding frequently leading to death.

Although there are countless TV shows and movies focused on the more riveting aspects of medicine, the extended study needed to enter the field is almost exactly the opposite of dramatic. Medical school is hour after hour of monotonous rote learning, memorizing a never-ending series of facts that can seem completely disconnected from the act of caring for actual human beings.

Years of exams merge together until you almost forget why you chose to go into medicine in the first place. Surrounded by highly competitive people, you can easily become distracted by which specialties are the most prestigious or the most lucrative. During that time, Lassa became a symbol to me of something different, of foreign adventure and unquestionable need.

I knew that my trip was risky, some had told me even foolish, but the mix of danger and adventure surrounding the mysterious virus compelled me toward it. I had studied for years to swear an oath to care for the sick. In my eyes, confronting Lassa seemed to be the ultimate test of such moral fortitude. It meant that I had not yet lost a few threads of idealism, to which I so desperately clutched throughout my training.

As I had researched the trip, I learned that the Freetown physician to whom Mikhail referred had contracted Lassa from a patient returning from southern Sierra Leone, where the disease is endemic. The doctor's and his patient's horrific deaths, their bodily fluids pouring like flowing tap water from every orifice of their swollen corpses, had caused panicked patients and staff to flee the Freetown hospital.

Admittedly, Mikhail's comment disarmed me for a moment. I didn't want to be reminded about the past physician's death. To me, at that time, medicine was supposed to be about tales of human triumph. I thrived on stories of success, tumors removed and lives saved, not failure.

I did my best to turn the topic to a more pleasant subject. 'So, what do you do for Merlin?' I asked Mikhail.

'Fix problems,' the big man answered. 'I'm in charge of logistics for Sierra Leone, moving stuff and people around the country.'

'You just got here?' I said.

'Yeah, last week. The post has been open for several months, and they were pretty anxious to fill it, given the fighting in Liberia.'

'And before?'

'I was back in Kosovo, where my wife and twin girls are. I worked for Merlin there, transporting medical supplies. But the pay is higher here as an expat.'

'It's a move up, then?'

'Yep. And I'm already looking forward to buying my girls matching tricycles for their birthday,' Mikhail answered, with a twinkle in his eyes.

Then, just as quickly, that glimmer disappeared. With a sharp grunt, the Macedonian slammed down his empty beer bottle. 'Time to go,' he said, before herding the driver and me into the Range Rover. Assuming the wheel, my temporary guide proceeded to drive us a short distance down the dark Freetown streets to the Merlin guesthouse. As we approached, a growing glow from the building illuminated high walls – broken bottles, cemented on top, glinted beneath rolls of barbed wire.

A group of more than fifteen armed security guards soon unlocked the gates to let us enter the compound. The African men wore winter hats and thick jackets, along with threadbare pants and sandals. 'They think it's cold at night,' Mikhail whispered to me, perspiration clearly beaded on his own forehead.

As I greeted the near battalion of guards, the nearest man cheerfully grabbed my arm and proceeded to teach me the Sierra Leone handshake. We began with the normal Western grasp, then spun to clutch each other's thumb, and then back to the ordinary grip. I bit back a smile as each guard shook my hand the same way, the eldest with methodical dignity.

Mikhail eventually led me through the small, dark house to my room for the night. 'We should have a ride for you in a couple of days,' he informed me. My final destination was Kenema, a southern town close to the border of warring Liberia. Merlin sponsored a ward there, the only one in the world solely dedicated to treating Lassa fever.

I unpacked a few things and got into bed, but sleep eluded me. My comfortable mattress, where I had last laid my head in one of London's towering high-rises, seemed a distant memory. More than space and time separated me from that place — in between sped a river of differences. Concealed under the cover of night, I clung tightly to my makeshift pillow and silently hoped that the rising torrent wouldn't sweep me away.

2

THE RAINS

July 1, 2003

Wham! A sudden explosion woke me, and it took me a second to realize that it was the corrugated-iron roof, above my head, that was pounding with deafening thunder. Through the window, I could see rain outside, pummeling leafy plant life into swift submission. It was as if a mad engineer had inexplicably moved the shoddy Merlin complex directly underneath a waterfall.

Awed, I walked down crumbling cement stairs to what turned out to be a connecting garage, for a better view. The guards were all huddled inside the bay. *There's little they can protect from there,* I thought. But it was hard to imagine any thief brave enough to venture outside.

The water poured down without a moment's respite. 'How long will it last?' I asked the guards.

'Four, maybe five, months,' the nearest one told me. The guards all laughed at the joke. It was the beginning of the rainy season. But despite the smiling faces around me, I had a sinking feeling that they were partially serious.

The dirt courtyard outside our recess had already become a wild torrent, the water running higher than my knee as it flooded out beneath the gate. I shook my head in amazement. 'Chillin,' the same guard told me, 'they die now, every year.'

'The children?' I asked. 'How so?'

'Freetown's hills be steep,' the guard continued. 'Sometimes they get all the way to the sea,' he said, pointing down out to the coast. It took me a few moments to register the magnitude of the tragedy that the seasonal rains brought to the city.

'Really?' I said.

'Sure, sure,' the guard said, his voice low for a moment. 'That how death be here. Easy, like a sigh before bed.'

There was a shortwave radio in the garage, and it suddenly started chirping with a call from Merlin personnel in neighboring Liberia. The garage's inhabitants quickly gathered around the battered speaker, all eager to hear the latest news from across the border. Rebels there, the Liberians United for Reconciliation and Democracy (LURD), had been trying to overthrow Charles Taylor's government for several years. They had recently pushed closer to Monrovia, that adjacent nation's capital.

Much like a virus, Taylor's presence had infected much of West Africa for over a decade. His contagious influence had spread turmoil, via rebel groups, to Liberia's neighboring countries: Sierra Leone, Guinea, and the Ivory Coast. Now Taylor was starting to consume his own host nation, and Liberia was degenerating into chaos.

Kofi Annan, the head of the UN, had been calling for peacekeepers to mediate the crisis for several weeks. As a U.S. congressional charter had originally founded Liberia in the early nineteenth century, in order to have a place to send freed slaves, Annan had been urging the U.S. to spearhead the proposed intervention. There was ample historical precedent – Britain had recently led a similar rescue mission in Sierra Leone, and France in the Ivory Coast.

'We . . . need . . . supplies . . . urgently,' the radio crackled, going on to report that, although almost every other NGO had pulled out of Monrovia due to heavy fighting, the Merlin contingent was still attending to the ill and wounded. The group requested permission to raid the medical stores of the NGOs that had fled. Looters were stealing the abandoned provisions by the hour, and the Merlin workers wanted to try to save some of the supplies for humanitarian use.

The connection broke off into static before anyone could reply to the frantic appeal. While one of the guards tried to raise the besieged personnel again, the others recalled similar experiences during their own country's conflict. The men around me had all lived in Freetown the two times Sierra Leonean rebels, linked to Taylor, overran their capital. Pointing vaguely toward the mountains in the east, my new compatriots explained how the RUF had fought their way into the city, bullets spraying everywhere.

Through the rain, one of the guards pointed out the bush where he had personally hid with his young daughter, the two fearfully huddling together until the fighting had passed. The walls around me took on a new dimension as I surveyed the former battleground – the dirt beneath my feet almost certainly contained drops of spilled blood from the massive slaughter.

That evening, I ate dinner at a crowded living-room table along with ten other Merlin expatriates. Mikhail, a sleeveless white undershirt over his sweat-covered torso, sat to my left. Based in Freetown (the headquarters of the NGO for West Africa), he had spent the day arranging emergency supplies for the Merlin obstetrician in Kenema. 'You can take them with you when you leave,' the logistician told me.

I was excited to talk to the other humanitarian workers, most just passing through the city on their way to, or from, a posting. I had grown up an idealistic kid in Minnesota, drawn first to science and then eventually to medicine. Fantasies of humanitarian adventures in some distant, invariably warmer land had gotten me through countless nights of tedious study, and I was ecstatic to be finally turning those hopes into reality.

My new colleagues each had a special skill: malaria control, water improvement, health care unit setup, among others. I was just the new guy but found those around me to be like childhood comic-book heroes. Each one had his or her own 'superpower' to do good, and now I finally had the chance to become one of them. I was, as Mikhail had called me, 'the Lassa guy.'

The aid workers all knew each other well and recalled local anecdotes of West African life, as well as firsthand accounts of every hot spot in recent memory: the Congo,

Sudan, and East Timor. The discussion ranged from how to say 'thank you' in Somalia, a land that evidently has no such concept, to the twisting political nuances of the Balkans conflict. President Bush had just declared a premature end to the war in Iraq, and one worker had already been there for a brief assessment. Others were soon to join their colleagues in Liberia.

During a lull in the conversation, a British woman several years my senior asked what brought me to the troubled region. 'I'm working on my public health thesis,' I explained as the table turned their attention to me. 'It's a practical guide for the treatment and control of the Lassa virus.'

'It's amazing what white people want to do!' Daren, the Merlin medical coordinator for Sierra Leone, exclaimed immediately. He looked at me from across the table with exaggerated confusion on his face. 'You know Lassa can kill you, don't you?'

'I may have read that somewhere,' I said with a smile.

'White people do the craziest things,' the Nigerian physician continued, egged on by the group's good-natured laughter. 'On television, you can see them swimming with sharks and jumping off buildings with tiny parachutes. I mean, isn't there anything safe to do in America?' I also chuckled at Daren's impromptu routine, although finding it slightly ironic, considering he worked in a recovering war zone. But we each have our own personal fears.

The group had many questions for me, those gathered having heard of Lassa only secondhand. Freetown was near, but outside, the normal distribution area. Still inwardly anxious about my lack of real-world experience, I did my best to explain what I could about the deadly virus, based on my pretrip readings. I had yet to actually see an infected patient.

I told the attentive group how the Lassa virus, the cause of Lassa fever, was normally present only within certain parts of West Africa. In Sierra Leone, the disease is mainly in the southeast. It escapes that area only when someone contracts the virus there and then journeys elsewhere – thus spreading the contagious illness outside its normal habitat, as happened with the patient seen by the deceased Freetown doctor.

Lassa is really a rodent disease, infecting people only by accident. Human outbreaks originate from contact with *Mastomys natalensis,* a type of rat that scavenges for leftovers in and around village homes. The virus has little detrimental effect on these rodents but saturates their tissues and bodily fluids. Since, like all rats, *Mastomys natalensis* leave a constant trickle of urine wherever they walk to serve as a scented escape path, the rodents easily contaminate human food and dwellings with infective particles.

I had read that many of the poor West African villagers also encountered the virus more directly, by actually eating the rodents. The rural people evidently consider rat meat to be quite a delicacy.

'After doing so much reading,' I remarked, 'it'll be great to finally see things firsthand.'

'Well,' Daren said with a smirk, 'then I guess *you'll* think you picked a great time to come.'

He informed me that a World Health Organization (WHO) team had just been through Freetown on their way down to Kenema. The group was apparently investigating reports of a new Lassa outbreak among the Liberian refugee camps on the Sierra Leone side of the border. The UN High Commission for Refugees (UNHCR), the overarching world body responsible for refugee health, had just recently identified several cases.

From my background research, I knew the WHO team was all part of a pattern, starting after September 11, of increased attention on Lassa from the outside world. With a new focus on potential agents of terror, the US Centers for Disease Control and Prevention (CDC) had identified the virus as having one of the greatest potentials for causing fear and death if intentionally released. They gave the virus their highest rating (Class A pathogen) in part because both the US and the former Soviet Union had pursued methods to use the disease, in addition to Ebola, as an aerosolized weapon.

Although there was some Lassa research taking place in the West, all of it was in multimillion-dollar Biosafety Level 4 (BSL-4) labs, the highest degree of protection possible. Such facilities have sophisticated features to prevent accidental transmission of the virus. Like something out of a futuristic sci-fi novel, lab technicians work completely encased in sealed space suits, while vents filter the air into a special sanitizing system.

I understood that there was no way to support such infrastructure in war-torn Sierra Leone. And now, amid rumors of a new outbreak, I was acutely aware of how little I really knew about what I would encounter in Kenema. Not to worry, I tried to comfort myself a few hours later as I prepared for another night of restless sleep – I would find out soon enough. My ride was leaving in the morning.

3

YOUR DEED IS YOUR HISTORY

July 2, 2003

The four-wheel-drive Range Rover clutched at the road while its continuously honking horn strained to shield us from oncoming traffic. My driver and I wound through the mountains that surround Freetown. Almost unconsciously, I leaned toward the cliff face that was just outside my window, silently urging my slight weight to keep us on the precarious trail and out of the deep ravine below.

When our car dropped out of the mountains and entered denser jungle, the road became indistinguishable from a riverbed. Our car wipers feebly protested the coffee-colored puddles that serially splashed onto the hood and over the rooftop, while I listened to our medical supplies and my rucksack bounce around the back of the vehicle.

Pedestrians peered at us through the raindrop-splattered windshield and occasionally waved a hand. This was my first time in sub-Saharan Africa, and I was surprised to find the sporadic traditional sarong mixed among secondhand Western clothes. I watched stray pieces of my American childhood walk by in the rural African bush as a pair of acid-washed jeans and a Mr T I PITY THE FOOL! T-shirt threaded past.

Motorcycles worked their way along the supposed road, their drivers holding umbrellas overhead while weaving between the small lakes. Packed vans, the closest thing to public transit, also intermittently sped by. The front of each offered a few philosophic words hand painted by its owner: WORK HARD EXPECT HARD; FEAR NOT THE WORLD BUT THE PEOPLE; GOD SENTENCE NO APPEAL; YOUR DEED IS YOUR HISTORY.

We passed through several baby blue checkpoints where piled sandbags and rolls of barbed wire lined alternating sides of the road. United Nations Mission in Sierra Leone (UNAMSIL) troops guarded most of the main thoroughfares. They were in charge of disarmament and power sharing in the country, helping to maintain the fragile Lomé Peace Accord, which had officially ended the Sierra Leonean civil war between the government and the RUF. Barely slowing, my driver weaved through the blockade like a slalom course, my white face and the insignia of our car sufficient for a security pass.

As we passed farther into the countryside, we came across magnificent cotton trees, their leaf-covered limbs stretching out like giant gnarled arms across the horizon. Underneath them labored countless undersized children, their bellies huge and swollen. Despite having been prepared for the presence of the ill kids by countless late-night commercials in America, they still struck a deep chord within me.

But our car passed the same portrait so many times that the ailing kids eventually merged into the background, as if I were just flipping through TV channels. Guarded only by the silent branches high above, the starving children became simply another part of the terrain – they were an obligatory but unremarkable piece of the accepted Sierra Leonean landscape.

Three hours into the trip, the trail morphed into a wide patch of black asphalt that donors had built before the war. Having come across the only decent strip of road in the country, my driver happily gunned our engine without hesitation.

I held on to my seat as we proceeded to hurtle through the rain, sending villagers literally diving into the bush on either side. The section lasted only a few minutes, but my would-be chauffeur made the best of his short opportunity, an instinct that came naturally in a country with one of the world's shortest life spans.

Soon after the road returned to the now familiar potholes, our car began to sputter. My driver angrily pumped the gas but proved unable to save the engine. After one last gasp, we coasted to a halt with only the sound of crunching gravel beneath the wheels.

With a low grumble, the driver exited the car and looked under the hood as raindrops pattered lightly on the surrounding vegetation. Tall grasses waved at eye height, framing the road on either side. I watched a few villagers walk by in the distance, the loads on their heads silhouetted by the afternoon sun, while wondering what would happen if the driver couldn't get the car to start. Would I sleep in the jungle for the night?

After a half-hour of the driver's diligent work, I was relieved to hear the car slowly coaxed back to life. Two more break-downs and subsequent repairs later, we finally pulled into Kenema. The town was dark when we arrived, with only indistinct buildings visible around a main intersection.

As we turned onto a small side street, my driver suddenly slammed on the brakes and our car skidded to an abrupt stop, only inches away from a cowering African woman. She lay collapsed on the ground in front of us, with ineffectual hands guarding her head. It took me a few moments to register that a large man, standing above her, was screaming incoherently while beating her with his hands and then feet.

'My god! What is he doing?' I yelled, unconsciously open-ing the car door to help. But before I got very far, I noticed that there were four onlookers, all watching calmly from the side of the street, and realized I had no idea what I was jump-ing into. The powerless woman tried feebly to escape, but the attacker pulled her back onto the ground and began hitting her again. 'Do something!' I finally shouted in frustration at my driver.

The driver vigorously honked our horn, which startled the assailant into staring up at us, his mad eyes reflecting back red flickers from our headlights. My chauffeur proceeded to roll down his window and lecture the attacker while the hurt woman limped off into the underbrush. Although unable to make out the driver's exact words, I was able to grasp their meaning. He was telling the assailant not to block the road again in the future.

Our car finally pulled past more guards and barbed wire, into the small courtyard of the Kenema guesthouse. After thanking my driver for the eventful ride, I carried my bag into the bigger of the two buildings, where the sound of a radio bounced off cement walls. On my way in, I heard a British broadcaster announce that President Bush was still considering whether to intervene in neighboring Liberia. Acknowledging the growing chaos, the president called for Taylor to resign. However, the US was pointedly avoiding any talk of direct intervention.

In the living room, I found three expats just finishing dinner, and I introduced myself around the table. All stood to greet me: Mohammad, a squat Egyptian obstetrician/ gynecologist; Lila, a rather plump Moroccan midwife; and Dr Nassan, a tall Ethiopian pediatrics professor. My entrance had evidently interrupted Mohammad, who ran the Kenema maternity ward, in the middle of a heated speech.

'I guess I have some supplies for you in the car,' I told him.

'Now they send it!' the fiery obstetrician said in exasperation. 'I'm sure that will be a lot of help since I'm leaving tomorrow for a week in Freetown.'

'Uh . . . sorry,' I said, a bit taken aback.

'That's always the way it is,' chimed in Lila.

'Well, it's certainly not your fault,' Dr Nassan said to me. 'Come, sit. Let's get you some food.'

When I sat down at the table, I realized I was ravenous from the long drive. The main dish consisted of mashed greenery, with ample salt scarcely covering up a strong, pungent flavor. 'Potato leaves,' Lila said, after noticing my reaction. 'In most places, people only feed them to their pigs,' she continued before rolling her eyes and briefly reminiscing about a café near her former residence in Paris.

The group quickly returned to their prior discussion, which evidently had been about techniques to obtain blood donations for their patients. Dr. Nassan explained to me that there was no organized system in the country, meaning that caregivers had to find a donor whenever someone needed a transfusion, and he had recently run into trouble trying to locate blood for a critically ill child.

'I know these people will not donate,' Mohammad stated with conviction – it was apparently a frequent issue in the maternity ward after surgery. 'The families always sneak away whenever there is talk of giving blood.'

'You can't be so nice,' Mohammad continued, looking at Dr Nassan. 'Lock the room before requesting donations and do not let them out until you get one!' the Egyptian emphatically urged, gesturing with both hands in the air.

'Well, I guess,' Dr Nassan answered, 'it just seems . . .'

'People can be so selfish,' Lila muttered.

Mohammad listed for Dr Nassan some of his other strategies for compelling blood donations. The obstetrician's ideas were contrary to those espoused in the West, and I was sure an American ethics committee could sit around for days debating the appropriateness of his techniques. But given the local circumstances, the Egyptian explained, it was either force the issue or let the patients die.

Mohammad, who I soon learned was a devout Muslim with two wives and several children back in Egypt, excused himself to attend to his evening prayers. Dr Nassan also left for bed, leaving Lila to show me to the next-door annex. 'It's barely waterproof,' she said, referring to the first room, 'but you can sleep here for now.'

'Thanks,' I said.

'I had to move in to this place after my boyfriend dumped me,' the midwife continued.

'Oh. I'm sorry to—'

'He was from here, although we met in Paris.'

'That's very—'

'Anyways, the caretaker is fixing up a spot for you in the main building,' Lila finished. 'You can move in there when he's done.'

'Thanks,' I said. 'Really, anything is fine.'

'It's about the same, though,' the midwife uttered with a depressed sigh before leaving me alone in my room.

A beat-up bed, a dilapidated desk, and the remnants of an old locker took up the small space of my new home. While nervously eyeing the barren quarters, I unpacked my few things and set up a mosquito net underneath the questionably waterproof ceiling. Eventually, I climbed into bed and lay there listening to the unfamiliar night sounds that whispered outside a broken window screen.

There was a lot to process, but I found I couldn't keep my mind from repeatedly replaying what I had seen upon my arrival to Kenema: the man's angry fists raining down from high overhead onto the cowering woman. I remembered one of the expats in Freetown had mentioned that she worked on 'female violence.' However, at the time, I hadn't given it much thought – it had been just another of the many humanitarian job descriptions.

'That's nice,' I had replied. 'I do Lassa fever.'

4

JUST SAY NO

July 3, 2003

The next morning I met Sela, a local woman who functioned as the guesthouse maid and cook, and she cheerfully supplied some bread and jam for breakfast. I ate in the living room, eyeing a mother cat and her kittens through the window screen as they purred loudly to get my attention. The house 'rat-control strategy' seemed more intent on my food than their intended prey.

Daren had told me the WHO team would be meeting that day at the hospital. So as soon as I finished my quick meal, I had Chris, a local teenager who was also the guesthouse security guard, radio the Merlin car. I set off to find the team, hoping that I had not missed my opportunity to work with them.

As the driver took me toward the hospital, I had my first daytime glimpse of the town. Artillery fire had destroyed most of Kenema, and almost nothing stood taller than a single floor. We passed the sole exception partway through our journey, a half-demolished three-story building. Its floors were sandwiched together in the middle, as if a giant had used it for a large sofa.

Billboards lined the streets, advertising the shops of various Arab diamond dealers. A few Lebanese families, the merchant class of the region, owned most of the businesses stretching across West Africa. Through the store windows, I could make out cheap boom boxes, televisions, and stereo systems. The night before, Mohammad had mentioned that the local people immediately traded in any diamonds that they found for entertainment equipment. It was a jackpot economy – there was no point in saving for college.

Interspersed among the signs for Jawad's Diamond Trading House and those of his compatriots were placards for the NGOs. Kenema was the base for much of the humanitarian work in the south of the country, and the colorful insignia of UN branches mixed with other well-known aid groups.

We soon pulled up to the hospital entrance and past a pack of parked motorcycles. Young men lounged around the shiny vehicles in 2Pac T-shirts and dark sunglasses, looking like trouble waiting to happen. They gave me a very confident looking over as we passed by, and I briefly wondered if I should worry about my safety. None of them had visible guns, but they had the look of those used to carrying them.

'Rebels,' my driver explained after we were securely within the hospital complex. 'Former combatants' was the more politically correct term used by the aid organizations. The RUF fighters had turned in their arms as a condition of the cease-fire, and several NGOs were attempting the difficult task of integrating the insurgents back into society. But from the look of disdain on my driver's face, I was doubtful about the success, at least so far, of such efforts.

Although I had heard the many infamous stories, this was my first time seeing the rebels in person. I couldn't help feeling a mix of both fear and interest, as if I were encountering a dangerous animal in the wild. Unlike opposition groups in other parts of the world that sympathized with their local populace, the RUF had taken the reverse approach during its troubled reign. Rebel forces had instead committed countless atrocities to cause a fearful exodus from the diamond-rich areas that they subsequently plundered.

One of the better-known incidents occurred after the Freetown administration called on the citizens of Sierra Leone to 'use their hands to vote,' as a show of support for the government. The RUF fighters had responded by chopping off the arms of everyone they found – a camp of amputees near Freetown attested to their horrendous efficiency.

Several people had told me another chilling tale: the rebels bet on the sex of unborn children, then used machetes on pregnant mothers to determine the winner. I'm not sure if the often repeated story is true. But the fact that it seemed so plausible to everyone who lived through the violence was chilling enough.

My driver slowly navigated through the hospital complex, which consisted of a handful of one-story buildings scattered around a gravel courtyard. After passing a few chickens pecking unattended, we stopped next to what appeared to be a rudimentary pharmacy, where posters on the wall warned of the local health hazards in both English and Krio.

One sign for Lassa fever depicted a happy cat eating a rat. A newer illustration had a man and a woman holding hands. KEEP TO ONE PARTNER, it said. DON'T GET AIDS. Pictures of military ordnance, on another, alerted kids that the un-exploded armaments were not toys. A final placard had an image of a little girl holding up a diminutive hand to a large man sitting in a bed. Underneath it read, CHILDREN SAY NO TO SEX. I did a double take on this last one, shocked that some health worker evidently thought it was the young girls' fault that they were being sexually abused.

Exiting the car, I got directions from the driver and then headed off to what I hoped was the conference room. I walked by people who sat or lay on an open-air sidewalk that connected the buildings. IV bags hung from an overhead awning that protected the walkway from rain, and I weaved through their plastic jungle, toward what I hoped was the WHO team.

Suddenly, a screaming African woman ran out of a building across the street. Waving her arms high in the air, she darted past a huddled crowd, then continued down a dirt road off into the distance. I stared in the direction of her fading shrieks, con-templating what trauma had inspired such universally recognizable grief. 'I'm told that's the pediatric ward,' someone said behind me, in a crisp British accent. I turned around to find a man of Indian descent, wearing wire spectacles. He had just stepped out of an adjacent complex to squint briefly at the midday sun.

'I wonder what happened,' I said.

'One can only imagine,' replied the slender gentleman, who turned out to be Trent, the English virologist in charge of the WHO team. I had caught his group just as they were about to start their session. 'The hospital medical director is sick,' he said, 'but we're using his conference room.'

Trent introduced me to the twenty-some people present inside. The Sierra Leone Ministry of Health, the UNHCR, and the Merlin Outreach Team all had representatives. American, English, French, and African accents intermingled.

I was surprised to find such an international congregation in remote Sierra Leone, since only a handful of people in the world worked on Lassa. I had carried to Kenema every scientific paper ever written on the infection. The three-inch stack was heavier than I would have wished, but minuscule when compared to the research done on other diseases. HIV or malaria studies could fill whole libraries.

Dr. Conteh, the Sierra Leonean doctor who ran the Lassa ward, was present as well, and I was thrilled to meet him. 'Daren mentioned you would be arriving soon,' the grandfatherly physician said in a steady voice after standing up to greet me. He was shorter than I was but carried himself with distinguished stature. Dr. Conteh was the main reason I had traveled to Kenema. Internationally renowned for having treated hundreds of Lassa cases, he was the perfect resource for my paper.

The topic of the meeting was the WHO project, which aimed to assess the spread of Lassa by surveying for its antibodies in the refugee camps and surrounding communities. Positive antibody results would indicate that individuals had survived a past infection, which would give an idea of how much contact the populace was having with the virus. No one knew the exact distribution of the disease, since the poor transportation infrastructure in the area meant that many of those infected with the illness never made it to a medical center.

Trent and his WHO group had been setting up the study over the past week. They were planning to draw blood for the next two days before leaving with their samples. At the end of the meeting, I asked Dr. Conteh if he would be joining the WHO group on their outings.

'No, I am needed in the Lassa ward,' he said.

'Then I can start there as well,' I said.

'Everything in due time,' the physician said, with a gentle pat on my back. 'You should go with the WHO team while they are still in Kenema.'

'You're sure?'

'Yes, the Lassa ward and I will still be here when you finish, and it will be a great opportunity for you to see the countryside.'

Dr. Conteh told me how, in addition to coping with rebels, AIDS, unexploded ordnance, and child molesters, the people of Sierra Leone frequently had little choice but to care for their Lassa-stricken family members at home, thus further spreading the disease. The deadly virus regularly hopped along the traditional bonds of kinship. 'It spreads quite quickly from mother to son to daughter to father,' the experienced physician said. 'I have seen whole families be wiped out within a single week.'

5

LITTLE BUDDHAS

July 4, 2003

The air hung saturated with moisture from recent rain when dawn broke the next morning. Those of us who made up the WHO team gathered into three groups at the hospital, each one to head to a different study location. I was excited to get started, and my boots splashed through scattered puddles that swirled with reddish mud as I got into the designated Range Rover.

My group included Trent, looking a bit anxious, along with a handful of local laboratory technicians who had volunteered to draw the blood. With one of the local drivers behind the wheel, we headed off for the Jimmy Bagbo Refugee Camp, where the Lassa virus had recently struck. The most recent outbreak had started with a young boy and quickly spread to several other refugees, all of whom had swiftly died. The fatalities had been the impetus for the most recent international interest and the current WHO team.

While we bounced along the dirt road, we listened to

news on the car's static-filled CB radio. Fighting continued in Liberia between Taylor's forces and the LURD rebels. The UN, Britain, France, and various African nations were continuing to pressure the US to take a more active role in quelling the unrest. However, President Bush was now saying that he would consider sending in American troops only if Taylor first left the country.

This essentially meant that the conflict had to be over before help would arrive. It was a catch-22 that I was sure my government had not overlooked. Much like Lassa, Taylor was a deadly virus that everyone was afraid to treat. I shook my head, silently ashamed of the actions of my own nation, while trying to gauge the reactions of my local compatriots. But they sat looking silently ahead, as if holding much lower expectations for my homeland.

It was my first time visiting a refugee camp, and I was looking forward to seeing the outpost, since I had been studying about public health in conflict areas for the last year. Although I had taken numerous classes on the topic, the closest I had previously gotten to an actual camp was via CNN. Trent, on the other hand, had more experience. Although the virologist spent most of his time in a London laboratory, he had been touring the region for the last week. From his stories, I had the feeling that the day would be an eye-opening experience.

Rows of tents, emblazoned with the UN logo on their plastic tarps, began to dot the lush grassland. Flying directly in front of us was what initially appeared to be an American flag. But as we came closer, I realized that there was only one star amid the corner sea of blue. It was the Liberian banner, a close copy to that of my homeland and a vivid reminder of the long history connecting our two countries.

Our car stopped next to a huge crowd waiting by a rusty shed. Two wooden fences squeezed their dusty bodies into an aisle that looked like a conduit for herding cattle. When they saw us, the line began to surge back and forth, the people suddenly jostling for position. Children scurried among adult legs, trying their best to avoid being violently trampled.

I must have been staring with wide eyes, because Trent turned to me in explanation. 'They normally give the food out here,' he said. Trent had observed an actual ration distribution a few days earlier. 'You should have seen it then,' he continued, as if today's shoving refugees, in comparison, were an orderly checkout line at a neighborhood supermarket.

But, in truth, I had little desire to have seen it earlier. The current view was a deep enough look into a world where desperation had overwhelmed human decency. Denial is a strong human defense, and not having to see people at their worst means, in part, that we can avoid thinking about the basest parts of our nature. In the modern world, we live safely protected from any doubts about that darkest part of our makeup. A brief glance was more than sufficient for me.

We got out of the car and unpacked our equipment. The boxes of gloves, needles, and vials seemed utterly out of place amid the African bush. As we entered the shack, the chaos outside subsided, each person seemingly having found his or her appropriate place amongst the competing horde. Done with pushing one another, the refugees stood calmly inside the wooden dividers. Soon they began happily chatting and watching us expectantly.

The day before I arrived in Kenema, Trent had visited the camp on a sensitization campaign, which had – in theory – given the refugees an explanation about what to expect for the day. Trent's plan was to pick families at random from a camp list, and one member of each chosen family would have blood drawn to test for specific antibodies, indicating past Lassa exposure.

Later analysis of these samples would produce a picture of viral spread. By comparing the percentage of people with Lassa antibodies in the different camps and villages, the team would be able to pinpoint exactly where the outbreaks were originating, which would help focus public health measures.

Since we had the resources to test only a small portion of the refugees, it was going to be necessary to use statistics to extrapolate the overall exposure to the larger populations. The key to such mathematics is randomization, one of the basic tenets of any study and the bane of many a researcher. Trent had tried to explain this concept to the poorly educated local populace during his earlier visit. But he had found it close to impossible.

If we tested only the relatively healthy group that clamored to the front of the barricaded line, while those potentially debilitated by Lassa lay in their tents, then we would find a falsely low percentage of people with antibodies to Lassa. This would lead to the incorrect conclusion that there had been little infection in the camp, and resources would mistakenly be sent elsewhere.

In any country, nothing gathers a crowd like a crowd. In a refugee camp without real work or amusement, we were the next best thing to a functioning television. It seemed clear that most of the refugees had gathered just to watch the foreigners at work, along with the resultant commotion, and I doubted whether they understood much of our reason for being there.

We started with one of our workers randomly picking the first name from a bag and reading it out over a handheld megaphone. The family came forward, amid confusion over the change in normal protocol – there was no reason to stand in line, a concept that sunk in slowly.

The Liberian father and mother approached with their daughter, son, and small infant. I grabbed four handmade playing cards, one for each person over five years old. One of the paper squares had an X on the bottom; whoever received that card would be the person randomly chosen to give a blood sample.

I shuffled the cards and then dealt them out facedown as the two kids stared at my pale face with wide eyes. The mom passed one to her son, since he was too scared of my ghostly hands to take it from me. He stared at the foreign object before slowly turning it over. It bore the single large X.

Then, with sudden swiftness, the technicians got the parents to pin their son down on a makeshift table. The child lay there limply until we pulled out a needle, at which point the boy cried and struggled with shocked surprise. With experienced skill the tech swiftly drew our sample. We then moved on to the next family.

I found it painful watching each time as the parents and children chose from the deck. Inside, I kept rooting for the adults to pick the X, one of the reasons why we were not ourselves deciding who to test. If left in my hands, I would have stuck only the adults, thus ruining the randomization scheme and keeping us from detecting if any kids had been exposed to Lassa.

Passing out the cards was unnecessary for the many children who came up alone, the only members left of their family. The fighting surrounding Charles Taylor had struck an almost mortal wound – they had lost everyone else along the tortuous journey out of Liberia. Their youthful faces gazed up at mine, with deep adult eyes betraying that they had witnessed too much during their short lives.

After our team drew the blood, we sent the family to one of the researchers, who was a physician. Each household received a quick medical checkup, along with a packet of medication. The pills included aspirin, antibiotic eyedrops, and albendazole, a drug to treat worm infestation.

The utility of the last medication, albendazole, was clear from the children's bellies, which protruded roundly like those of little Buddhas, with intestines presumably chock-full of worms. The medication would kill the gastric intruders, although I knew that the poor sanitation of their living conditions meant that the kids would likely become reinfected within only a few months. However, that brief interval gave important time for growth and development.

Unfortunately, we did not have sufficient resources to supply medicine to the unselected refugees. Although the information we gathered would ultimately help address the possible spread of Lassa in their camp, those families would receive no immediate benefit from our visit. I looked out at the people, all of whom were in dire need of assistance, and acutely felt the pain of being able to offer such little help in the face of such great need.

My eye kept jumping to a smiling toddler who stood at the front of the onlookers. Shirtless, with a taut belly protruding over tattered shorts, he reminded me of the Happy Buddha, the golden statue that sits in front of countless Chinese restaurants. We had not yet called his family, and I asked Trent if we could give the child some medication.

'I don't know,' the virologist fretfully answered, clearly a bit more at ease in a BSL-4 isolation lab than in the African countryside. 'I think it might cause a riot,' he concluded.

'Why's that?' I asked.

'I don't know,' Trent said, 'but I think that if we start treating kids out of turn, everybody here is going to start demanding a visit with the doctor.' Both Trent and I knew that was something we unfortunately lacked the resources to provide.

'You're probably right,' I said, remembering the morning chaos. However, my heart ached every time I glanced at the child's dirty face. Throughout the day I continued to hope that the young boy's family would be called next, but at one point I looked up to realize that the Little Buddha had disappeared into the crowd, thus taking a small part of me with him.

As we called out the names and went through our list, it became clear that some of the families were absent. Our technicians tried to persuade the people around us to bring those missing to the survey station, but the crowd cared little about our need for randomization. They felt it was unfair that we were trying to recruit other people while those who wanted to contribute were already there waiting.

This, along with a growing fear of the blood drawing, quickly diminished the awaiting crowd. Rumor had spread among the refugees that we were stealing blood to sell elsewhere. The populace had never had venous blood samples drawn before, the kind done for any routine lab test. They had experienced only sticks on the tip of the finger.

By the end, only ten Liberians remained in the dusty stalls. The small group was there to see a physician about past Lassa infections. Most had previously been patients in the Lassa ward and had been lucky enough to survive with Dr. Conteh's vigilant treatment. But they were all deaf, a possible complication of even the mildest cases.

One man came up to me while pointing to both his ears. 'No fine! No fine!' he kept yelling, along with a torrent of words in the local dialect, which I couldn't understand. He repeatedly motioned from his ears to the scattered equipment we had brought with us, his hands pleading like a beggar.

It took me a while before I eventually understood that the man was asking for us to heal his Lassa-induced deafness, assuming we had brought with us a cure for him and his fellow victims. But I unfortunately knew of no therapy for this devastating outcome that, in his poor society, relegated an intelligent person to the role of village madman.

I kept doing my best to explain to the man that I was unable to help, with apologetic hands and words eventually progressing into futile shouts. But no matter what gestures I made or what I yelled, the man continued to fail to understand my message. He either could not, or would not, believe that he was destined to remain in unnatural silence for the rest of his life.

At first, I was not sure if I should pity or admire the deaf man's persistence. But when people are faced with so much tragedy, hope is perhaps the only savior. In the end, I wished it brought him, and all the others, what solace it could.

6

RISKY BUSINESS

July 4, 2003 (continued)

'I think we have a problem,' Trent said to me, looking worried, while I was trying to communicate with another deaf refugee.

'What?' I said, looking around at the nearly empty stalls. 'Did all the refugees leave?'

'That too, but more importantly, one of the sampling teams has a woman with Lassa symptoms,' the nervous virologist told me.

'Oh?'

'. . . and they drew her blood.'

'That's not good,' I said. Trent agreed, shaking his head back and forth anxiously.

Our group evacuated the shed while Trent radioed the Lassa ward ambulance for the ill woman. The Englishman's concern was not only that we had found a Lassa patient, although that was disturbing in itself, but that we had belatedly identified her. A tech had already drawn blood from the potentially infectious individual: sitting somewhere in our coolers, mixed with all the other samples, was a vial possibly teeming with the deadly virus.

Our group quickly decided to return the next day to obtain the rest of the samples. We apprehensively departed, leaving the doctor, who was keeping a generous distance, to wait with the sick woman. On the way back to Kenema, I could hear the samples, sealed in two coolers, bounce in the rear of our car.

Back at the hospital, Trent gave a quick talk to the WHO team, stressing early identification of future cases, before everyone headed home for the night. 'Remember,' he said, clearly distraught that things had not gone according to his carefully outlined plan. 'It's Lassa. . . . It can kill you.'

I ate dinner with Trent at the UNHCR guesthouse, where he was staying. The virologist was worried about having to deal with the potentially infectious samples in the local facilities. He reminisced about the sophisticated lab that had been present in a nearby town before the start of the Sierra Leone conflict and had contained much better infection-control infrastructure.

Earlier in his trip, Trent had visited the remnants of that lab with some of the local technicians, to see if there was anything to salvage. 'They destroyed everything,' he told me. 'There wasn't a building left standing, just rubble and smashed equipment.'

One of the techs confided in me that Trent had cried

when he saw the lab wreckage, earning the fretful virologist a place in the technician's heart with that involuntary gesture. Amid such tragedy, small things sometimes can hit the strongest chords, the enormity of it all being too great for anyone to fully comprehend.

Trent would have to work with only the substandard facilities left in Kenema. 'It's going to take all night,' he said, with a mixture of fatigue and concern written across his face.

'Why don't I help?' I replied, the words out of my mouth before I really analyzed them. It seemed unfair to make Trent do everything all by himself.

'You sure you want to do that?' Trent asked.

'I know how to use a pipette,' I continued, not mentioning that the last time I had been in a lab, I had been growing algae for a college ecology experiment. It was obvious that I had not been working on a BSL-4 agent in the African bush.

For a moment, Trent's restless gaze focused on me with a long and searching stare. I swallowed with a suddenly dry mouth as I thought about what I had just volunteered to do. But I hadn't come halfway across the world to back out in the end – I was already too far in.

'Okay,' the virologist finally said with a shrug, 'I guess it's your choice.'

It was dark by the time Trent and I arrived back at the hospital complex. The Lassa ward sat apart from the rest of the buildings. A high fence provided a physical barrier, although a psychological one seemed to extend much farther. I wondered to myself if the enclosure was there to keep people out, or in.

After we knocked at the front entrance, a security guard opened the gate for us. Then, uneasily crossing my hands over my chest to avoid touching anything, I followed Trent across a small courtyard and into the dark ward. An odor of bleach and some other substance hung in the hot, unmoving air – after a few moments, I realized it was the ferrous smell of spilled blood.

Trent and I eventually passed through a quiet hallway into a back room, which contained a lone desk and a solitary lightbulb that flickered with the whim of a generator. Another door opened into the adjacent 'laboratory,' a similar space that contained an old centrifuge, a few boxes of supplies, and a new refrigerator, the last of which the WHO team had brought specifically for the study.

Our sealed coolers sat in the middle of the room, with the vials still inside. Trent put a full duffel bag on the desk and pulled out several special containers. They had BIOHAZARD written in bold letters across the top, along with intimidating pictures. The British virologist was planning on shipping the samples by special arrangement from Freetown to his lab in London, where he would perform the antibody tests. But we had some work to do first.

The vials contained whole blood, which consists of both serum (the fluid portion of the blood) and the clotted blood cells. We needed to separate off and save this liquid portion before the cells broke apart, something that interferes with antibody testing.

Since clot is denser than serum, it naturally falls to the bottom of the tubes. But we still needed to centrifuge the samples in order to separate the two layers as thoroughly as possible. We would then take off the floating serum portion and seal it in a new container for transport.

After Trent explained the plan, we dressed in personal protective equipment (PPE): a surgical gown, two pairs of gloves, eye goggles, and a special face mask. It seemed like a lot of gear, but compared with a BSL-4 lab, it was like playing with the virus in only our underwear.

Before we began, Trent pulled me aside to caution me. 'The percentage of people who die from Lassa infection increases dramatically when it is transmitted directly from a blood stick,' he said, slightly muffled through his mask. I blinked a few times while staring at his carefully garbed figure, then nodded my head to convey my understanding. Exposure to higher levels of the virus results in worse mortality rates – needle injuries or punctures from shards of glass would undoubtedly have devastating results. I had to almost physically suppress the urge to shudder.

'I'm worried about the centrifuge,' Trent went on to say. The old thing looked as if it might fly apart, even to my untrained eye. 'If it breaks, it's going to spray all over.'

'Yeah,' I mumbled back. The masks we were using were far from ideal, and the possibility of aerosolizing a highly infectious VHF and splattering it around the room was enough to give anyone nightmares.

'There's no reason we should both be at risk,' Trent told me. 'I can do the centrifuge work and you can pipette out here.'

'Okay,' I said with a twinge of guilt. It was a potentially life-altering decision. Slightly safer, I would work in the second room, taking off the serum from the finished tubes.

Trent and I worked rhythmically in the ghostly light: find a tube, label a new one, centrifuge, take off the serum, seal it up, and do it again. It was an elaborate game played by humorless adults: you can touch this, you can't touch that, pour the blood this way, don't touch your forehead, beware of glass and needles.

Somewhere in the middle of this process, I turned behind me to see the ward security guard quickly approaching. But before I could say a word, the man nonchalantly glided past my full-suited figure to enter Trent's lab room. I froze, eyes fixed on the closed door, while the centrifuge whined away behind it. A few seconds later, the guard came out and strolled past me once again.

I waited for the centrifuge to stop before entering to see Trent's still stunned face. 'He came to get his water,' my partner told me, pointing to the new refrigerator where we were beginning to store our samples. 'I told him we'll have to talk about that later,' the virologist simply said.

Trent and I finished the last vial about two hours later. The centrifuge had survived and so had we. Dead tired, we peeled off our sweaty gear before passing through the dark recesses of the ward to the cleansing safety of light rainfall.

Quietly huddled under umbrellas, the two of us hiked back along the dirt road to our respective shelters. With weak flashlights, we dodged puddles and avoided the occasional motorcycle, the lonely headlamps half obscured by the downpour.

After escorting Trent safely to his compound and wishing him good night, I headed to my own. Halfway there, I looked up from mud-covered boots to see a solitary headlight coming down the middle of the road. Without much thought, I put my head down and continued along the side.

As the light grew nearer, the ground began to shake softly and I suddenly found myself eye to eye with a lumbering construction truck. As I belatedly jumped to one side, the side-view mirror of the massive vehicle tore through my lagging umbrella, the spokes snapping like uncooked spaghetti before my flimsy protection fell beneath the rear wheel.

Shaking and with rain pelting my unprotected face, I eventually struggled out of a muddy ditch that ran alongside the road. I watched the single functioning headlight slowly fade away as my heart pounded in my ears and my hands trembled uncontrollably.

Stunned by the swiftness of my sudden peril, I stared off into the darkness long after the jungle had again returned to darkness. My new home clearly contained more than just viral hazards. Indeed, the growing list of potential dangers seemed almost never ending.

7

THE MEASURE OF THINGS

July 5, 2003

I was still wiping sleep out of my eyes when I met the WHO group the next morning. Trent was going to return to the Jimmy Bagbo Refugee Camp to collect the missed samples. But I decided to join a different team going to the Jimmy Bagbo Village, the community neighboring the refugee camp. It was my opportunity to see up close how typical Sierra Leonean people lived.

The community was only a mile from the camp, and so most of the drive was familiar. Our team eventually pulled into the village, past rickety huts of bamboo and mud, which were topped with palm-leaf thatching. The lodgings were familiar replications of the many scattered throughout the countryside.

Our cars stopped next to an open-air gazebo in the center of the village. Clearly built by an NGO, the building had a concrete floor and long wooden benches. My new team had previously talked with the community members during a town meeting there, and the villagers had promised to return to participate in the study at the appointed hour.

Despite our punctual arrival, the village center was empty except for a toothless old man, who happily waved at us from the front pew. One of the technicians went to talk with him and returned to report that the town crier had neglected to remind the village of our visit. Everyone, besides our patiently waiting greeter, had either forgotten about us or assumed we were not coming – the villagers were all out in the fields working.

It was the WHO team's last day in southern Sierra Leone, and this posed a significant problem for the survey. It was impossible to come back the next day, with the cars, drivers, and staff all needed elsewhere. While thinking how disappointed Trent would be if we returned empty-handed, I asked, with little hope, that our new friend try to round up anyone he could.

After setting up our gear, our group waited impatiently. I spent my time kicking rocks around in the dirt. Eventually, a crew of seven kids trickled in, all too young for fieldwork. They ran around barefoot with belly buttons sticking out like half-bananas. The children were covered in dirt, the lucky ones also wearing T-shirts and tattered underwear. One little girl's shirt read I HAD MY BIRTHDAY AT SKATE PALACE, with a few fading snowflakes drawn on the front. For a few moments, I tried picturing the cute little dirtball at one of the ice rinks where I had played hockey during my youth, but the image was too ludicrous to imagine.

One boy, clearly the class clown, kept sticking out his tongue at me, only to run away laughing. As I watched his antics, a smaller child, who could barely walk, wobbled toward us from the bush, dressed only in a pair of oversized underwear hooked precariously over one hip. I thought back to my days of lecturing parents in the States, during a pediatrics rotation, about 'baby-proofing' their houses – that image contrasted starkly with the abandoned children scattered around me.

When this last child finally saw me, he stopped abruptly, bunched up both fists, and proceeded to bawl. I didn't know the cause of the outburst but wondered if he was seeing a white person for the first time. One of the Freetown guards had jokingly confessed to being scared of Caucasians as a child – he had thought they were ghosts who had come to eat him.

The other kids ran around the little one, some teasing with taunts and others trying to comfort him with awkward hugs. I walked over to help but stood mesmerized by the toddler's powerful lungs. Then the child grabbed my pinkie finger and abruptly ceased crying.

The two of us looked as if we were about to go for a walk, and the young gang ran circles around us, howling with laughter. I tried to withdraw my hand, but each time I did, my new friend burst forth into renewed tears. So we stood chained together in the remote African bush.

The group jester, not appreciating his loss of attention, eventually ran up with a devious smile. Grabbing the toddler, he hoisted him overhead before running off at a gallop toward the distant huts and, I hoped, the child's absent mother.

There were still no adults anywhere, so I entertained myself by performing magic tricks for the kids. Although my clumsiness bordered on malpractice, they remained fascinated nonetheless. The 'disappearing rock' trick – I stuck it down the back of my shirt – turned out to be a big crowd-pleaser.

Even better was my next stunt: I flicked my thumbnails against my teeth, behind concealing hands, to produce a bone-crunching sound while I pretended to break my nose. However, this last joke proved too popular, and the children were soon rolling around in the dirt, trying to grab each other's noses. I had to avoid eye contact with them for some time after that, as almost any glance instigated additional scuffles.

It was just after I discovered this 'darker side' of magic that I looked up to see a whole village walking toward us. To the surprise of everyone on the team, our elderly friend had come through with our request.

The villagers quickly gathered around us in the main gazebo. The women all had one or two children strapped to their backs with colorful shawls. Some babies were so small that their tiny heads barely emerged. The larger kids' feet stuck out, to straddle their mothers as if riding large ostriches.

Our team quickly divided into two groups and immediately started taking samples. Again I took the job of passing out the playing cards. When my first family arrived, before even asking for the ages, I excluded one child from the process. The youngster appeared to be about three years old, just big enough to start riding a tricycle.

'What about him?' the lab tech said, pointing to the child I had skipped.

'They have to be at least five,' I explained. The tech asked the mom for the child's age – the boy was six years old.

Intellectually, I understood the concept of stunting. But it was not until child after child passed me that its reality sank in. My best guess for every child's age was several years off. Sixteen-year-olds were prepubescent. Ten-year-olds looked as if they were five. Three-year-olds appeared too small to even walk. Malnutrition and infection had exacted an enormous toll on the populace that surrounded me.

It occurred to me that everyone I had met in Sierra Leone was shorter than I expected. One of my friends back home, whose family was from West Africa, towered above me. However, close to his ancestors' homeland, I was taller than almost everyone.

As the families passed through my group, I began to realize that the villagers were actually worse off than the neighboring refugees. While the camps were far from luxurious, they provided regular food and limited health care. In the village, the nutrition was far worse and the health access nonexistent.

The local dynamics highlighted a contrast well known in international health circles, between 'emergency' and 'development' situations. Donor funds are the basis of humanitarian aid, and people are much more willing to give in emergencies. Sponsors consider refugees to be a temporary problem: since their stay is finite, it is conceivable to supply food, health care, shelter, water, sanitation, and all of life's other necessities.

In contrast, donors are much more reluctant to provide the same things to people living on their own land, because such assistance seems unsustainable. The sad truth was that changing all of the Sierra Leonean countryside into a refugee camp would have been an improvement for the vast majority.

Our team proceeded to sample the waiting throng over the next few hours, before finally coming to our last two subjects: a muscular man with dark sunglasses and a frail boy in a tattered shirt. The other group had the healthy-looking man, who had a cocky air that made me think he must be the son of the chieftain. He dwarfed the little child, who was much smaller than his six years could justify.

When the two lab technicians pulled out their needles to draw our final samples, color drained from the macho man's face. His big eyes clenched and he arched backward in his chair, which caused the surrounding crowd to laugh loudly in amusement.

In contrast, while the needle was still in his tiny vein, the little six-year-old giggled at his muscular compatriot's contorted face. I had to smile along with the fearless child. Size is not so important after all, I realized – in most things, it is the stature of spirit that matters.

11

THE LASSA WARD

8

FIRST FEE

July 6, 2003

The next morning, I caught the WHO team before they headed back to Freetown. They were happy with their mission – all the expedition groups had successfully obtained their needed samples, and no one had repeated the mistake of drawing blood from an active Lassa case. 'Take care of yourself,' Trent told me as he got into his car to depart.

'I'll do my best,' I told him.

'Out here,' he said through the open window, 'it seems you never know what's going to happen.' He smiled and shook his head. Then they were off, leaving only a trail of dust behind them.

Back at the guesthouse, Sela served a typical Sierra Leonean lunch of rice covered with orange palm oil, mixed with an unidentifiable meat. I ate alone, already missing the company of Trent and the rest of his crew. I had not seen the other Merlin expats for a couple of days.

Dr Nassan was staying in a room next to the Lassa

outreach office while his new girlfriend, a white South African woman who worked for one of the other NGOs, visited. Lila, who could be a bit of a gossip, had mentioned that the pediatrician began his yearlong position with Merlin shortly after a difficult divorce – Dr Nassan's ex-wife had quickly remarried, taking their teenage daughter with her.

The midwife herself frequently spent several consecutive days teaching traditional birth attendants (TBAs) to deliver babies, and I assumed she was out on an excursion to one of the surrounding villages. Mohammad, I knew, was still on his work-related trip to Freetown.

I listened to the radio, which reported that the Economic Community of West African States (ECOWAS), a group headed by Nigeria that had previously intervened in Sierra Leone, was offering to send three thousand soldiers to Liberia if it could get US backing. In response, Taylor had also announced that he would resign from office, although there was considerable doubt as to his willingness to follow through. It seemed likely that the fighting would continue until he truly renounced power.

As I finished my meal, Sela mentioned that Lila had not eaten any food for the last couple of days. 'She be wanting any?' the cook asked me.

'She's here?' I replied, surprised that I had not seen my next-door neighbor around the guesthouse, despite my last few days of long hours with the WHO team.

I went to Lila's room to investigate the odd behavior, but there was no response when I knocked at her flimsy door. I pounded louder. 'Go away,' a faint voice said.

'Lila,' I replied, concerned. 'It's me . . . Ross. Are you all right?'

'Sleep' came the answer through the thin wooden barrier.

'Lila. Lila,' I said, 'what's going on?' But she didn't respond. 'I'm coming in,' I finally said, overcome with worry as I pushed open the unlocked door. The stuffy room was hot from the midday heat, with the lights off and a drape across the window. I could barely make out Lila, curled on her bed in the fetal position under several sheets and a jacket. 'Are you okay?' I asked her.

'Another blanket,' Lila moaned. Despite her objections, I pulled the cloth away from the window. My Moroccan colleague lay in a pool of sweat, which outlined her pale body like chalk from a murder scene. 'Put it back,' she protested weakly. 'I'm so cold.'

I touched Lila's forehead with the back of my hand – she was burning. With verbal and physical prodding, I soon learned that my neighbor had been sick for the last few days, alternating between intense periods of fever and then chills. It was the classic pattern for malaria.

Ancient slave traders had named Sierra Leone the 'White Man's Grave' because so many foreigners had died from the parasitic infection along its coast, and the country continued to have a high incidence of the disease. But I had never personally seen anyone with the illness. The U.S. government had eradicated the parasite from its borders shortly after the end of World War II by using DDT to kill the malaria vector (the *Anopheles* mosquito).

Malaria spreads from person to person when an infected

mosquito injects its contaminated saliva into the human bloodstream. There, the parasites multiply in the red blood cells, later bursting the cells upon emergence to produce the characteristic chills. When a new mosquito subsequently bites the infected person, the cycle then continues.

'Lila,' I said, 'I think you have malaria.'

'Don't worry about it,' the Moroccan midwife muttered, delirious with fever.

'You could die,' I continued, my own heart starting to race.

'Well,' she replied weakly, 'you know how it is.'

With that, I became even more worried. Lila clearly was not thinking straight – I couldn't imagine her giving up on her own life so easily if she were in her right mind. It looked as if my neighbor was developing cerebral malaria, one of the most dreaded effects of the disease. *Plasmodium falciparum,* the most dangerous of the four malaria species, evades the immune system by making infected red blood cells sticky, which causes the cells to clump in the capillaries of the circulatory system. If severe, the growing masses can block blood flow to the brain, thus leading to seizure and death in about half of those with full-blown symptoms.

Lila needed help quickly. One of my medication handbooks identified the necessary intervention: intravenous quinine. An ancient Peruvian treatment from the bark of the cinchona tree, the drug was the best option given the urgency of my neighbor's symptoms and the regional malaria resistance to other drugs.

I shook the ill midwife. 'Is there medicine anywhere?' I demanded, trying to retain a physician's calm demeanor despite my lack of experience. I had no idea how to procure the necessary supplies.

'Just let me die,' Lila feverishly rambled. 'It's the easiest thing to do,' she mumbled before passing out completely.

I quickly searched the guesthouse for provisions. There was no quinine, but I found a malaria testing kit in one of the cabinets. Lila didn't even flinch when I pricked her finger. Two lines immediately appeared as her blood dripped onto the disposable plastic strip, thus confirming my initial diagnosis.

I ran outside to find Chris, the security guard, but he was also clueless about the location of any medication. Then I remembered the pediatric ward at the hospital and had Chris quickly radio the car. Lila was clearly sick and my natural instinct, as a medical student, was to find a real doctor to save her – I hoped desperately that Dr Nassan would be there to help.

When I finally arrived at the pediatric ward, I found a large group of women and children huddled outside the facility, their bodies spilling out onto the dirt avenue like pilgrims awaiting a messiah. Wading through the waiting masses, I made my way to the dim doorway.

As I entered, soft cries and moans washed over me. Children filled an enormous room, with cots packed closely together. A narrow passageway snaked between the beds, each cot crowded with three or four emaciated kids, their IV lines intertwined overhead. For a few moments I stood aghast at this manifestation of the worst child mortality rate in the world: one third of the children in the country died before their fifth birthday.

I eventually recognized Dr Nassan across the ward. The professor sat at a small table, with a nurse at his side, surrounded by the throng of humanity. He wore a necktie and a long white coat, a beacon of hope amid a nation's worth of disease.

I hesitated for a second. Nothing seemed more important or more urgent than the needs of the children lying around me. Thoughts of Lila, though, and the malaria coursing through her body pushed me forward. As I approached, Dr Nassan's gentle face looked up from an emaciated boy he was examining. 'Ross,' he said, surprised. 'So nice of you to visit.'

'Lila,' I told him immediately, 'she's sick and I think she might have cerebral malaria.' I quickly summarized the midwife's condition, feeling a cathartic release as I delivered the story to more experienced ears. 'She doesn't look good,' I finished, relieved that I had passed on the responsibility for my neighbor's life into Dr Nassan's accepting hands.

Dr Nassan nodded his head – we both knew the dangers of Lila's condition. 'We had better get her some IV quinine quick,' the professor said. Dr. Nassan had his nurse prepare a bottle of the medication. The fluid sloshed in a glass bottle as the driver rushed me back to the guesthouse, where I found my neighbor still shivering in her room. After threading an IV needle into a vein in her arm, I hung the lifesaving drip on a loose nail in the wall.

Dr Nassan had predicted that the quinine would have a swift impact, but I was still amazed at how quickly Lila's fever broke. It seemed almost as if I could see the medication diffuse through her body, slaughtering parasites along the way. Only an hour later, I was overjoyed to find that, although she was still weak, the midwife's temperature had returned to normal.

I spent the rest of the day neurotically chasing mosquitoes around my room. Lila knocked on my door just before night-fall. She caught me perched on top of my desk while stalking a particularly clever one. Despite a ringing in her ears, the main side effect of quinine, my neighbor felt much better.

'I brought you some Moroccan peanuts,' she told me with a rare smile. 'They can be your first medical fee.'

9

DR. CONTEH

July 7, 2003

'These pills are horrible,' Lila complained over breakfast the next morning as she stared down at a small bag containing her white quinine tablets.

'Horrible?' I asked.

'I can't take this constant ringing,' she said. Part of me thought it was probably a good sign that the midwife had returned to her customary, albeit sullen, temperament.

'Cerebral malaria,' I pointed out to her in my best doctor's voice, 'is clearly much worse.'

'. . . they're more bitter than potato leaves,' she continued.

'Just take them,' I said as sternly as I could, trying to ignore the fact that Lila was almost a decade older than I was. Since the medication killed the parasite only in its bloodstream stage, she had to take the drug for the next several days to clear the infection completely. Untrusting, I personally watched her take the next dose, her face puckered up like a child forced to eat green vegetables.

After finishing the meal, I jotted down a few notes for my slowly growing paper, then decided to get a little exercise and walk through town to check in with Dr Conteh at the Lassa ward. I thought hiking on foot might give me a better feel for the town.

Chris opened the front gate for me with a confused look on his face. 'No problem to drive you,' he assured me as he undid the padlock.

'It's okay, I'll walk,' I said.

'But we have a car,' Chris responded, pointing at the vehicle to make sure I understood the point. 'You can ride.' He clearly could think of no reason to walk when the luxury of a car was available.

I insisted on declining the ride and exited through the steel doors to walk along the ravine-engraved road, where I had witnessed such violence upon arrival. Women did chores in their yards: some washed laundry with ribbed boards while others cleaned away the daily rubbish.

As I passed, the women looked up to smile and wave. They wore sarongs wrapped around their waists, many with nothing but the shimmering sunlight to clothe their exposed breasts. The more modest among them used lacy, secondhand lingerie for bikini tops, making them look something like an exotic spread from a Victoria's Secret catalogue. Although there was nothing actively sexual about the display, as I waved back I still had to suppress a juvenile grin at the liberal exhibition, so different from the customs of my own culture.

Children stopped playing in the dirt, or with an unlucky

chicken, to run up and give me high fives. 'White man! White man!' they yelled excitedly, pointing at me with big pearly smiles, as if informing me of my complexion. I was a celebrity by the very color of my skin. I could have been no more popular if I had just won the World Series.

I made my way on the main road into town, careful to avoid honking motorcycles and the occasional car. Stalls sold all of the local necessities, and I chuckled to myself when I found the clothing section. I had observed people throughout the country wearing the old Western outfits, but seen together, the clothes seemed to compose the strangest vintage shop in the world. Platforms of jungle saplings, lashed together, supported piles of recycled American attire, Pepsi T-shirts and Disney shorts, heaped high upon their wooden platforms.

At least half of the pedestrians had something perched on their heads, and packs of bundled wood jogged past. An old man, carrying a shovel, almost speared me, the spade portion lying on his curly locks with the handle extending far out front. Little kids precariously balanced jugs of water. One girl carried her book bag on her braided head, ignoring the use of the more conventional straps.

A platter of raw cow hooves was the most unappetizing item that graced anyone's head. Another salesgirl carried peanuts piled high on a steel plate, and I imagined what would happen if she tripped. I saw one woman balancing four crates of eggs and was sure she was just showing off.

A sewer ran next to the road to accompany me for most of the trip. Between dodging vehicles, I watched its color change from milk gray to neon green. Kids played nearby, their happy faces reflecting in the swirling waste while unknowingly confirming that environmental degradation is more than just a first-world issue.

A few undersized mutts with open sores limped across the road. Tsetse flies swarmed greedily around them. One canine lay unmoving in the street, its legs sprawled out as if it had been hit by a car. Only when a child ran up and mercilessly kicked it, causing the hound to yelp, did I realize that the dog was still alive.

Pairs of men sauntered down the dirt road, happily talking amongst themselves while grasping each other's fingers. At first, I was surprised that homosexuality was so open in Kenema. That was not something I had expected. But it took me only a few minutes before I realized the masculine duos were not gay – holding hands just seemed to be a local custom between close friends of either sex.

In the middle of town, I came upon a group of yelling men. In the center, two combatants held each other with out-stretched arms, the other fists cocked high overhead. All heads turned to watch me as I passed, until the shorter contender connected with a hooking sucker punch. Although part of me wanted to watch the fight, I moved on quickly.

The former rebels still lounged at the front of the hospital, and I approached them apprehensively. I wondered at their odd choice for a hangout. Perhaps, I decided, the fighters had developed a predilection for trauma during their previous escapades.

'Sssssss . . . ssssss,' one hissed loudly as I neared their shiny motorcycles. I did my best to ignore him, keeping my eyes focused firmly on the ground.

'Sssssss . . . ssssss,' another one hissed. I kept going.

'Sssssss . . . ssssss,' a third one said, and I finally looked up to meet his gaze.

'Hello . . . friend,' the third man said with a big grin.

'Hello,' I said, not stopping. The former combatant turned to his associates, smiling, as if he had won a bet.

Inside the hospital compound, the Lassa ward was hard to miss during the daytime, with signs covering its high fence to warn the unsuspecting against coming too close. When I got to the front entrance, the guard stationed there retrieved the head nurse for me. She was a motherly woman several years older than I was.

'What's na you name?' I asked the nurse when she stepped outside. I was trying to practice the few words of Krio I had learned. She responded with a strange jumble of sounds that I found impossible to articulate.

After I made several butchered attempts, she finally said, 'Call me Amie,' her mouth lighting up with a healthy smile.

'Thanks,' I said. 'I'm Ross.'

'Oss?' the nurse replied.

'Ross,' I corrected.

'Rue's?' she asked.

'Not quite.'

'How about I call you Momo? It be a common Mende

name,' Amie said, referring to the local tribal dialect around Kenema.

After briefly wondering if the nurse was making fun of me, I decided it was best not to argue. 'Sure, that'll work just as well,' I finally replied. I had worked in medicine long enough to know that nurses make either wonderful allies or horrible enemies. I was on a different continent now, but I doubted that that general rule had changed.

Crossing my hands again across my chest, I entered the dark ward for the second time. Amie led me to Dr Conteh's 'office,' where the physician sat behind two flimsy walls that had been hammered together to form a small room in the corner of the entrance alcove. Stacks of medication dominated the tiny space, barely leaving room for a desk, two chairs, and a dusty bookshelf.

On the desk, a computer keyboard and monitor peeked out from under a pair of dusty scrubs. 'A new gift from the UNHCR,' Dr Conteh told me, noticing my gaze as he turned around to greet me. 'I guess they wanted to thank me for taking care of so many refugees,' he continued, referring to the UN refugee body.

'That's nice of them,' I said.

'Actually, I might ask you to show me a few things on it, later,' the physician said.

'I'd be happy to,' I answered.

Dr Conteh motioned me to sit, and his eyes, slightly opaque with the dull shimmer of cataracts, calmly evaluated me for a few moments. After taking a notepad and pen out of my pocket, I held the pair uselessly. I had traveled across half the globe to talk with the distinguished physician but suddenly had no idea where to begin.

'I'm not exactly sure what goes on out here in the ward,' I said, almost to myself, 'but I'd like to learn as much as I can about Lassa.'

Dr Conteh said nothing, but his gentle smile encouraged me to continue. 'It seems amazing that this place even exists,' I said. 'How did it ever start?'

'Well,' my new teacher said with a contemplative rub of his chin, 'some stories are told best from the beginning.'

In 1969, Dr Conteh explained, a mysterious outbreak in Lassa, Nigeria, first brought the hemorrhagic fever (later named after that town) to international attention. After numerous villagers unexpectedly became sick with high fevers and copious bleeding, three American nuns, working as nurses at a missionary hospital in the area, began to develop the same symptoms. Two of them eventually died in the far outpost before parishioners evacuated the third back to the States.

In the US, researchers eventually isolated a hitherto unknown virus in the sole surviving missionary. But despite standard precautions, the illness spread to two lab technicians who had worked on the blood samples. Both became gravely ill, one later dying. After the ensuing panic settled, the government limited all further studies of the clearly dangerous Lassa virus to BSL-4 facilities.

Although rural conditions hampered field investigations,

antibody studies, similar to the one performed by the recent WHO team, eventually demonstrated the presence of the virus in multiple areas across West Africa. In 1976 a CDC team identified southern Sierra Leone as a major disease center and began a research program there, doing much of the seminal work on Lassa diagnosis and treatment.

Dr Conteh was raised in one of the many small villages that dot the Sierra Leonean landscape. His father was village chief, but his mother died when he was only a teenager. This forced him to move to Freetown, where he started working to support his siblings. While there, he attended school, finding a love for biology and chemistry, and eventually becoming a teacher.

In 1968 Dr Conteh left teaching for medical school in more technically advanced Nigeria. After graduating, he worked there for several years before returning to his home-land in 1979. Still a young physician, he joined CDC researchers at the Nixon Memorial Hospital in Segbwema, the same facility Trent had earlier visited. There, he worked with the noted American Lassa researcher Joe McCormick, who headed the CDC team. The following year, Dr Conteh was promoted to medical director.

When the Sierra Leonean conflict began to flare years later, in 1991, the hostilities drove out the CDC and destroyed the hospital. 'I was so shocked. I had no idea what to do,' Dr Conteh told me. 'There was no food or even a safe place to sleep.' Hungry and in a state of perpetual danger, he wandered for months around the countryside. 'At some point,' he said, 'I even became numb to the fear.'

The rootless physician eventually arrived in Kenema, without any specific plan. In between the bouts of fighting, he ended up caring for his poor countrymen. Soon a small clinic built up around him. Many times, he thought about fleeing the country – he was, after all, a physician with marketable skills, and he had friends abroad. 'But how could I leave?' Dr Conteh asked softly, almost to himself. 'My people, they had no one to help them.'

At one point, Dr Conteh identified a patient with Lassa and mentioned his finding to a passing aid worker. Suddenly, everyone suspected of having the deadly disease was being referred to the Sierra Leonean physician, all other experts familiar with the illness having left the country.

The new Lassa ward eventually grew out of donated supplies and borrowed funds, but there was never a discussion as to who should run it. Besides Dr Conteh and the few nurses he trained, no one else could be convinced even to come close to the contagious patients.

In the rural African ward, there was no way to use space suits or fancy ventilation systems. The staff prevented transmission to health care workers by adapting barrier techniques to the local situation and using bleach solutions to clean the simple equipment. It was far from ideal, but the best anyone could manage.

During Dr Conteh's subsequent tenure in the ward, Kenema had been overrun by hostile forces several times. Movements of rebels, refugees, and governmental forces, along with the nearby diamond mines and the Liberian border, provided continual sources of conflict. The nearby hospital buildings had been looted and burned, but Dr Conteh and his ward had survived surprisingly well. Ironically, the fear everyone had of the disease had ensured the safety of the medical team and the facilities.

Dr Conteh had married and raised six children in Kenema. Over the last nine years, Merlin had helped support his work while the ward received an increasing number of displaced persons due to the deterioration of the neighboring Liberian conflict.

Dr Conteh told me he felt a particular bond with the refugees, since his eldest son was now stranded somewhere in Monrovia. The doctor and his wife housed several families at any one time in their modest home. The aged physician told me he had few complaints, although he hoped the Liberian conflict would one day end and he could enjoy some time alone with his wife in a less crowded residence. 'Always so much noise,' he said with a rueful smile.

For most of the past decade, Dr Conteh explained, the Lassa ward, like the disease itself, had been an overlooked stepchild. Despite a steady stream of cases in the region, the illness garnered little international attention until a refugee, UN soldier, or expatriate fell ill.

'They will forget about us again soon enough,' Dr Conteh told me, referring to the recent interest that stemmed from the possible spread of the disease into the refugee camps. Lassa affected the most dispossessed people in one of the poorest countries in the world – it was an affliction of the unfortunate amidst the deprived. Only a faithful few battled against it.

10

THE LASSA WARD

July 8, 2003

Blood-soaked sheets covered the unmoving body as wails pierced the thin walls of the Lassa ward from outside. The boy had died early that morning, just before I arrived. Like a punctured water balloon, his body had spouted fluid out of every orifice and former IV site. The child had drowned as the liquid quickly filled his lungs.

Our guard didn't allow the boy's family to enter. Their precious youngster had transformed into a mass of infectious waste, potentially spreading disease to anyone who touched him. His parents would never again caress his face or hold his small body on their laps. There could be no good-bye kisses.

The father brought a shawl to the front gate and handed me the clean white cloth. I took it in hands that faintly trembled from the sight I had just witnessed, one that undeniably made me want to flee far from that place. We exchanged no words, and I again closed the door. What was there to say? Through a crack in the fence, I could see the man's wife standing next to him, paired rivulets streaming down her cheeks – there was no end to them.

Amie put on the ward's personal protective equipment (PPE) while showing me how as she went: boots, gown, mask, eyewear, cap, and gloves. Dressed like a surgeon marooned in a distant land, she proceeded to prepare the boy's body for burial.

While Amie cleaned, I talked with Zuri, the ward's local lab technician/nurse. With his friendly face framed by a carefully trimmed goatee, he was seemingly unaffected by the morning's tragedy. The two of us talked of small things, the weather and what he did around the ward, not wanting to dwell on the spilled misfortune in the other room.

'Your centrifuge looks a bit hazardous,' I remarked at one point.

'Always fixing it,' Zuri agreed. 'And one time, it blow up big-time,' he casually related.

'Really,' I said, 'what happened?'

'Blood be all over the lab,' Zuri continued, gesturing around the ward. Trent's and my previous concerns had evidently been well founded.

'Were you all right?' I asked him, surprised by his nonchalant attitude.

'No problem,' Zuri said with a ready grin. 'I be immune.' The lab tech had been one of the patients fortunate enough to survive the disease while in the ward, before he started working there. Zuri told me Amie's husband had also been a patient at the same time. But the man had not survived Lassa's devastating effects – Dr Conteh had subsequently given

Amie a job at the ward in order to help the distraught widow provide for her three young children.

Luckily for Zuri, however, like chicken pox and measles, the viral infection presumably could not strike him again.

'That's nice,' I said. 'But don't forget about HIV.'

Dr Conteh came out of his office after Amie finished cleaning, and the four of us gathered to see patients. The grandfatherly physician explained that they put on PPEs whenever they touched people or their secretions, and wore masks and eyewear when patients had a cough or excreted copious fluids. These precautions were slight compared with those used in the West — I knew that British doctors had treated a recent Lassa patient through a sealed plastic bubble.

Small rooms lined the back hall, and I nervously squeezed into the first one with the rest of the group. However, Zuri impeded my efforts to hide in the back by graciously ushering me to the 'best spot' in the front, next to Dr Conteh. This made me even more anxious since, especially after what I had seen that morning, I wanted to stay as far away as possible from anyone infected with Lassa.

Three patients lay in separate beds, the fourth one empty. I concentrated on not brushing up alongside anything while silently hoping my vigilance would guard me against infection. A woman wearing a plastic smock and gloves was wiping one boy's head. 'Does she have Lassa too?' I distractedly asked Dr Conteh.

'Actually . . . no,' he said.

I gave him a questioning look.

'When I first set up the ward, I tried to maintain a complete quarantine, without any visitors,' Dr Conteh explained. 'However, after a few people died, there were no more villagers to treat.'

'Why?' I asked.

'Here in Sierra Leone, family members normally provide most of the nursing care, even in the hospital,' he said. 'So when we kept the other people out, everyone assumed that there was no one in the ward to care for the patients – that they were just being left to die.'

'People stopped coming then?' I said.

'Yes,' Dr Conteh answered, 'and no one would believe me when I tried to tell them otherwise. After a few weeks with an empty ward, I had to compromise: one family member per patient.'

'We train them,' Amie said, referring to the PPEs. Zuri nodded his head proudly in agreement.

'It hasn't completely eliminated the secondary transmission to the family members,' Dr Conteh said, 'but it seems better than having an empty ward.'

The four of us made our rounds, discussing each person's treatment from bedside to bedside. Zuri carried a sheet of paper that functioned as the patient chart, and wrote down Dr Conteh's treatment directions. It was a routine surprisingly familiar to me – the same thing occurs every morning in hospitals across America.

The patients slept or sat quietly in their rooms. They were fairly representative of Sierra Leonean society, with almost no one above the age of fifty. One 'older' man in his late forties, named Steven, had such strong tremors that he could no longer walk. He lay in bed profusely apologizing for not being able to sit up.

Dr Conteh pointed out to me the Lassa patient that the WHO team had discovered in the refugee camp a few days earlier. I was happy to see that the woman had done well after treatment with ribavirin, the main therapy for Lassa infection. Like many of the patients in the ward, she was simply waiting to finish her ten-day IV course.

Dr Conteh asked the woman a few questions, utilizing another patient as an interpreter. The Liberians spoke American Krio, a language I could barely distinguish from the English Krio of Sierra Leone. But the two groups could barely communicate. 'They be sounding so silly,' Zuri told me, with unnoticed irony. 'Like babies.'

The ward had only twenty beds and was spacious compared to the pediatric ward, but far from optimal given the circumstances. As we stopped by each patient, I found myself thinking that over a fifth of those I saw would die within the dark recesses. But, still new to the Lassa ward, I was unable to guess who would live and who would die.

After we finished rounds, the four of us gathered in the entrance alcove to see a little girl named Amber. Our new patient lay on the examination bed with a massively swollen face distorting her youthful features. She didn't look well, and my heart couldn't help but go out to her.

Half of Amber's head had been shaved, and an IV stuck out just above her left ear, evidently a common place to find venous access in Africa. Instead of inserting the IVs in arms, as in the States, the local nurses liked to put them in a vein that runs across the temple. I was unsure why we avoided this practice in the States but guessed it probably related to a desire to avoid shaving patients' heads, which can look somewhat scary.

After getting a quick history from Amber's mother, Dr Conteh pronounced the daughter a classic case of Lassa fever, who needed immediate therapy. The IV in the child's scalp had stopped working, so Amie trimmed the hair on the other side of Amber's head to put in a new one, giving the little girl a Mohawk. Amber lay listless throughout the procedure, her lack of crying betraying the severity of her illness. She did not even whimper when the needle pierced her skin.

While Amie and Zuri got the IV flowing into the little girl, Dr Conteh explained to me the Lassa staging system he had developed. The incubation period starts first, a three- to twenty-one-day delay between exposure to the virus and the first onset of symptoms. People are not contagious at this stage, but the infected individuals can get to almost anywhere in the world before becoming sick. A handful of cases had made it to other continents over the last few decades.

Next, Dr Conteh divided symptomatic Lassa progression into four stages. Stage one begins insidiously with fever, weakness, and general malaise, the kind of nonspecific complaints that anyone feels when coming down with a cold. After a few days, the patient transitions into stage two: this consists of flulike symptoms, such as a sore throat, headache, and cough. Chest pain, vomiting, diarrhea, red eyes, or body aches can also occur.

Stage three starts around seven days after the first onset of symptoms, and it is a critical moment in Lassa progression. During this phase, the virus begins to overwhelm its host and causes fluid leakage throughout the body, frequently with swelling around the face and neck. In many, fluid pools in the lungs and impedes breathing.

Clotting problems also lead to bleeding from the nose, mouth, vagina, rectum, and old puncture sites. Neurologic sequelae, a shaking in the mouth and hands, can also lead to intractable seizures. At this point, people either recover or continue into the final symptoms of stage four. The respiratory dysfunction can quickly be fatal, as in the case of the boy who had died that morning. In others, bleeding in the brain leads to coma, or fluid losses everywhere cause shock. The end result is the same.

'The key,' Dr Conteh said, placing a gentle hand on my shoulder and looking me directly in the eye to make sure I understood his point, 'is initiating antiviral therapy before the onset of stage three.' I nodded my head slowly to assure him I got the point.

'If we give ribavirin early enough, most patients do well,' my new teacher said. 'However, once stage three takes hold, it is frequently too late, even with the treatment.' Ribavirin is the only medication known to mitigate the deadly symptoms of Lassa. The drug interferes with the virus's ability to replicate itself, but it does little good if the viral levels have already grown too high.

'And how about her,' I said, motioning to our new patient, Amber, as Amie and Zuri finished with the IV. 'How will she do?' I asked.

'In her case, it is hard to say,' Dr Conteh said. 'She is just now starting to cross that deadly line.' I looked over the child's body, which I could now see betrayed the start of stage three, with Lassa's characteristic swelling.

The pediatric ward had admitted Amber still in stage two, the ideal time to start antiviral therapy. But Lassa is a great impersonator of other illness in its first two stages: malaria, typhoid, and other tropical infections often present with the same clinical picture.

The local laboratory was of little help during this critical time for accurate diagnosis and treatment. Malaria studies were useless, as almost all local children had some amount of malaria parasites in their blood. Testing for Lassa was ideal, but the local facilities lacked the equipment needed to perform that sophisticated analysis.

This was why the pediatric staff had initially started Amber on malaria therapy, a reasonable choice given the circumstances. Ribavirin was in limited supply and had significant side effects – the ward could not give it to everyone with a fever.

After Amber had failed to respond to the antimalarial and antibiotic medications used in the pediatric ward, her Lassa diagnosis became more certain. 'Make sure you give her the first dose of ribavirin right away,' Dr Conteh told Amie and

Zuri. With precious time already lost due to the poor diagnostic facilities, every minute mattered. Amber would continue to get the medication three times a day for the next ten days, if she made it that long.

As I walked to the guesthouse at the end of the day, I kept thinking of the blood that had slowly oozed from beneath the white sheet that covered the boy who had died that morning. When I got back, I started to wash my hands, then decided in favor of a shower. As the unheated water poured down around me, I wondered if coming to Kenema was a brave idea or just insanely stupid. But, at that point, there was little I could do to change my fate. Only time would tell if I had made a dreadful mistake.

11

TECHNICAL DIFFICULTIES

July 9, 2003

I munched on Sela's breakfast the next morning while listening intently to the news. President Bush continued his strident demands for Taylor's resignation but still refused to commit US troops. The Nigerian president, Olusegun Obasanjo, was helpfully offering Taylor safe exile in his country if the Liberian dictator promised to stay out of politics. But Taylor seemed little interested in letting go of the remnants of his past empire.

The broadcaster eventually announced a satellite connection to an aid worker in the middle of the fighting. 'The rebels are surrounding the city,' the besieged man reported over the radio. Despite the crackling connection, the humanitarian worker's thick Eastern European accent was easy to recognize: Mikhail, the Merlin logistician, had somehow gotten himself to Monrovia.

'We need food and medicine urgently,' Mikhail reported over the static, and suddenly the nearby war seemed even closer, with someone I knew and had just heard now at its epicenter. I pictured the big 'problem fixer' stuck in the middle of the continued fighting, with bullets and shells randomly flying, as I had heard spoken of on the radio. Silently, I wished him the best of luck.

When I later arrived at the ward, I found Amie working alongside Bryan, the third and final nurse brave enough to work in the Lassa ward. I had not previously met the nurse, who was in his early twenties.

'Do you also work somewhere else?' I asked him.

'In the maternity and peds wards,' Bryan self-assuredly answered.

'Oh,' I said, 'do all of you do that?'

'No, only I have a degree. I be trained in Freetown.' Unlike the rest of the staff, whom Dr Conteh had unofficially educated, Bryan had received a year of formal nursing training.

The two nurses were readying the morning doses of ribavirin, which a Chinese pharmaceutical company had donated. They broke the tops off the glass containers and drew the clear fluid into a syringe. I was amazed at the quantity – a starting dose for one adult was almost twenty vials.

Afterward, Zuri, Amie, Bryan, and I joined Dr Conteh for rounds. We started with Steven, the patient who had previously been unable to stand, and were able to get him to balance himself under his own power. The man was shaky but held the bed with the beginnings of hope on his face.

'That's a big improvement,' I said.

'Most do well once they make it through the acute infection,' Dr Conteh told me.

Next, we entered Amber's room to find her swollen face unchanged from the day before. The child sat in bed with her IV sticking out of her now bald head – someone had shaved off her Mohawk, transforming her appearance from hard rocker to angry monk.

Amber shared a room with a boy called Little Sia, who slept quietly on the adjacent cot, his angelic face crowned with a few wisps of curly hair. The patients' two mothers chatted quietly between our intermittent questions. Dr Conteh tried to board the more definite cases together, to limit possible spread among patients. Little Sia was also receiving treatment for Lassa infection.

Amber stared at me accusingly throughout the whole process. 'She no like you,' Amie said to me with a chuckle as we turned to leave. I smiled back at the young girl, happy that the child had not precipitously worsened. I had witnessed only one death in the ward so far, but it already seemed like more than enough.

'She put the IV in,' I replied slyly, pointing at Amie. But Amber didn't seem to buy it.

A bit later, Dr Conteh brought me into the office to look at his new computer. 'Actually, the man who delivered it gave me some directions,' the physician said, 'but I am still unsure about a few things.'

'Where should we begin?' I asked.

'First,' he said with innocent delight, 'I would like to know how to turn it on.'

I soon learned that neither Dr Conteh nor any of his staff had ever used a computer. The Lassa physician was one of the most educated men in Sierra Leone, yet the most he knew about computers was from looking over the shoulder of the occasional aid worker. Ten years of fighting meant the region had missed the computer revolution – it knew only the kind with guns and bullets.

Amie, Zuri, and Bryan gathered around as well as I undraped the computer. They all remained silent, tilting their heads from side to side, as if at an art exhibit. I pointed out the On button, which, I realized, was neither labeled as On nor particularly easy to identify in the plastic molding.

'What is this "Windows"?' Dr Conteh asked me as the group watched the multicolored logo appear on the screen.

'It's how the computer works,' I explained, and my new colleagues nodded their heads in false accord. 'It's . . . the way we look into the computer,' I continued, only to confuse the matter further.

Whoever had assumed that the ward would be able to use the local fortune worth of equipment had done little assessment, but they had made some minor efforts. Beneath the Word icon were the words 'For Letters & Reports' and under Excel, 'For Math & Statistics.' That this was far from adequate was apparent when I explained how to use the mouse. I named it five times, between giggles, before everyone was clear.

'It's an *arrata*,' Bryan proudly explained to his colleagues when he understood, using the Krio term for rat and pointing to the picture on his LASSA CONTROL T-shirt.

'See, here is the tail,' I said, indicating where the electric cord joined the computer. They found that comment particularly amusing.

I had the group practice moving the arrow around the screen to rewarding *ooh*s and *aah*s, but clicking proved slightly more problematic. I had never before appreciated the dexterity needed to keep the mouse from moving when flexing the index finger.

Although the single click was eventually manageable, the double click became the bane of my teaching experience. I cringed as my maladroit students, in misguided attempts to open documents, cast icons about the screen and inadvertently renamed them. It was amazing that these same people effortlessly threaded needles into the tiny veins of children. In life, there are few substitutes for experience.

The arrival of a new patient eventually interrupted our technology session. We left the computer to gather in the front alcove, where a UNAMSIL medic, from the Nepalese division, accompanied one of his privates.

The UN had troops from Pakistan, Nepal, Bangladesh, Nigeria, and Zambia stationed all around the country. The exact reason for this seemingly random assortment of countries eluded me. But, as was becoming increasingly clear from the ongoing Liberian situation, it was certain that the armed forces were not going to be American.

Dr Conteh explained to me that over the last year the UNAMSIL forces had referred more than thirty Lassa cases to the ward, and I was surprised that the soldiers had such a significant exposure to rats or ill locals. 'Most come from the Zambian camp,' the Lassa physician told me quietly. The hygienic standards there were rumored to be poor, and this had presumably led to rat infestation.

Since the Nepalese private did not speak English, the accompanying medic translated his story for us. Four days prior, the private had been sleeping in his tent when he awoke to feel something crawling on his shoulder. He had grabbed what turned out to be a rat and flung it across the room, but not before the rodent managed to bite him. The soldier dutifully showed us the healing puncture wounds on his hand.

The private had not thought much of the incident until he developed a fever and a cough three days later. The soldier had then talked to the medic of his battalion, who discussed the issue up the chain of command and eventually decided to bring the man to the Lassa ward.

Our new patient's temperature was slightly elevated, but he did not look particularly sick. We had him describe the rat for us and lamented that he had thrown away the carcass. It sounded like a *Mastomys natalensis* (the species that transmits Lassa), but it was impossible to be sure. After some debate, Dr Conteh decided to err on the side of safety and start the soldier on a prophylactic regimen of ribavirin.

We put the unfortunate man in his own room, away from the other patients. His case was a reminder that, in Sierra

Leone, Liberia, and elsewhere, the majority of wartime deaths are not directly from bullets or bombs, but from the spread of infectious disease that historically accompanies a society's breakdown.

The medic eventually excused himself after promising to return with the private's personal belongings later in the evening, and the Lassa ward staff left the private sitting on a dilapidated bed. As I headed home for the night, I wondered at the experience that the man was going to have in the run-down ward while he received his ten days of treatment. I could only selfishly hope that the same would never happen to me.

12

GOD'S WILL

July 10, 2003

'Do you see?' Dr Conteh softly asked me while pulling down Amber's lower eyelid with a gloved hand.

'See what?' I said.

'Come closer,' he insisted, and I inched forward, trying to suppress an urge to run from the contagious girl. Although Little Sia's condition was unchanged overnight, the boy's roommate had not fared as well. The swelling in Amber's face had slightly lessened, but her respirations had noticeably increased.

'Do you see?' Dr Conteh asked again.

At his direction, I peered down at the inner surface of the girl's eyelid, realizing that it lacked the normal pink shine of healthy tissue. Instead, it was dull gray.

'She's anemic?' I finally said.

'Yes!' Dr Conteh agreed excitedly. She had the character-istic sign. Too few red blood cells circulated in Amber's blood, thus reducing her ability to transport oxygen from her lungs to her tissues. Mild anemia causes fatigue, but if the problem becomes severe enough, the body can literally suffocate despite adequate oxygen in the air.

'That's the ribavirin,' Dr Conteh said confidently. 'We see the complication quite frequently.' The drug was known to destroy red blood cells, but Dr Conteh had noted much more severe side effects than those cited in the Western literature. This was likely because his patients started treatment with low baseline levels of red blood cells and required the high dose of ribavirin used for Lassa treatment.

Continuous malaria infection, along with a diet lacking in iron, meant that over half of the country's general population met WHO criteria for chronic anemia. The ribavirin treatment pushed some of these unfortunates over the edge, an emergency that only a blood transfusion could alleviate.

Zuri pricked Amber's finger for a hematocrit – it was the sole diagnostic lab test available in the Lassa ward. A marker of anemia severity, the test measured the percentage of the blood that was made up by red blood cells. Zuri transferred Amber's blood into a thin glass tube before retreating to his lab to spin the cells down with the centrifuge.

'Actually, during electricity outages,' Dr Conteh told me, 'Zuri swings the tubes around his head with a special rope, to get the same effect.'

'Really?' I said.

'They probably do not do that in America,' the Lassa physician said.

'No,' I agreed, 'they definitely don't.'

When the red blood cells had settled, Zuri showed us the

vial in the light. We compared the crimson clump of cells at the bottom to the layer of clear fluid on top. In a healthy American, red cells make up more than 40 percent of the tube. Dr Conteh said he was happy with anything over 18 percent, a level that would have been cause for severe concern back in the States. Amber's result was 13 percent –

it was so low that I had to look twice before I believed it.

While Zuri went to arrange a blood transfusion for Amber, Dr Conteh, Bryan, Amie, and I continued rounds. A soft melody emanated from one of the far rooms, and we passed through its door to find Steven gently singing. 'He is feeling much better,' Dr Conteh told me, 'even walking around without assistance.'

Our patient was evidently looking forward to going back 'home' to the refugee camp. Dr Conteh told Steven he could possibly leave in a few days, and a sheepish grin crept across the man's face – not even the dark walls of the ward could put a damper on it.

Next door, our small group found the UNAMSIL private alone in his room. Families normally provided most of the necessities in the hospital, but no one had come to bring the soldier any supplies. 'He have no food and be sleeping in his uniform,' Amie reported sternly.

Our patient smiled politely at us, nodding his head without comprehension as we discussed his predicament. Medically, he was doing fine and was without complaint – it looked as if his accommodations were going to be the only thing causing him discomfort.

'Chop-chop?' Amie said to the soldier, motioning with her

hand to her mouth. The man continued to nod his head in polite affirmation.

'What are you saying?' I asked the nurse.

'It be how we tell children to eat,' she told me politely.

'Oh,' I said.

'He no be talking English good,' she continued, 'so we need to speak simple to him.' I doubted that baby Krio was going to breach the language gap but lacked the heart to criticize Amie's altruistic attempts.

'Yes. He does need some food,' Dr Conteh agreed.

'And some pajamas too,' Bryan insisted.

A half-hour after finishing rounds, Bryan returned with some clothes for our abandoned soldier. The nurse proudly showed us his purchase, holding up a bright pair of blue and yellow terry-cloth shorts, along with a matching top.

I had to bite back a smile when the private, having changed out of army fatigues, marched around the ward for us in his eighties beach attire. 'They look very nice,' I told Bryan, who beamed with pleasure at the compliment. 'We can even wash them in bleach,' I continued, 'and use them for the next patient.'

'Do you see?' Dr Conteh uttered at my remark, as if he had stumbled upon a great epiphany. 'Do you see how the white man thinks!' Bryan and my fascinated mentor stared at me, nodding their heads in affirmative synchrony while I smiled back, unsure if they thought I was stingy or clever. How did the white man think?

Although I hadn't considered it earlier, it was definitely possible that I thought differently from the people I had met in Sierra Leone – we did come from wildly disparate cultures and environments. However, I hadn't really noticed any overt antagonism regarding my pale skin. West Africa was one of the few places in the world where America was still held in high regard, despite our recent Iraqi invasion. Our two countries had a shared history, having both been British colonies, and there seemed to be few feelings of past injury.

Racial tension, a frequent undercurrent at home, appeared to be mostly absent. In many ways, the atmosphere actually felt much freer than the race relations in the States. Black people far outnumbered white, so now I was the minority, and there were not the same generations of injustice lurking silently in the background. When the Sierra Leoneans felt oppressed, as they often did from their leaders or the many fighting groups, it came from people who looked like they did, not people who looked like me.

Although I didn't really understand the meaning of Dr Conteh's words, it surprised me mostly because of how infrequently the very forthright West Africans had commented on my ethnic background. It could have been a constant source of discussion, but the local people seemed more interested in my culture than in my race.

The people I had met in West Africa all had stories of distant relatives who had gone to America and become immensely wealthy, regardless of their skin color. Whether or not any particular story was true, it was an aspiration that almost all of them shared. Ironically, our greatest export, the

American dream, lived on, if anything even stronger abroad than it was at home. It transcended race, even a far continent away.

The ward was quiet for a while after that, with Dr Conteh away at a hospital meeting and Bryan off at work in the pediatric ward. I was trying to work on my research paper using the new computer when Zuri entered the office later that afternoon. 'Sia be seizing,' the tech casually reported.

'What?' I said.

'Little Sia be seizing,' he repeated.

'Now?' I said.

Zuri nodded his head.

I jumped to my feet and ran the few feet through the alcove to Sia's bedside. Amie was there, watching the two-year-old boy shake from head to toe, with only the whites of his eyes showing, as if possessed. Sia's mom stood next to him, crying fearfully, as Amber and her mother looked on from the adjacent bed.

Dr Conteh was away, so I waited for Amie and Zuri to respond. Although short seizures are not really emergencies, if they last too long they can lead to permanent disability and even death. But the nurses' lack of reaction became increasingly worrying. Were they waiting for me to do something? I had made it clear that I was just a medical student doing research. Although I had helped out with Lila's malaria episode, my place was normally squeezed into the far back corner of the room during any hospital emergency.

'So . . .' I said, trying to spur them into action. 'What do you guys think?' My heart pounded in my chest, and the adrenaline now coursing through my veins had wiped my mind blank. I tried to remember the standard medical regimens used for seizures in the States, but I had been doing public health work for the last year – my past clinical work suddenly seemed a vague memory.

'Well, sometimes we give Valium,' Zuri said. 'Should I get some?'

'Uh . . . yeah . . . that's right,' I said, feeling stupid that I had not remembered the name of the drug. 'Go get some,' I continued, with growing anxiety at Little Sia's continued seizure.

Zuri leisurely strolled out of the room.

'What other emergency supplies do you have?' I asked Amie urgently.

'Like what?' she said.

'Like where's the Ambu bag?' I asked, her blank face forcing me to continue. 'You know, the bag valve mask,' I added. 'The thing you put over someone's face to breathe for them.' It was a simple device: a rubber bag that, when squeezed, forced air into the lungs through a mask placed over the face. In the States, every hospital room had at least one in case someone stopped breathing.

'We do not be having anything like that,' Amie said sternly, looking at me as if I were from another planet, and I began to think I was. A few terse questions proved that the Lassa ward had no real emergency equipment or drugs.

I tried to think of what to do. What was causing the

seizure? I quickly put on PPEs and felt Little Sia's forehead. The child did not seem to have a fever, the most obvious reason. Too little sugar in his blood was another possibility. I had Amie give the boy a dose of sugar water through his IV, since it could do little harm.

We waited, but the nutrient had no effect. Little Sia had been seizing for at least five minutes by the time Zuri returned with the Valium. I was worried that the seizures were beginning to last long enough to prevent oxygenation of his young brain.

'Okay, let's give the Valium,' I said hesitantly.

'How much?' Zuri asked, handing me the vial.

'How much do you normally give?' I replied, while flipping hurriedly through a small medication handbook that I always kept on me. I wished Dr Conteh was around – the nurses' vague answers inspired little confidence, and I clearly was in over my head.

Valium's main side effect, decreased respiration, would be fatal if we administered too much of the medication. The ward lacked any equipment for artificial ventilation, making breathing cessation immediately lethal. Even old-fashioned mouth-to-mouth was not feasible, since Little Sia was highly infectious with Lassa.

'Two milligrams?' I said, before timidly drawing the liquid into the syringe. No one objected, and I slowly injected it into Sia's IV.

I waited, for what felt like an eon, with his mother standing next to me quietly sobbing. Mesmerized by his quivering body, I wondered if I had given too much. Would I cause the small child to stop breathing and die right before my very eyes? Or was I not being aggressive enough, and was I watching him develop more and more brain damage in front of me? Just as I was about to give some more Valium, the seizures abruptly stopped.

I waited with held breath to see if he would keep breathing. The child lay with his abdomen rapidly pumping up and down in his oversized bed, and I let out a deep sigh of relief. However, Little Sia was still unresponsive. I was worried and had Amie and Zuri go over his chart with me. It seemed the child was getting all that the Lassa ward had to offer from its limited armamentarium.

'I wish we had oxygen,' I said aloud to myself. I had taken the ubiquitous machines for granted in the US, where we use them reflexively on so many patients that it doesn't even seem like part of therapy.

'I think we have one of those,' Zuri said to me. I looked at him questioningly, and then around the pitiable room. Half-broken screens dangled from the windows, and tattered bed nets hung from the ceiling. What was he talking about? The nurse might as well have told me that he had one of the bulky tanks in his pocket.

Nonetheless, I followed Zuri to the storage room, where he rummaged through equipment in the back. Under a dust-covered box, the nurse revealed a portable oxygen concentrator, the same kind used in the States when people need oxygen at home.

'Zuri, you're a genius!' I said. 'Where on earth did you get that?'

'Donated,' Zuri told me with a big grin. He offered no further explanation.

The three of us plugged in the machine, and I showed them how to turn it on, finding its low purring hum more beautiful than Mozart. Stashed in a back compartment there were even rolls of the requisite plastic tubing for connecting it to the patient. I couldn't imagine how the device had gotten all the way to Kenema.

Zuri and Amie were both excited to learn about our 'new' piece of equipment. Although it only had two buttons, one to turn it on and one to set the speed, they had not known what to do with it previously. I gave them an impromptu lecture on the 'amazing' properties of the gas, feeling like a professor on a seventies science show. 'Nothing could live without oxygen,' I told them sagely.

With some creative handiwork, we were able to set up the machine for Sia. The pronged cannula barely fit in his petite nose, and the plastic tubing stretched awkwardly across the ward, but at least we were helping his breathing.

After that, there was little else to do. I found it hard to relax and went into Sia's room repeatedly to stand quietly next to his mother. By her side, I watched the undulations of the child's smooth belly.

Dr Conteh eventually returned from his meeting to find me still at Sia's bedside. I immediately felt relieved that the ward was back under his capable supervision and that I could return to my safe role as a medical student. But it still took my mentor's simple words to finally pull me away. 'Not in our hands anymore,' he said with the wisdom of many years. 'Now God will have his way.'

13

FRIDAY RITUALS

July 11, 2003

I passed through the hospital gates the next morning and approached about twenty people mingling outside the Lassa ward's fence. 'What's going on?' I asked the guard after weaving through those gathered. He simply opened the door and pointed inside, through the inner courtyard, to an unfamiliar woman who lay convulsing on the front examination table.

The woman's thrashing body lay uncovered. Short, hurried breaths brought foam to her mouth, which dribbled past a piece of rubber jammed between clenched teeth. As I approached, I could make out unseeing eyes that stared, with a reptilian glow, at the ceiling.

Amie and Zuri both hunched over an arm, trying to start an IV line, while one of the patient's relatives, who I guessed was a sister, paced worriedly in the corner. Yards of tubing stretched awkwardly across the hall, and the oxygen machine purred away gently. A brief moment of parental pride swept over me as I realized that the nurses had set up the equipment without my assistance.

'She just get here,' Amie told me.

'Is Dr Conteh around?' I asked hopefully.

She shook her head. 'But we send someone for him.'

I was uncertain what was causing our new patient's vicious symptoms, but such notable jaundice was uncharacteristic of Lassa. My mind was working better than it had the day before – I was not quite so shocked to be left alone. Amie informed me that our new patient had been sick for the last week. At first, the woman's family had brought her to a traditional healer. After she had worsened, the concerned relatives transported her to the Lassa ward.

Amie and Zuri worked quickly, a noted difference from their earlier performance. I had spent much of the night thinking about seizures and also felt more confident about what to do. But I still breathed a sigh of relief when Dr Conteh arrived, just as we finished putting in the IV line and readying to give the first dose of Valium.

I gave Dr Conteh a quick summary of the situation, and he agreed with my plan. However, just as Amie connected a syringe to the IV port to push the first dose of medication, the woman had a massive paroxysm. She thrust back her head and heels into the bed as her chest and pelvis arched violently upward. Her glistening body held the contorted posture for several seconds before gently unwinding, her muscles relaxing one by one.

After a single deep breath, our patient exhaled in a long, slow sigh. We waited awkwardly, but there were no more respirations to follow. In the States, the commotion of CPR and other emergency procedures would have filled the room. But we had no bag valve mask or other resuscitation equipment. There was nothing we could do.

As the four of us stood immobile with the oxygen machine quietly humming in the background, it slowly dawned on me that the woman before us was dead. I had worked in medicine for several years but had never experienced anything similar. In the States, doctors in essence 'choose' when people die, and only after a protracted attempt at resuscitation. In Sierra Leone, nature made that final decision instead. After my high-tech training, it felt like more than just poor medical care – it seemed almost sacrilegious.

I turned off the oxygen machine and closed the eyelids of the woman, whose name I did not know. The 'sister' trembled in the corner. Her eyes darted from each of us to the motionless body and back again. Then, after a few moments of hesitation, the distraught relative ran out the Lassa gate to be embraced by the waiting crowd. We stood in a half-circle around the dead corpse as their waves of mourning washed over us.

Zuri and Amie methodically put on their PPEs and started to wrap the body. Dr Conteh and I discussed the possible causes of death, an exercise that proved unsatisfactory. 'Some kind of hepatitis?' I suggested.

'Maybe,' he replied. 'Or could be yellow fever.' Without autopsy or diagnostic facilities, the cause of death remained completely speculative. The whole situation rested uneasily with me, particularly because it would have been so easy to find out in the States. Just dropping it like that would have never happened at home, but Dr Conteh, with a shrug of his shoulders, was ready to move on without further questions.

How can we just leave it? I wondered. I could see no way to improve without knowing such answers. But perhaps it was my expectations that were most unreasonable. Did it really matter? The ward obviously lacked many resources. Not knowing what had killed the woman lying before us was arguably not the first priority.

However, the nameless death continued to haunt me afterward. It was like reading to the end of a book but finding the last few pages ripped out. I had had a glimpse of the woman's life through the eyes of her relatives and had witnessed her passing with my own. Priests and shamans hold no monopoly on the explanation of death – the medical profession has its own. But the Lassa ward denied me the comforts of those traditional answers. In my mind, it felt as if the woman's body were destined to go unburied.

On the subsequent rounds, our group found Amber breathing better after her blood transfusion and Little Sia sleeping quietly next to his mother. Amie had gotten the private some food, and it appeared that all the other patients were also doing fairly well.

Still reeling from the morning commotion, I did not notice until after rounds that Dr Conteh and his staff were not dressed in their normal Western clothes. Instead, Amie wore a colorful African dress of handspun, woven fabric. Dr Conteh, Zuri, and Bryan all had shirts and pants made from similar, brightly hued materials, along with matching caps.

'How come everyone looks so nice?' I asked.

'Muslims dress up on Fridays,' Zuri explained, clearly pleased with my compliment.

'*Everyone* be dressing up on Fridays,' Bryan corrected him.

'He be Christian,' Amie explained, referring to Bryan.

'Sure, but Muslims *have* to dress up,' Zuri continued.

Zuri and Bryan debated who had to do what in each religion, and I was surprised at their candidness. In Sierra Leone, unlike other conflict regions, faith had played little part in the violence. The combatants had not aligned themselves with any particular sect. In a show of religious egalitarianism, Muslims and Christians had made no distinction as they killed and tortured their fellow believers and nonbelievers.

Zuri even had a Christian brother, whom missionaries had converted several years earlier. Locally, the two religions seemed to be more similar than different, in part due to an intermingling with tribal animism.

'The big difference,' Zuri told me, 'is that Muslims get *four* wives and Christians only *one*.' Zuri clearly felt that polygamy was a big selling point for his religion. He already had one wife and was looking for a second, a likely reason, I decided, for the tech's frequent forays around town with the ambulance.

'Not a big deal,' Bryan replied, shrugging his shoulders. But he was clearly a little envious.

'Don't worry,' I told the Christian nurse, trying to cheer him up a bit. 'In America you can only have one wife, even if you're Muslim.'

Zuri looked at me in complete disbelief. 'Only one?' he asked dubiously.

'Yes,' I told him with a smile. 'In America, one woman is a lot of work . . . Two would be impossible.'

A new patient arrived later in the day, but Dr Conteh quickly decided the man probably just had a mild case of malaria. While examining our visitor with Zuri and Bryan, I noticed particularly distinctive scars on the man's chest. I had seen the inch-long horizontal marks on the cheekbones and torsos of many local men, including both Zuri and Bryan, but hadn't inquired about their significance.

'What are those things?' I asked the two of them when we finished, but the nurses seemed not to hear me. Zuri went to get something from the storage room, and Bryan became intent on untangling some IV tubing. 'Bryan, what are they?' I persisted.

'Better not to ask,' he told me.

'What, is it a secret?' I continued sarcastically.

Bryan suddenly remembered a task in another room.

Zuri didn't seem to be around for the rest of the day, so I kept pestering Bryan to explain the marks to me, but each time he found work somewhere else in the ward. As it neared sunset, I made a joke about the scars being from overly excited women, and the nurse finally turned to me, exasperated. 'I cannot tell to you,' he whispered. 'They be very secret.'

I looked at him in disbelief and Bryan sighed, pointing to the fine scars over his cheekbones. 'You and I both be males, but these make me more,' he continued in a low voice. 'They make me "male-plus."' The nurse looked surreptitiously around the room. 'I should not tell you even that . . . We cannot talk about it.'

Realizing I had put Bryan in an awkward position, I dropped the subject, only a little hurt when I realized that I could not be 'male-plus' myself. I didn't know the exact significance of his particular marks, but I was familiar enough with African scarring practices to know they bore some kind of tribal significance. Belatedly, I recalled having read somewhere that such scars had added to the ethnic violence in some regions by visibly marking – and thus identifying – people from disparate tribes.

From what Bryan had hinted, I assumed that the marks also had some kind of sexual significance. This made sense, since most of the scarring rituals were related to a child's coming-of-age, at which point he or she was considered to be an adult. However, if the fine marks that Zuri and Bryan so proudly bore were all that they had received to become men, then they had gotten a much better deal than the women.

One of the reasons I had not initially connected the scars with African coming-of-age rituals was that most publicity focuses on the parallel rites for females. In West Africa, initiation into womanhood frequently includes genital mutilation, normally around the ages of four to eight. Girls are held down by their older female relatives while, normally without even basic anesthesia, a midwife removes the clitoris with an unsterile razor, knife, or even machete.

After tissue removal, the girl is stitched up, and her legs are bound for weeks. Serious bleeding and infections can result, sometimes leading to death. Those who survive frequently have long-term gynecological and obstetric problems, including permanent sexual dysfunction. But for those who practice such rituals, this is thought to be one of its advantages. One of the 'beneficial' reasons cited by practitioners of female mutilation is that it reduces a woman's desire for sex and therefore her inclination for infidelity, thus preserving her family's honor.

A few NGOs were trying to change the practice but had found it surprisingly difficult to achieve. Health threats in this impoverished country included more than just overwhelming infections such as the unclear illness that had killed our jaundiced patient that morning. Many of the maladies stemmed from poor education and maladaptive customs.

As proudly as Bryan and Zuri wore their marks, the mothers and grandmothers of Sierra Leone stubbornly continued the practice of genital mutilation, concerned that their daughters would never become women and would forever be unsuitable for marriage without the horrendous scars. The caring relatives wanted the best for their progeny – they wanted them to be 'women-plus' as well.

14

A FOREIGN FUNERAL

July 12, 2003

The Lassa ambulance waited leisurely outside the ward while a gentle breeze blew over an adjacent group of patients. Children blinked rapidly under the light of the morning sun, their mothers chatting quietly amongst themselves. Steven hummed to himself a quiet ditty. The small gathering of former patients was going home, and their every action spoke of thanksgiving.

Amie and a young man whose body had barely outgrown the awkwardness of adolescence handed out tattered pamphlets to those assembled. The nurse rubbed her assistant's curly hair with an affectionate hand when I arrived. 'This be Ossay,' she said to me. 'He be my patient before.'

'Really? And he still made it?' I said, trying to make a joke.

'No,' Ossay replied in all seriousness, 'Amie be a very good nurse.'

Amie and I laughed. 'Well, I stand corrected then,' I said.

'Ossay be in the ward for too many weeks, when just a

chillin,' Amie told me. 'And now he be in charge of the outreach team,' she finished proudly.

'After I survive Lassa,' the young man said with overflowing enthusiasm, 'all I ever want to do is fight it.' I learned that Ossay's sister and parents had died in the war, but that had not prevented him from pursuing his dream of working for the Merlin Outreach Team.

The pamphlet that the pair was handing out had pictures, along with text in English, Krio, and Mende. The part I could read said:

Although you have recovered from Lassa Fever you remain infective for the next 2 months. This means that the Lassa virus is present in your body fluids and may be passed on to anyone who comes in contact with your blood, urine, stools, vomit or semen. In order to reduce transmission of the disease, you must:

- *Use latrines. Do not urinate or defecate outside or in the bush.*
- *Spillages of blood, urine, stool, vomit or semen must be cleaned up immediately using blue soap.*
- *Use blue soap or any other chlorine soap for washing and laundry purposes.*
- *Do not share food with other people. Have a separate bowl for yourself.*
- *If any family member or close friend becomes fevered, they must be brought to a health center for examination and a health worker informed that Lassa Fever is a possibility.*

An outreach team will visit you at your home to check on your progress and ensure other members of your family and household remain healthy.

Ossay continued the pamphlet distribution while Dr Conteh began rounds with Amie, Zuri, and me. But before we got very far, the ward's guard interrupted us to report that the medical director of the hospital, who had been sick for several weeks, had just died.

My three colleagues paused to shake their heads somberly. 'Was he young?' I asked.

'No,' Dr. Conteh replied sadly, 'almost fifty.'

After witnessing several deaths over the last few days, in addition to the many sick children, I was surprised at everyone's reaction. It contrasted with the normal businesslike attitude regarding death and illness in the ward. Up until then, my colleagues' responses to such overwhelming circumstances had been quite guarded, as if having witnessed so much suffering made them impervious to its further effects.

But now I could see by the cracks in their normally stoic expressions that I had gotten it all wrong. Their faces were clearly filled with grief and, as the group discussed the director's life, I began to understand why. Years of work had drawn an invisible barrier between the caregivers and their patients, something perhaps necessary to allow the workers to function despite the heavy burden of constant loss. But the director's death allowed a glimpse into their deeper souls – he had been both a colleague and a friend.

★ ★ ★

Our group took a break from rounds to gather in the dirt courtyard outside the Lassa ward, along with workers from other parts of the hospital. The medical director had worked and died in the adjacent building. Local culture required burial of the deceased before sunset, so people were hurriedly arranging transport for the body and its mourners.

Mohammad arrived shortly afterward with the Merlin car – the Egyptian obstetrician had returned from his trip to Freetown the night before. 'You should come to the funeral to pay Merlin's respects,' he told me before emphatically yelling at hospital workers to squeeze over in an adjacent vehicle.

'Really?' I said, not knowing the proper formalities.

'Of course, of course,' Mohammed said while physically pushing me toward the nearby car. 'You just listen to me. I will be there also, soon.' Following his lead, I jammed myself into the crowded car, apologizing as I crawled over laps to a mirage of space in the back.

After waiting a while in the rising heat, we finally started down a surprisingly smooth road to the director's neighboring village. The car weaved through motorcycles, trucks, and vans, careering around blind corners and plowing through jungle foliage.

Since I had traveled out to the villages several times with the WHO team, it now felt like an ordinary ride. Thus the demeanor of my local companions consequently surprised me as they tensely clung to the seats and roof while muttering anxious prayers. I smiled at my neighbors, and they laughed back nervously. We were more than a half-hour into our journey before it finally struck me: it was possibly the first car ride for some of them.

When we pulled up to the village, the locals silently pointed our car toward the deceased director's house. After getting out to stretch my legs, I heard a faint sound wafting over the hills, like sirens in the distance. The noise grew as we hiked up a winding path, following the villagers' guiding fingers.

As my group crested the hilltop, I looked down to find a house with around fifty people in front. '*Yaaaaaaaaaah!*' Yelling bansheelike cries, my previously calm female colleagues suddenly, as if a gun had gone off, hurtled themselves down the hill. I watched in disbelief as the women raced at breakneck speed, waving their hands high in the air like giant antennae. Two of the sprinters crumpled to the ground, rolling down with a trail of dust.

Welcoming wails surged up from the awaiting crowd as people abruptly dashed chaotically in every direction. The awaiting masses bounced off one another like a mad game of pool while screaming at the top of their lungs. Several people threw their bodies into the dirt and then jerked about as if seizing.

Men chased their female counterparts to capture them in massive bear hugs. The women squirmed within their grasps, hitting with ineffectual slaps before slowly submitting to the calming embraces. One big man ran about shouting until surrounded by his fellows – they restrained him from an angry fight, his enemy nowhere in sight.

After several minutes, the scene began to normalize. Like visiting dignitaries, the Kenema men and I calmly walked down. We shook hands and paid our respects to those gathered below. There were several folding chairs in a half-circle, and everyone encouraged me, as an honored foreigner, to have a seat.

People proceeded to talk quietly about the director's life and death. Despite the foreign jungle scenery, it felt like a normal stateside funeral. The mood was such a distinct change from the prior hysteria that I found it hard to regain my bearings. It was as if I had experienced some kind of hallucination, everyone suddenly screaming and then pretending nothing unusual had happened.

Being the clear outsider, I wondered what a 'normal' response to death really is. Why shouldn't people yell and run around at a funeral? There was surely nothing more starkly in contrast to my stoic midwestern upbringing, but in many ways the Sierra Leonean approach made more sense. These were emotions with which we could all identify.

Although I had been starting to believe I understood my new Sierra Leonean friends, what I had just witnessed truly revealed how foreign things really were. I found myself second-guessing all the other assumptions that I had made about the inhabitants of my new world. Did I really under-stand them at all, or was I just assuming a shared human experience? Were we, at heart, similar or nothing alike?

After thinking about it for a while, I started to convince

myself that I hadn't really witnessed such an odd spectacle. Maybe my mind was just exaggerating everything after the long drive. However, my doubts vanished when the second hospital vehicle arrived half an hour later. I sat calmly in my plastic chair as the fracas repeated itself around me, with bodies hurtling back and forth.

After it abated, Mohammad came down with the second group of men, gave his condolences, and joined me to sit in the adjacent chair. 'A little melodramatic, don't you think?' was all the obstetrician said.

Mohammad had brought with him several hefty bags of rice that he presented to the director's widow. He had been in Sierra Leone for two years and was well versed in the local customs. The growing cluster of men also donated to an increasing stack of money. Together, the food and cash made up a kind of community life-insurance payment to help the director's family survive the difficult times ahead.

While the crowd of mourners talked among themselves, other villagers passed by in the distant bush. Each one moaned loudly, to share viscerally his or her grief with the deceased's family. 'All types of crying do for burying' was a local saying – each person shared pain in his or her own way.

While we sat, Mohammad and I quietly discussed the probable cause of death, a morbid habit shared by many in the medical profession. 'It sounds like no one knows what he died from,' I said.

'He's been getting sicker for months, and a lot of doctors saw him,' Mohammad said.

'He kind of wasted away then,' I said.

'Yeah, and he had almost every kind of treatment,' Mohammad continued with a meaningful look.

'Right,' I said. Although we never said the word aloud, AIDS was on both of our minds. The director had traveled extensively, a known risk factor for contracting the illness.

HIV was a growing problem across Sierra Leone and the neighboring region. Although there were few reliable statistics, most experts thought about 7 percent of the population had the disease. This was slightly below the average for sub-Saharan Africa and not yet the sky-high rate seen in some areas, but a considerable burden nonetheless.

HIV was one of the biggest challenges for the country as it began the difficult transition out of war. However, the signs were already boding poorly. Conflict had left almost half of all soldiers infected with the disease. Yet less than a tenth of the local populace was even aware of how the virus spread.

The Sierra Leonean government had only recently begun to formulate an HIV/AIDS policy. There were neither condoms nor antiretroviral treatment available in the country, and testing was limited to a small facility in Freetown. Although each year of delay would increase the final catastrophe exponentially, it took time to muster the political will to address such a difficult problem.

Nations across the globe, including the US, had followed a similar pattern as their citizens died, much like the fated director. People ignored HIV at first, then blamed it on someone else: the foreigners, the homosexuals, the drug users, or the sinners. Finger-pointing invariably continued until it was too late – the virus was a disease not of one single group, but of the entire country.

III

ALONE

15

AN UNEXPECTED DELIVERY

July 26, 2003

'They are lucky I am a good Muslim, or I would strangle them all!' I heard Mohammad yell through our shared wall, as I readied for bed. From the questionably better quarters in the main guesthouse, where I had moved a few days earlier, I could easily make out the sounds of my new neighbor angrily throwing things around his adjacent residence.

Time had blurred the last few weeks as I worked each day under Dr Conteh's patient tutelage at the Lassa ward. Meanwhile, across the nearby border, the LURD forces had pushed into the heart of Monrovia, fighting their way into the capital. The humanitarian emergency and daily casualties there had continued to increase, with civilians suffering the brunt of the casualties.

Despite a greedy power struggle between the rebels and Taylor's forces, both combatant parties had surprisingly requested American assistance, an unusual move in modern civil war. But the US continued to resist the growing Liberian and global pressures to intervene.

My upset colleague, Mohammad, was a skilled obstetrician with deeply held religious convictions, who provided free equipment and training to a country with one of the highest maternal mortality rates in the world. During his stay in West Africa, the Egyptian had repaired over three hundred gynecologic fistulas, a horrific injury that occurs after unsupervised delivery, causing feces and urine to drip continuously out of the vagina. It is an almost unheard-of complication in the Western world.

Although distraught women had traveled even from neighboring countries to have Mohammad's life-altering operation, the surgeon had been having problems with the staff at the maternity ward since his arrival in Kenema. The workers there disliked my good neighbor's intrusion into their affairs. They wanted him to leave and had even threatened to strike to get him to do so.

The maternity personnel had been quite open about the crux of their displeasure: Mohammad was not charging his patients for his services. Medical care in Sierra Leone was theoretically free to its citizens, but a decade of fighting-induced separation from the Ministry of Health in Freetown had broken the system. The local staff in Kenema regularly charged their patients for medical treatment.

I had heard horrible stories of hospital workers refusing to get up from their chairs to see emergency cases unless a family member first supplied a stack of money. Mohammad was inadvertently challenging this status quo by providing his services for free. To the dismay of the staff at the maternity ward, the obstetrician's altruistic acts had driven down what they could charge as fees.

I pursued the commotion next door to find Mohammad shaking with anger. 'What happened?' I asked him.

'These people!' he yelled, kicking in frustration at clothing strewn across the floor. 'And that stupid CMO!'

It took me a few minutes to calm Mohammad enough to learn the cause of his latest outburst. Eventually, I was able to piece together the story. The obstetrician had evidently instructed his chief medical officer (CMO) to do an emergency cesarean section on a patient the day before. But when my neighbor recently returned to the maternity ward after finishing his evening prayers, he was appalled to find that the woman had still not gone to surgery.

'She has repeat eclamptic seizures despite maximal medication!' Mohammad said furiously. It was a true emergency for the expectant mother: the condition could end up killing both her and the unborn baby. Delivery was the sole cure – but this pregnant woman did not have enough money to pay for surgery, and the CMO was quite literally bargaining with her life.

After relaying the exasperating story, Mohammad grabbed his gear to return to the hospital for immediate surgery. Since it was the middle of the night, I offered to help, and my friend gratefully accepted. Only minutes later, we sped down the dark streets with a humid breeze blowing through the car windows, and I had only a few moments to think back to the last time I had worked in an operating room (OR).

It had been more than a year ago, when I was on an

obstetrics and gynecology service at a state-of-the-art facility in LA, a place where pampered Hollywood celebrities routinely deliver their children. New Age music wafted out of candle-covered speakers, and plastic balls, normally used for abdominal exercises in the gym but also a fad among the famous for use during labor, bounced haphazardly down the hospital halls. I had no doubt that the night ahead would be considerably different.

Mohammad and I marched through the doors of the maternity ward to find an open room containing about twenty beds. Several women lay next to their bundled newborns, while others looked ripe to deliver. Even from the doorway, I could pick out our sick patient. She lay unattended, slumped over in one of the far beds.

Three nurses sat gossiping at a table in the middle of the room. Although Mohammad had asked them to urgently prep the patient, nothing had happened. The obstetrician threw up his hands in anger. 'Does anyone care that this woman is going to die right here on this bed!' he yelled at them.

Mohammad and I ran to a beat-up gurney that sulked in one corner. After shoving it next to our patient's cot, the obstetrician jumped up on top of the two beds. Straddling the gravid woman, he picked her up by the waist and thrust her over to our shaky transport. Then we were off, rolling down the hall while hoping our patient would not seize again.

Slamming through the OR doors, our small procession scared up a cockroach. We followed its scurrying antennae down the long hall to a room with only an ancient surgical table teetering in its center. Long-deceased equipment occupied a sole corner of the near-barren room, and a forgotten poster on the wall listed the initial ten steps for war trauma. I could only imagine what the place had seen over the last decade of conflict.

Using an unconventional argument, Mohammad cajoled a trailing nurse into functioning as an anesthesiologist. 'We all know this patient may die on the table,' the obstetrician said. 'So do not worry . . . If she does, it will not be your fault.'

Mohammad quickly gave our ailing woman some medication through her IV and then put a tube down her throat. The obstetrician had a modified bag valve mask that the nurse started squeezing at regular intervals to breathe for the woman during the procedure. I manually set the IV by timing its drops with my watch, a skill I knew only from an old EMT class, as automated bedside machines had long since taken over that function in US hospitals.

While the nurse watched our patient, Mohammad and I changed into scrubs before draping on top plastic butcher aprons, an item absent from practice in the States. After washing our hands with a tired piece of soap, we held them in front of us to maintain their questionable sterility. We then dressed in gowns that frequent 'resterilization' in a local oven had imbued with a brown tinge.

I was happy to find that we had disposable surgical gloves, one of the items Mikhail had bought and I had earlier transported to Kenema. Throwaway caps, torn from repeat use, completed our tattered ensemble. We had no masks or eye protection but were ready to begin.

Given the fortuitous consistency of human anatomy, the act of surgery itself was almost normal in comparison to the setting. Mohammad used a scalpel to make a several-inch incision just across our patient's bikini line. Then the two of us dug through yellow lobs of fatty tissue underneath to arrive at the fascia, a pale white membrane.

We had no electrocautery to stop bleeding vessels, but Mohammad was experienced with the primitive conditions. He made a small cut, and we proceeded to separate the fascia from the twin rectus muscles (the long bands used during sit-ups) that ran underneath. Then I pulled the parallel muscles apart, exposing the translucent cellophanelike film of the peritoneum underneath.

Mohammad carefully incised this coating with a scalpel, exposing the bladder and uterus beneath. I had to jump a few times to keep bodily fluids from splashing on my unprotected face while Mohammad quickly cut above the bladder. This allowed me to push it downward with a retractor, a metallic shoehornlike device. We then had a better look at the uterus, a large gourd-shaped organ, which the obstetrician quickly cut at its base.

Suddenly, like an upside-down jack-in-the-box, the recognizable head of a baby popped into the surgical field. It surprised me – it always does, even though I know intellectually it's coming. A human face somehow seems almost shockingly recognizable amid the peculiar background of our inner anatomy.

I quickly used a small suction bulb to clear fluids from the baby's nose and mouth. Then, with a slight push on the mother's abdomen, the rest of the infant's body came out. After clamping and cutting the umbilical cord, I handed the baby boy to the nurse. The whole process had taken only about a minute since first incision. I sighed with relief when I heard the child cry.

Mohammad and I then proceeded to remove the placenta and sew up the uterus before closing the tissue layers in reverse order. Everything went smoothly, and eleven minutes later we sutured closed the outer skin without complication – both the baby and our new mother had made it through alive.

While Mohammad took care of some postoperative details, I took a walk outside. It was almost two in the morning, and relatives slept on the raised concrete sidewalk, no one stirring from fitful slumber. I thought about how similar everyone's insides are, regardless of the geography. After a simple cut through that first superficial layer of skin, color and cultural differences are so quickly left behind. To the trained eye, human anatomy is universal, as is human emotion.

Outwardly, of course, the differences between Sierra Leone and Los Angeles were too numerous to count. In the States, people think delivery is so safe as to make it almost akin to a fashion statement. Expecting parents choose from a seemingly endless menu of possible ways to bring a child into the world. 'Epidural or no epidural?' they might fret. 'Cesarean or vaginal?' It has become almost like deciding between Coca-Cola and Pepsi.

Of course, in California everyone wants it to be as 'natural' as possible. But I had just witnessed nature's true face: absolute fear in our expectant mother's eyes and the very real danger of death for her and her baby. In many ways, it is only because of modern medicine's many successes that Americans have the luxury to question each small detail. One out of every fifty pregnancies in Sierra Leone resulted in the mother's death – it was the highest maternal mortality in the world. There was nothing, or perhaps there was everything, natural about that.

I eventually passed under a familiar Ministry of Health sign that hung on a nearby wall, illuminated by the building's meager light. It was similar to ones I had seen displayed all over the hospital. The poster encouraged women to come to the maternity ward for childbirth, but I had never paid attention to the crude white paint brushed over a few of its words. I scratched off the covering with a disappointed shake of the head. 'Come to the hospital,' it read, 'for a safe *and free* delivery.'

I eventually wandered into the courtyard to gaze up at the countless twinkling stars overhead. How different things were in this distant country, I thought, and yet, how similar. Outwardly, everything seemed so foreign, so unlike anything I had ever experienced. But underneath that disturbing exterior dwelt causes that I recognized all too easily.

No matter where I go, the results of greed remain the same.

16

SCARCELY TALLER

July 27, 2003

Joyous music dove through my window from the building next door, and I woke to whoops and hollers. The tambourines and cymbals intermingled with soulful voices sounding like a marching band, a church choir, and a Mardi Gras party all rolled into one. From bed, I enjoyed the unexpected Sunday extravaganza and rubbed the sleep out of my eyes from the late night before. It was amazing how happy people could be amid so much misfortune.

Given the circumstances in Sierra Leone, I had expected the populace to be in an almost continual state of mourning. But in every war-torn town, stranded refugee camp, and downtrodden village, I found warm smiles and hearty laughs. The West African people were full of life despite having so little.

'You must repent!' a deep voice abruptly declared after a stop in the music, suddenly changing the tenor of the unseen gathering next door. An emphatic preacher proceeded to berate his unprotesting masses and declared that their suffering was of their own making. Such pain was a just penance for their misdeeds, he proclaimed. 'God is punishing you for your sins!'

The vehement words almost physically accosted me as I lay undressed in bed, shielded only by my thin bed net. It was not an idea unique to religion – I had heard the same sentiment, expressed more subtly, even in the ivory walls of higher education.

I could feel welling up in me a growing anger at the unseen preacher, and those like him. 'Let them sing! Let them dance!' I found myself wanting to howl back into that faceless void. With so many lives afflicted by unthinkable violence and disease, blaming the victims added only insult to injury.

As I later walked along my habitual route to the Lassa ward, the preacher's voice echoed in my thoughts. I could picture his righteous admonitions reflecting off the faces of the many locals I now recognized. What unique sin, I wondered, had these people committed?

Due to my late night, I arrived at the ward later than normal, and Dr Conteh had already finished his rounds. He sat in his office talking with Ossay, the outreach coordinator I had previously met.

'What's up, guys?' I said upon entering.

Ossay got up and excitedly shook my hand. 'We plan the health care training,' he replied. 'Will you come? I would be so happy to show you!'

'When is it?' I asked.

'Tomorrow, in Kono,' Ossay continued. 'We head out this afternoon.'

In addition to visiting the villages, the outreach team also gave occasional seminars at the primary care units (PCUs) that provided most of the little health care available in Sierra Leone. The team taught how to diagnose a Lassa case and refer it to the Lassa ward, as well as how to prevent the spread of the virus to health care workers.

After several weeks with Dr Conteh, I was beginning to feel comfortable with the basic treatment of a typical Lassa case. My research was also supposed to cover the public health components of Lassa management, including how to control the virus on a larger scale using outreach programs and hospital education. The upcoming training seminar was exactly the kind of experience I needed to be able to address those topics further.

'It would be great to join you,' I told Ossay, delighted at the invite. The young outreach coordinator beamed at the prospect, but I noticed Dr Conteh's normally tranquil face develop an odd expression.

'Actually,' the physician said, 'it would be better if you stayed here at the ward.'

'Oh,' I muttered, surprised by my mentor's words. 'Okay then,' I mumbled. I hid my disappointment better than Ossay's clearly dejected face, but I was still hurt that Dr Conteh did not want me to go. I could not imagine any reason for the restriction – up to that point, the Lassa physician and the rest of his team had been overly accommodating.

I made some excuse to check on Little Sia and distracted myself in his room, where the child still remained with his mother. Amber, his former roommate, had successfully completed therapy and left for home a week earlier. She had departed the same day as the Nepalese private, who had finished his uneventful stay without ever developing Lassa symptoms.

Dr Conteh found me later as I sulked in the supply room. 'I apologize for wanting you to stay here,' he said, correctly recognizing that I was upset. 'It is just that the ward could use your help.'

'Oh,' I said, surprised.

I was flattered, but also skeptical. I had done my best to help out as I learned about Lassa under Dr Conteh's dutiful tutelage, but the Sierra Leonean physician had run the place for over a decade without my presence. Certainly, my absence for a four-day trip was not going to make or break the care. I was supposed to leave in a month and felt I had to partition my time as best I could.

Reading my disbelief, Dr. Conteh slowly shifted his weight back and forth from one foot to another like an over-sized child, his hands deep within his pockets. 'It is just . . . Of course you are welcome . . . It would be nice if you could come with us . . .' he trailed off.

'What do you mean?' I asked, puzzled. 'You're going too?'

'Four days is just a long time to leave the nurses alone,' he finished. 'I thought you could look after the ward while I am gone.'

As Dr Conteh's words started to register, my questioning

stare began to melt, and its cold runoff pooled in my stomach. I could feel my heart beat progressively faster, the pounding in my chest unable to compensate for my increasingly clammy entrails. I had to suppress a nervous laugh – the look on Dr Conteh's face defied humor. 'You want me to stay without you?' I finally said in disbelief. 'But I'm only a med student!'

Dr Conteh smiled for a moment before putting his hand on my shoulder. 'And how many years of school have you finished?' he said gently. I just looked at him without an answer. We had already discussed the differences in my American medical training. After high school, I had completed four years of undergraduate, three years of medical school, and one year of a master's in public health. It was much more time than for physicians in West Africa.

'But that's really not the point,' I finally protested. In the U.S, I would not accept sole responsibility for patients for another four years or more. 'I'm not supposed to yet . . . It's just . . . I'm just not ready.'

However, no matter how I explained it, Dr Conteh patiently persisted. 'Things are different here,' he said with a meaningful gaze around the dilapidated ward, as if pointing out the obvious. The aging physician did not really want to go to Kono – the roads were horrible in the rainy season, and the travel hurt his back. But, even though it would briefly take him away from the ward, he thought that helping to train the hospital staff there would ultimately be doing the greatest good for the greatest number. In his mind, I could see, that was simply the end of the matter.

As it became apparent that I could not prevent my instructor's departure, my protests grew progressively weaker. A wave of fear gripped me for a second time, and I thought for a few minutes that I might actually throw up. My previous confidence about the workings of the ward evaporated. I felt completely unprepared.

Dr Conteh packed some last-minute items in his office while I pestered him with questions and madly drew out flow sheets of possible patient scenarios. For what sin was I now being punished? I wanted to repent my earlier self-assurance, to atone for hidden transgressions, to do anything to make him stay.

'But what if . . . you just can't . . . what do I . . .' I mumbled as the Lassa ward's sole physician walked toward the door.

Dr Conteh paused under the exit, turning to look at me one last time. 'No matter how low a cotton tree falls,' he said quietly, 'it is still taller than grass.' In shocked disbelief, I watched my mentor's retreating back as he passed through the outside gate.

I was all alone.

17

ALONE

July 28, 2003

After a fitful night, I arrived at the ward with the early sun. The tall gate appeared even more foreboding than normal, and I walked through its ominous door with an unrestrained shudder. Passing from the bright courtyard into the building, I was enveloped in darkness.

When my eyes finally adjusted, I recognized Amie perched on the front stool. 'Morning,' I said.

'Morning, Momo,' she replied.

Krio removed 'Good' from 'Good morning,' 'Good afternoon,' and 'Good evening.' The proper greeting was simply to state the time of day. I cynically found the custom appropriate that morning – it was as if we were withholding judgment.

'How did we do?' I asked.

'Tanks God,' the nurse answered.

'Everyone made it through the night?' I asked. The nurse nodded.

'Tanks God,' she said again.

I tried busying myself in Dr Conteh's office until Zuri eventually found me. 'Should we see the patients?' he asked.

'Now?' I said.

Zuri smiled back a big pearly grin.

'Fine,' I reluctantly responded, desperately wishing there was some way around it.

Amie, Zuri, and I started in one of the back rooms. I stood at the front of the group, in Dr Conteh's traditional place, and an adult woman sat on one of the cots, watching me expectantly. Zuri and Amie gathered behind me, waiting respectfully for me to speak. But, despite all my years of schooling, I couldn't think of where to begin.

'What's her story?' I finally said.

'Day nine of ribavirin,' Zuri answered. The woman needed only twenty-four more hours of Lassa treatment before we could declare her cured.

'Does she have any problems?' I continued hesitantly. Amie said something quickly in Mende. With a torrent of words, the woman gestured expressively to her belly, head, and arms.

'No,' Amie replied.

'All right,' I continued, not daring to ask what I had missed in translation, lest it lead to some problem I couldn't solve. 'So what do we normally do?'

'Give her one more day of ribavirin?' Zuri proposed cautiously.

'Well, then that's what we'll do,' I replied.

I went from room to room while Amie and Zuri followed with polite answers to my poorly thought-out questions. I feared making even the most minor decision, each an unwelcome opportunity to cause harm to those now solely in my care.

My gaze kept searching the ward, sure that at any moment a real doctor would appear. I could picture someone in a long white coat forcefully throwing me out the front gate while swearing about my stupidity. 'You're only a med student!' they might yell. 'What are you thinking?' But patient after patient went by, and I could only be saddened that no one was there to rescue me from the overwhelming responsibility.

We found Little Sia in his room, lying across a plastic apron on his mother's lap, with porridge dribbling down the side of his face. His devoted caregiver tried to scoop more gruel into his weak mouth, but he barely moved it. Although the child had finished his ribavirin treatment a week prior, he and his mother had remained a permanent fixture in the ward.

'I don't get it,' I said, acutely conscious of my new role. 'Isn't he supposed to be cured by now?'

'Not eating well,' Amie replied forthrightly.

'That's definitely true,' I agreed.

I looked over my small patient, diligently listening to his heart and lungs with my stethoscope. Everything seemed fine except that he was obviously very weak. 'Is anything else going on?' I asked.

'He have a rash,' Amie said, before instructing Sia's mother to turn the boy over.

His mother pulled down her son's pants, revealing an angry red swath. It extended over his groin and up his back, with flakes of broken skin impregnating his dirty diaper.

'Wow!' I said. 'When did that start? How come no one told me?'

Amie and Zuri stared back at me with blank expressions – I guess it was my job to know.

'What do you think it's from?' I asked, as much to myself as to the two nurses. It was so huge, I couldn't decide. I wished Dr Conteh was there to answer the question for me, feeling disturbed yet again by his absence.

'Lassa?' Zuri answered hesitantly.

'I don't know about that,' I said. The tech seemed to be trying to make the symptoms fit the diagnosis, instead of vice versa. There was sometimes a rash associated with Lassa, but it was normally only an incidental finding. Little Sia's skin problem appeared much more dramatic.

'Bad nutrition?' Amie suggested. 'He come first from the feeding center.' Zuri nodded his head sagely in agreement. That must be it, they concluded.

'Hmm,' I said, still unsure.

Having been trained in American hospitals and, except for the occasional textbook picture, never having seen severe childhood malnutrition before, I felt ill prepared to judge. But the rash looked a lot like a staphylococcus infection to me. 'Staph' is a bacterial organism that attacks skin damaged from less serious problems, such as Lassa or malnourishment. If it was such an infection, then it was one of the worst I had ever witnessed.

'What antibiotics is he on?' I asked.

'None. All done,' Zuri cheerfully replied. Little Sia had already finished a full course of ampicillin and gentamicin, the two standard drugs in the ward. But staph infections are notoriously hard to treat. The bacteria have enzymes that can break down most medications, thus predisposing the organisms to antibiotic resistance and necessitating special treatment.

'Do we have vancomycin or oxacillin?' I asked, naming a few of the drugs that might work. Amie looked skeptical, and a search of the supply room confirmed her hunch. They had been out of oxacillin for three months, the nurse informed me, displaying the sheet of paper where she kept track of the ward's supplies.

I was unsure what to do and felt wholly inadequate. Was the rash a staph infection or solely the result of poor nutrition? I felt a growing anger at Dr Conteh for having abandoned me without any assistance. The rash looked very serious, and I was sure the child before me could easily die because of my lack of knowledge. What could the physician have been thinking when he left?

Our small group finished rounds with Little Sia's limp body still hovering in the back of my mind. In comparison, the other patients were all fairly straightforward, most in various stages of recovery from Lassa. They needed only their standard dose of ribavirin with little input from me.

While Amie and Zuri were dispensing the daily medications, I returned to Sia's cramped room to stare further at his rash. I eyed his skin, wishing it could talk, but the lesion remained stubbornly speechless. The more I looked, the sicker the child appeared and the deeper his mother's trusting eyes dug into me and my own fears of inadequacy. I was essentially doing nothing to help him.

I felt so alone and wished desperately that there was a doctor in the ward to tell me what to do. Then it came to me that there was still a physician in the pediatric ward, along with an overabundance of malnourished children. Surely Dr Nassan would have some advice.

'I'll be back in a sec,' I told Amie, before leaving the Lassa compound and jogging through light rain to the pediatric ward. It was as crowded as ever when I arrived, and I found Dr Nassan in the back area used for the sickest patients.

The gentle professor stood in his white coat, looking down on a naked baby boy. In medicine, we develop an unusual love of crying children, since their howling means that they are unlikely to be critically ill, but this baby lay too quietly in a small wooden cot in the middle of the room. Even upon superficial inspection I could see that the tiny infant was panting rapidly, the spaces between his small ribs indenting with each breath.

'Dr Nassan,' I said, to waken him from his reverie.

'Ross,' he answered after looking up. 'Didn't see you there.' The professor's eyes wandered back to the minute patient before him. 'Have you seen NEC before?' he asked quietly.

'No,' I answered softly.

I had read about the disease, necrotizing enterocolitis, in which bacteria attack and sometimes ulcerate a premature infant's intestines, but had never seen it in person. 'They get a fair amount of it out here,' the pediatrician continued, shaking his head sadly. 'The child's mother fed him formula.'

Infant formula had been a problem in the third world since the 1970s, when large multinational companies launched a massive marketing campaign there. Advertisements displayed fat, healthy babies drinking from bottles, to convince the local women that formula was healthier than breast milk. The companies then flooded the markets with free samples to get the infants hooked on their artificial drinks.

In the third world, formula feeding not only greatly increased the likelihood that premature babies, who lack the specialized care they receive in the West, would develop NEC, but also caused massive disease and death in otherwise healthy infants. When the mothers ran out of the free samples, most were unable to afford any more. However, the women frequently had already stopped lactating and could no longer produce breast milk.

The recurrent result was that the mothers would dilute the remaining samples to make them last longer. This, in turn, caused slow starvation and electrolyte disorders in their newborns. The practice also gave the children an early exposure to drinking water contaminated with *E. coli* and other bacteria causing diarrheal infections, which are the leading killers of children in the developing world.

'See how rigid his abdomen is?' Dr Nassan said to me, pulling me back to the present. I pushed down gently on the taut, doughnut-sized belly. It barely budged.

'Not good,' I mumbled.

Treatment in the developed world for such severe NEC

was immediate surgery. Even then, the prognosis was poor. In Sierra Leone, the infant's illness was almost certainly fatal. Death permeated more than just the Lassa ward.

At least the infant will die in the hands of a real doctor, as opposed to my charges, I thought to myself. It was small consolation, but somehow comforted me. Dr Nassan was doing all that any physician in his situation could do.

'I have a two-year-old with a rash,' I said, pulling my gaze away from the doomed baby. Dr Nassan's face assumed a receptive expression universal to the practice of medicine. Like two connecting modems, we shared information about 'the case': history and then physical findings, just as I had been trained to do back home.

'Does it sound like malnutrition to you?' I asked the professor.

'You tell me,' he replied, before escorting me to the therapeutic feeding section of the ward, where he kept the most severely malnourished.

The pediatrician tenderly lifted a tiny boy up by the armpits. The child looked fragile enough to break, with wrinkled skin hanging loosely off a skeletal body to sag where his buttocks used to be. 'Classic marasmus,' Dr Nassan told me, naming the malnutrition syndrome associated with insufficient calorie intake.

Dr Nassan put the boy back down and gently pulled a girl, wide-eyed with fear, away from her mother. 'Kwashiorkor,' he noted, pointing at her puffy face and distended abdomen. The girl's desperate body had eaten away her abdominal muscles and swelled with retained fluid, the result of too little protein in the diet.

'Does it look like this?' he said, pointing to patches of shedding skin that faintly covered her body like flakes of paint.

'No,' I replied, 'it's much redder.' The girl's rash looked different from the angry one that covered Little Sia's back. 'You can come take a look if you want,' I continued, desperately hoping for the reassurance of an experienced eye.

'I'm sure you're doing a fine job,' Dr Nassan replied. 'If you don't mind, I think I'll leave that place to you.'

'Are you sure?' I pleaded.

'Sorry,' Dr Nassan said, 'I've never been in there, and I'm pretty sure I don't ever want to go.' Although the pediatrician occasionally referred Lassa patients to the ward, he was still very fearful of the highly contagious virus. I realized then that even the best of heroes have a weakness, a kryptonite that limits their powers to do good. It is, perhaps, the difference between superheroes and gods.

I looked at the malnourished girl's rash a little longer. It didn't look very similar to Little Sia's. 'I think my kid has a serious staph infection,' I finally said. 'But we seem to be out of oxacillin.'

'Yeah, we're out of it too,' Dr Nassan replied. I felt lost, never having heard anyone discuss what to do for staph infections without anti-staph medications. It was like knowing the correct answer for a test question but being given only the wrong answers from which to choose.

'Well,' I said, disillusioned, 'I guess I'll just give him what I have.'

'What? Ampicillin?' Dr Nassan said. 'You should try the market first.'

'The market?' I said, staring at the professor's unassuming face for a few moments without comprehension. I had seen the open aisles filled with mangoes, dried fish, and second-hand clothes, but the idea of finding an obscure antibiotic in the colorful stalls of the marketplace had never occurred to me.

'Yes. The market,' Dr Nassan assured me. 'We just bought some there for one of our own patients.'

'Really?'

'It's something like three dollars,' he said, before going on to explain that the families could sometimes scrape enough together to pay for needed drugs if the hospital was out.

Armed with this new knowledge, I hurried back to the ward, wondering at the world in which we live. A few dollars to save a child's life – the notion was sadly absurd.

18

TWENTY-FOUR HOURS

July 28, 2003 (continued)

Amie was sitting on her customary perch when I returned to the Lassa ward. She lacked the electronic monitors that nurses would use in the West, yet seemed to be somehow in touch with all of her charges. 'Zuri be off with the ambulance picking up a patient,' she informed me.

I marched past her to Little Sia's room. 'We're going to get him better,' I said determinedly.

The two nurses had been right – Little Sia was definitely malnourished. After visiting Dr Nassan, I could make out the characteristic signs that the professor had illustrated. However, the rash was much more dramatic than it would have been from starvation alone. Sia did have multiple breaks in the skin from malnutrition, but staph must have overgrown one of those underlying lesions.

With this new understanding, it was clear to me that Little Sia was in a descending spiral. His poor nutritional state aggravated his ongoing infection, which in turn sapped his energy to eat. Combined, they made the poor child grow ever weaker. I worried that he might readily die from the destructive mixture.

'At the peds ward, they said you can buy medications in the market,' I told Amie.

'Of course,' she said, looking at me as if I had just explained that the sun rises in the east.

'Can you send someone to see if they have any oxacillin?'

'Sure.'

'Can they afford it?' I asked, with difficulty. It seemed crazy that I was even discussing the cost of a simple medication that could easily save a young child's life and return him to vibrant health. I felt dirtied by even having to vocalize the underlying question: how much was Little Sia's life worth?

'Yes,' Amie said confidently.

'Good, send someone then,' I said. 'And while they're getting it, we need to put in an NG tube.' I outlined my plan to Amie. In addition to treating Little Sia with oxacillin, I also wanted to improve his nutritional status. This included putting a nasogastric (NG) tube down his nose and into his stomach, to feed the boy more aggressively.

Amie and I quickly gathered the supplies needed to insert the plastic tube. The nurse then proceeded to hold Sia's tiny shoulders down onto the cot, her gloved hands enveloping the child's fragile body. Sia squirmed only halfheartedly under her grasp, far too weak for my liking.

Since inserting an NG tube is a fairly simple procedure, nurses typically do it in the States, and I had initially been unpracticed at it upon arrival in Kenema. However, since

the ancillary staff had so little training at the Lassa ward, Dr
Conteh normally placed tubes himself, and he had demonstrated the proper technique to me on several occasions.

I was still angry at Dr Conteh for having left me alone
with all his ill patients, but momentarily grateful that the
Lassa physician had taken time to show me the technique
before leaving. Feeling the hands of the ward's absent doctor
guiding mine, I carefully threaded the tube into Sia's nostril.
As I fed more and more of the plastic tubing into his body,
my small patient gagged and swallowed reflexively.

After advancing it to what I thought was the appropriate
distance, I then listened with a stethoscope over the abdomen,
while Amie shot a syringe of air down the hose. Bubbles
gurgled just below the left rib cage, where the stomach is
located, and I knew it was in the proper place.

Amie soon began the tube feeding and, when the guard
returned with the oxacillin, gave the first dose of the
medication. After treatment had started, I felt a bit more
relaxed and drew a big circle with a pen to outline the ugly
lesion. I left Sia lying quietly in his mother's lap with the tube
protruding from his nose. He was very ill, but at least we were
helping.

Zuri soon returned with the ambulance and a new patient.
'You're back already?' I said, having barely had a moment's
rest.

'Sure be,' Zuri said happily as he helped a twenty-
something-year-old woman onto the examination table.

I could feel our new patient's fever almost from across the room. Below struggling eyelids, yellow slits gazed up at me through pools of sweat when I approached. She reminded me of the woman who had seized and died several weeks earlier.

Amie spoke quietly in Mende with the patient's accompanying mother, who had entered to hover hesitantly by the door. It almost looked as if they might be old friends. 'This be Binta,' Amie eventually told me, motioning to our new patient and shaking her head sadly. I silently agreed with my nurse: Binta did not look particularly well.

Amie translated for Binta's distraught mother, who told us that her grown daughter had been in good health a week prior, before the sudden onset of flulike symptoms. Over the next few days, Binta's body had quickly acquired a golden glow. Despite treatment for malaria and a visit from a traditional healer, the daughter's symptoms had only worsened.

Looking at my patient, I knew the dramatic jaundice was undoubtedly from abnormally high levels of bilirubin, a yellow substance that is a natural waste product of red-blood-cell birth and destruction. In healthy people, the liver continuously breaks down this complex particle and then excretes it in the feces. Damage to this organ was the most common cause of symptoms such as hers.

'Does she drink alcohol?' I asked while pressing on Binta's abdomen. She didn't look like a drinker, but it was the most common cause of such symptoms in the first world. Amie translated the question, and Binta's mother shook her head no.

Binta's liver felt larger than normal, a nonspecific sign of dysfunction, but I didn't know what had attacked it. Bacteria, viruses, parasites, and chemicals were all possible culprits. Back in the States, I would have ordered a series of lab tests to elucidate the cause, but I didn't have access to any of them.

'Well, what are we going to do?' I said quietly to myself. Binta did not appear to have Lassa, although she clearly had some other, serious process going on. I wished again that we had figured out what had killed the seizing woman a few weeks before. Were we doomed to repeat our mistakes, since we hadn't learned from them?

'What?' Amie said, while Binta's mother looked at me expectantly.

'Never mind,' I said. 'Let's start with amp (ampicillin), gent (gentamicin), and Flagyl.' I hesitantly named all three of the Lassa ward's antibiotics. Together, they covered most bacterial infections.

'Empiric therapy' is the term for prescribing medications to treat multiple potential sources at the same time. In the developed world, physicians frequently consider the practice poor form, since it means you don't really know what is causing the illness. But without diagnostic facilities, targeting treatment to a specific cause is close to impossible.

If Binta was sick from a virus, I could offer her little help. Antibiotics would do nothing, and the majority of such infections lack specific therapy, with Lassa being one of the few exceptions. An alphabet soup of hepatitis viruses (A, B, C, D, and E, among others) can cause jaundice and fever but are rarely fatal in the early stages. Healthy people get sick but usually recuperate without assistance.

Yellow fever, a virus limited to parts of Africa and South America, was another possible diagnosis that hovered in the back of my mind. An excellent vaccine kept the disease out of the developed world, and I had never knowingly seen a case.

In affected areas, mosquitoes spread the yellow fever virus continuously among monkey hosts. The disease makes its way into humans when a mosquito bites an infected animal and then subsequently a nonimmune person. If yellow fever vaccination levels are too low in a given population, a secondary cycle can also develop, with mosquitoes transferring the virus directly from person to person. This can cause an outbreak of human cases and a slew of deaths.

I helped Amie put Binta into her own room in the back, underneath one of our less tattered bed nets, to help prevent possible transmission of her disease to others if it was mosquito-borne. In an attempt to find a potentially reversible cause of our patient's liver failure, I probed Binta's mother, via Amie, for possible exposures.

'Has she been swimming in the river?'

'No.'

'Eating any unusual foods?'

'No.'

'Exposed to any toxins or metals?'

'No.'

I found no obvious answers, and as Amie and I turned to leave our patient's new quarters, I asked the nurse one final question. 'Does Binta have any children?'

'Yes,' Amie replied. 'Two girls . . . they be two and four.'

In silence, we removed our hot protective gear and washed our hands in diluted bleach. Mortality is very high from full-blown yellow fever, and it lacks any specific treatment. There was no medical reason for my last query – it simply put things into better perspective.

I had barely gotten Binta settled when our guard poked his head through the front entrance to inform us that a nurse from the maternity ward wanted us to come look at one of their charges. I felt physically overwhelmed by the continuous torrent of patients and just wanted to sit down for a moment to try to come to terms with everything that was happening. But it seemed there would be no rest.

The day was turning out to be an unsolicited introduction to the realities of being a doctor. No longer could I hide behind a student status. Much like interns and residents in the States, I had been thrown into the medical cauldron, with little time to do anything but care for patients.

Despite having to make some of the most critical decisions of my life, I had so little time to think. Each potentially life-or-death choice deserved a week of diligent research and contemplation, yet I had undoubtedly put more thought into my last camera or computer purchase than the medical decisions I was suddenly forced to make on my own. As soon as one immediate issue was done, it was on to the next needy patient. Dr Conteh had made it seem so easy – there was no way to tell him now that I couldn't keep up.

'What do we do for maternity ward consults?' I asked Zuri when I found him in the back room.

'Very nervous about Lassa there,' he explained to me with a cheery grin. His untroubled attitude continued to amaze me, juxtaposed as it was with all the ill patients around us. Was he in denial, or had he simply come to terms with his work's stark reality?

'We should go now,' Zuri told me.

'If you say so,' I said. We gathered some gear while Zuri hummed a lively tune to himself. Then we were off, leaving Binta in Amie's care. Given the limited supplies at the ward, I could think of nothing else to do for the sick woman.

Beds with pregnant bodies, half naked in the afternoon heat, greeted us at the maternity ward. Mohammad was away operating in the OR, but his three nurses sat talking around the center table. The head nurse motioned to the back when we arrived, to indicate there was a patient for us.

'Over there,' Zuri said.

'Ask them for some history first,' I insisted.

It took some cajoling, but eventually Zuri learned a bit more of a story. Our new patient, Nini, was a twenty-one-year-old mother of four in her second trimester of pregnancy. Over the last week, Nini had experienced a classic Lassa account of a flulike illness followed by aching throat and the development of abdominal pains. Twenty-four hours earlier, the woman had begun to bleed from her mouth, nose, and vagina. Her family had then carried her from their remote village to the Kenema hospital.

At some point during the difficult journey, while bouncing in the back of a hired truck across pothole-ridden roads, Nini had entered into early labor. Upon arrival at the maternity ward, the distraught woman had promptly delivered a stillborn child, along with copious blood. The nursing staff had arrested the flow with difficulty and needed to coax a transfusion from one of her relatives to replace a portion of the lost fluids.

After putting on our protective gear, Zuri and I found our consult in the adjacent 'delivery room,' a separate area used for active labor. As soon as the nurses had entertained a diagnosis of Lassa fever, they had stopped attending to our new patient and had isolated her in the far back corner.

We found Nini lying abandoned and uncovered in a shoddy hospital bed. The woman shook feverishly, with a crimson trail of blood slowly leaking from her nose to a growing pool beside her sunken cheek.

'Hi,' I said softly, before examining Nini. She looked up at me but didn't respond, either because of the language barrier or because she was too sick. I felt her belly and worried about her appearance. Although arduous rides are clearly ill-advised for most pregnant patients, the sick woman's harrowing journey may have ironically been a blessing. It could possibly end up saving her life.

Pregnant women infected with Lassa have the highest mortality of any group. The placenta and fetus make up a vulnerable zone where the virus can rapidly multiply, walled off from a pregnant woman's immune system. Expulsion of the fetus, either spontaneously or via elective abortion, greatly increases the chance of maternal survival. Although Nini's horrendous car ride may have tipped her over the edge to miscarrying, it may have also prevented the virus from overwhelming her body.

We carried Nini to the Lassa ward on a simple tarp tacked between two wood poles. The sun had already set over the jungle-covered hills by the time we got Nini settled and started on ribavirin. I steadied myself at the front desk, my legs weak with a marathonlike fatigue: arriving at the ward that morning seemed a distant memory.

'Are we done now?' I asked Zuri.

'For today,' he said with a grin.

'I'm heading back to the house then. Come get me if there are any emergencies.'

'Sure, sure,' he said.

In a daze, I traipsed back to my lodging. Troubled by feelings of dread, I barely noticed the ongoing life around me on the dusky street. Sia, Binta, Nini, and all my other charges spun through my head like a visual game of Russian roulette. I wondered which face fate would stop upon.

In a fruitless search for hidden mistakes, I mulled over the many hurried decisions I had made throughout the day. Had I done everything I should? Dr Conteh had been gone only twenty-four hours, yet it seemed like eons. There was no predicting what would happen before his return.

19

BARELY MEDICINE

July 29, 2003

I woke the next morning, exhausted from my previous day of patient care. But without time to recover, I was off to the ward again. I felt like a sleepwalker drawn involuntarily to unknown catastrophe – I wanted to turn away, to rest a little more, but each step drew me closer.

Amie was absent from her traditional perch when I entered. I could hear a harsh, repeated rasp echo down the empty hall leading to the rear of the building. It was an almost mechanical sound, like a steam engine struggling up some forgotten river, and I followed the noise around the corner to the back room.

There, I found a gowned figure dressed in full PPEs, stooped at a sharp ninety-degree angle while sweeping the floor with a bouquet of foot-long bristles. When the covered head looked up, I recognized Amie's bottomless eyes from above a plaid green mask. 'What's going on?' I asked her, although deep inside, I already knew the answer.

'Small-small,' she replied. Directly translated, it meant that we had 'minor problems.' Amie nodded her head at the covered mass on the adjacent bed. 'Binta gone to heaven now,' the nurse continued. 'She die sudden in the night.'

Stunned, I was at a loss for words. 'Well . . . I guess you know what to do,' I eventually replied before retreating to Dr Conteh's office. There, I sat in front of a blank computer screen massaging a growing tumor of guilt. During my medical training and previous time at the Lassa ward, I had come in close contact with death, but this was the first passing of a life for which I felt solely accountable.

What was I doing? I asked myself. I wasn't even certain of Binta's true diagnosis. Was there something I could have done to save her? There was no one else to share the burden, no senior physician to bear the mantle of responsibility – in that, I was all alone.

Amie later interrupted my brooding with a hesitant knock at the open office door. I turned to face her and wondered if she could perceive the malignant cancer that I felt growing inside me. 'I have something to ask,' the nurse said slowly. I nodded my head for her to continue.

'You see,' Amie said, fixing her gaze high above me, on the dust-covered wall. 'Binta be my best friend's daughter . . . They live right next door.' I felt the tumor in my gut wrench suddenly on a vital structure as it dug deeper.

'I'm so sorry,' I mumbled, but the nurse continued without notice.

'You see, the ambulance be for getting patients,' Amie said, before looking hopefully at me for a moment. 'But Binta's home be very close.'

Amie paused, and it took me a few seconds to grasp her meaning. 'You want to use the ambulance?' I asked, finally realizing she wanted to use it for the funeral.

'Only for a half-hour,' Amie said.

'Of course,' I answered softly. 'Of course . . . just take a radio with you.'

The gratitude on Amie's face made my guilt seep all the deeper. It was such a small thing – I yearned for greater penance. 'You be sure go to heaven,' Amie said, nodding her head in confident affirmation.

But I was far from certain about that. Indeed, I had doubts about many things.

When Zuri and I later did our rounds, most of the patients simply needed another day of ribavirin treatment. This was true as well for Nini, the woman who had miscarried the day before. She had improved noticeably overnight and sat pensively in her room, gazing through a crack in the cement-covered window.

'How dee body?' I said.

'Dee body fine,' she replied.

Nini's symptoms were a dramatic turnaround from the previous day. The expulsion of her fetus and placenta, the likely location of most of the virus, probably accounted for much of her improvement. The antiviral medication we were giving her certainly was helping as well. 'Tell her I think she will be fine,' I told Zuri, trying to convey my words to Nini with an encouraging smile.

We found Little Sia in the room next door, with a much less certain fate. The tide of his rash was starting to recede from the ink line I had drawn the day before, but he lay limply in his mother's lap, barely moving.

I felt a desperate need to heal the small child, unsure if I myself could survive witnessing such an innocent death. There is something uniquely tragic about disease in one so young. Schopenhauer, an eighteenth-century German philosopher, gave the fact that children die as proof that God does not exist. Looking down at Sia's innocent face cradled in his mother's arm, I realized that witnessing his illness would likely test anyone's belief in a higher power.

Such tragedy challenges our faith in a just world. When confronting sickness in adults, we can imagine that there is some unknown reason guiding the hand of misfortune. Perhaps karma is righting unspoken transgressions. But what could a child have done to deserve such punishment? What sin, besides birth, could he or she have committed?

Somehow it seemed to me that saving Sia would begin to mitigate the guilt I felt over Binta's death. Having so recently, and with such questionable skill, been initiated into the full responsibility of holding another person's life in my hands, I felt a deep fear that I would again fail one of my charges.

'He's going to get better,' I said to the child's mother while simultaneously praying — for him, her, and me — that the words I spoke were true.

* ★ ★

Later in the afternoon, I received another call from the maternity ward – they had one more patient for us. Zuri and I walked over and again talked to the nurses. 'So, what do we have this time?' I said.

'Big bleeding,' the head nurse told us, staying firmly fastened to her seat.

We found our new patient, Mariama, in the same room Nini had previously occupied. The new girl was barely thirteen, and it was her first pregnancy. Similar to Nini, our new consult had bled from her nose, mouth, and vagina before arriving at the maternity ward. However, Mariama had not miscarried.

The young teenager lay flat on her back, her ripe belly sticking out past a sheet heavily soaked from fever. Pain wrinkled her youthful forehead, her childlike eyes swollen with fear. Zuri asked Mariama a few questions in Mende, but she barely answered, pointing only to her protruding abdomen.

The woman-child looked to be almost to term, although her smooth belly appeared even larger given the small size of her immature body. 'Does the pain feel like a contraction?' I asked. 'Does it come and go?'

'No,' Zuri translated, 'it always be there.'

'Hmm,' I said. 'How far along is she?' Zuri asked the girl in Mende, but Mariama just looked up at us with a blank face.

'When was her last menstrual period?' I continued.

Zuri translated, but Mariama just shook her head. Time

was different in Sierra Leone – it ran on a cycle divorced from conventional calendars. Birthdays were a foreign concept, and even ages were highly suspect.

In the States, we could have used an ultrasound to confirm pregnancy duration, through the calculation of fetal bone size. We typically measure the size of the skull and femur, along with a few other markers. But in Kenema, we were left with only the most rudimentary of estimates. 'Could you get me a measuring tape?' I asked Zuri. He found one on a nearby table and handed it to me.

'It's okay,' I tried to reassure Mariama, who cringed as I spread the strip from her pubis up to where I felt the top of her uterus, a few inches above her belly button. The length was thirty-three centimeters. Since this distance grows roughly a centimeter a week, I estimated that Mariama was around thirty-three weeks into her pregnancy.

Forty weeks is a normal delivery, and anything less than thirty-seven is technically premature. Being born too early greatly increases the possibility of complications and decreases the chances of infant survival, since the newborn organs are not yet fully functional. In developed countries, medical intervention has shifted the highest risk of infant complication and death to somewhere before thirty weeks. But in the developing world, each week before term still adds significant risk to the baby.

'Does she feel anything moving?' I asked Zuri, wondering if the fetus was still alive. He translated my question, but my adolescent patient lay flaccid on the bed, too fatigued even to respond. Zuri gave me a cheerful shrug.

'Well, I don't suppose you have a Doppler ultrasound lying around?' I asked the tech in half jest, naming the piece of equipment I would normally use to measure the baby's heart rate, which is the main indicator of fetal well-being. After finding the oxygen machine in the Lassa ward, I half expected Zuri to pull my new request out of a dusty cupboard, but he just looked at me blankly.

'What for?' he asked.

'To measure the baby's heart rate,' I said.

'We use this,' he answered, picking up what looked like a metal champagne glass from the same nearby table.

I turned the sturdy object over in my hands to find a hole in its base, which made the curious device function like a funnel. I had never seen anything like it before, and it was my turn to look dumbfounded. 'You listen,' Zuri said, showing me by holding the bottom of the thing up to his ear.

Sceptical, I proceeded to press the primitive tool to Mariama's belly, searching for the familiar pitter-patter of a tiny heart. To my surprise, as I tuned out her panting breaths, I heard a faint beating. It was a little faster than was best, but present nonetheless.

Lassa fever is one of the major causes of maternal mortality within Sierra Leone's hyperendemic area, and it seemed reasonable enough to imagine that Mariama had contracted the disease. Yet I was far from certain of her diagnosis. Without any lab tests, my novice clinical judgment was the full extent of the young woman's workup. My prior American training involved the analysis of so many studies for each patient that it seemed to be of little value, so different were the current facilities. I simply had to decide.

If the Lassa virus had infected Mariama, her retention of the placenta greatly increased her chances of dying. There were medications to therapeutically induce labor, which potentially could save the mother's life, but I had heard that Mikhail had been unable to procure those specialized drugs in Freetown for Mohammad, and there was no way the market in Kenema would have them either.

Over dinner, Mohammad and I had previously discussed the then theoretical possibility of doing a cesarean section on a pregnant Lassa patient for this very reason. But the obstetrician had emphatically concluded that it would be impossible to perform safely, given the limited equipment in the OR. Due to the copious amount of fluid released during the procedure, the chance of disease transmission to those performing the operation was unacceptably high.

If Mariama had contracted Lassa, I had nothing to give her but the standard ribavirin regimen. However, the US Food and Drug Administration (FDA) warned pregnant women against using the drug, since rat studies demonstrated damage to the fetus during the first trimester. Mariama was in the third trimester, when the fetus was much more resistant to toxins, but the risk was still significant.

If Mariama had Lassa, then giving her ribavirin would be best. It was the only remedy that could potentially save her life and that of the fetus. But if she was suffering from something else, then the drug was unnecessary and could potentially harm her unborn child.

'Let's bring her over to the ward,' I told Zuri. It was clear the maternity nurses had already divorced Mariama from their care.

'Sure, sure,' Zuri said.

Zuri retrieved the stretcher, and we carried our new patient back while I mentally debated the pros and cons of administering ribavirin. The bottom line was that I lacked enough information to decide properly. It was unlike the thousands of multiple-choice questions that I had completed throughout medical school – there was no correct answer.

Zuri tucked Mariama into a room while I paced around in the hall, unsure of what I should do. When he finished, I took another look at Mariama's hurried breathing. She appeared very sick to me.

'Nuke her,' I finally said.

'What?' Zuri asked, looking at me in confusion.

'Give her everything,' I continued.

I could think only of the mother of two who had died under my care that morning. Fearful of denying any potential treatment to someone so close to death's edge, I started Mariama on almost all the ward had in its small repertoire: ribavirin, ampicillin, gentamicin, quinine, and oxygen.

So crude, I thought, when I finally passed beneath the ward's tall gate and out into the town's darkening streets – it barely felt like practicing medicine.

20

IN DEEP

July 30, 2003

Two children, rolling a single metal hoop with wooden sticks, preceded me down the dirt road to the Lassa ward. They giggled with delight as their toy haphazardly wobbled along its perilous path. But the innocent laughter only echoed off the hollow chambers of my heart as I worried what catastrophes the new day would bring. A meek smile in their direction was all I could manage.

Amie was patiently waiting when I arrived at the ward, and her impassive eyes evaluated me, impossible to read. 'How did we do?' I asked, picturing an executioner's axe hanging above her head, in the dark corner of the crumbling ceiling.

'Tanks God,' she replied, and the shadows momentarily receded.

'Thanks God,' I agreed.

The nurses took turns staying overnight in the ward. This meant that Amie was just getting off and Bryan, who worked at three wards: maternity, pediatric, and Lassa, arrived shortly afterward to relieve her. It was the first time he and I had worked together since Dr Conteh's departure. 'Nice to see you,' I told him.

'Time to round,' he said.

Bryan and I started rounds with Nini, the first pregnant woman referred to us from the maternity ward. The Sierra Leonean woman lounged in her room without complaint, continuing two days of steady improvement. I began to scribble a quick note on the piece of paper that functioned as her chart. 'Wrong box,' Bryan pointed out to me.

'What?' I asked him, looking up.

'Should be here,' he said self-assuredly, indicating an adjacent area.

Zuri had been out with the ambulance picking up a new patient from one of the camps, but he returned before Bryan and I got any further. Zuri brought with him a woman in her early twenties. Beneath dust from the road, our new patient wore a shimmering rainbow-colored shawl neatly wrapped around her waist. It contrasted with the ward's dark walls, to which our new charge physically clung for support.

'What's going on?' I asked Zuri. He told me that our new patient, Fortuna, had been feverish for around six days before developing a sore throat and body aches. She had gone to the camp clinic two days earlier, where a health worker treated her with quinine and antibiotics, but the medications had failed to alleviate her symptoms.

Fortuna's early evaluation and swift referral was ideal. Based on her symptoms alone, it would have been hard to definitively diagnose Lassa fever. But knowing that her symptoms had not responded to conventional therapy made the chances of Lassa infection much more likely.

Zuri headed off to clean the ambulance, which left Bryan and me to tend to the patient. 'Fever?' he asked. Fortuna nodded her head.

'Sore throat?'

'Bleeding?'

'Weakness?'

Bryan succinctly listed Lassa symptoms while Fortuna nodded yes or no. I stood quietly nearby. The nurse exuded confidence, and I began to feel my heavy sense of responsibility lightening.

Sensing my continued hesitancy, Bryan happily took charge and put the woman in one of the far rooms. 'She can go there,' he said, pointing, 'and get ribavirin.' I nodded my head in agreement. It definitely seemed reasonable to begin treatment.

We checked next on Mariama, our most recent patient from the maternity ward, who still had a very high fever. The young teenager took rapid breaths, her oxygen cannula, which was supposed to be in her nose, pushed unhelpfully to the side of her face. 'Continuing ribavirin,' Bryan said, scribbling confidently on Mariama's chart. Meanwhile, I tried, MacGyver-like, to fashion some simple sheets of paper into an origami face mask to provide more oxygen. There was nothing more we could do.

Bryan and I continued on through several of the recovering patients, with the nurse doling out medications for headaches and nausea. I didn't argue with any of his decisions and, at some point, he stopped looking to me for confirmation.

When we reached Little Sia, I noted an improvement in his rash as it continued to withdraw from my inked line, but the child's NG tube was no longer in his nose, and he was coughing violently and running a low-grade fever. I listened to the boy's lungs with my stethoscope and, on the right side of his back, heard an abnormal sound with each breath, like ripping Velcro. Sia's mother reported to us that the plastic tube had fallen out sometime the previous day.

'We will put it back in,' Bryan said, ready to move on to the next patient.

'But how long has he had the cough for?' I asked, Sia's hoarse bursts punctuating my question. Amie had already teased me for spending an inordinate amount of time looking in on Sia, but I was unwilling to readily dismiss his new symptoms. I was determined to nurse the child back to full health.

'A day,' Bryan translated, looking annoyed at the delay and eager to see the next patient. 'After his mom feed him.' The nurse pointed to a bowl of yellow rice underneath the bed that attested to his mother's well-meaning attempts to nourish her lethargic child.

'Don't you think we ought to treat the cough?' I asked Bryan. I was concerned that some of Sia's food had in-advertently found its way into his lungs and formed a focus for infection. Termed 'aspiration pneumonia,' the problem commonly occurs in people who are unable to swallow properly. In Sia's weakened state, such an illness could easily be deadly.

'Fine, antibiotics to kill the virus,' Bryan said, before making a move to leave the room.

'Now that doesn't make any sense,' I answered a bit curtly, revealing my annoyance at the nurse's impatience. Most pneumonia is a bacterial infection, not viral, and antibiotics kill bacteria, not viruses.

'But *you* said *you* want antibiotics,' Bryan continued, pointing accusingly at me.

'Okay, okay,' I replied, feeling bad that I had been a bit terse. 'It's just that you said, "Antibiotics to kill the *virus*,"' I continued.

'Yes. Antibiotics to kill the virus,' Bryan insisted.

'The *virus*?' I replied.

'Of course, antibiotics to kill the virus!' Bryan repeated furiously.

I wanted to move on to the subject of how to treat Sia, but Bryan would not let the issue drop. Having listened to Bryan throughout the morning, I knew he was an intelligent man and was sure he was simply not paying attention. I saw Zuri walk by the doorway and headed out to the hall with the hope of changing the subject.

However, Bryan persisted.

'So, what do you think of giving *antibiotics* to treat *viruses*?' I finally asked Zuri, trying to end the discussion.

'Sounds good to me,' Zuri said with an affable grin.

'You guys don't really think antibiotics can kill viruses, do you?' I asked the pair, wondering what part was unclear.

'Of course they can!' Bryan burst out, before glaring at the floor in anger. I looked at the two of them in disbelief, slowly realizing the shallowness of their training.

The ward around me abruptly took on a new dimension, and I mentally surveyed it with fresh perspective. But for a few water-stained papers containing old Lassa criteria in Dr Conteh's office, the facility was empty of educational material. There was no Internet, no books, no other medical connection to the outside world. It was only through a certain naïveté that I assumed the nurses there had equivalent training to those in the States. I surveyed the scene around me and was suddenly unable to guess how much vital knowledge the Lassa staff members might be missing.

'Why can we not give antibiotics to kill the viruses?' Bryan persisted.

'Well . . .' I said, hesitating to go further. 'Do you know the difference between bacteria and viruses?' I feared hearing the answer.

There were only a handful of physicians spread out across Sierra Leone. Nurses with only a few years of basic training, like Bryan, were responsible for most of the limited care. I suddenly felt even more alone, as if I were sinking through murky water, unsure if I would ever find the bottom.

Bryan's muscular shoulders bunched with tension. My words had come out like an accusation and wounded his pride. I could see in his eyes that he felt I was indirectly accusing him of malpractice, of causing death and disability. He was clearly a bright man and the smartest nurse in the ward, but even his ample practical experience could not make up for a lack of formal training.

'I'm sorry, Bryan. Please forgive me,' I said, suddenly

hyperaware of my interloper status in the ward. 'Which antibiotics do you want to give?' I asked, doing my best to move on and diffuse the situation.

Bryan paused to eye me suspiciously for a moment. 'Gentamicin,' he answered guardedly.

'Why?' I asked, the question out of my mouth before I could catch it. I couldn't see any logic in his choice.

'You said he be very sick,' Bryan said defensively. 'We should use the strong medication.'

Further questioning revealed that Bryan and Zuri had no rational method for prescribing the few antibiotics that the ward possessed. They lacked the concept of choosing the drugs based on the groups of organisms they affected.

I felt a growing bond with the nurses as I realized they too were struggling to provide critical aid, despite insufficient training. We were stranded together, far from assistance and helplessly in over our heads. Suddenly, I wanted to teach them everything that they needed to know, just as I wished Dr Conteh was still present to direct me. It was a sin to let a lack of schooling hinder their heroic attempts to help their own people.

I looked at the pair and wondered where to start. I was unsure if they understood even the basic building blocks of biology. Did they know what a cell was or what the organs in the body did?

There was nowhere to begin, I realized, except with the present. 'When you give antibiotics, you need to think about what you're treating,' I said, before going on to explain the classification of bacteria at the simplest level: the 'Gram positives' and 'Gram negatives.'

In Deep

The antibiotics that we had in the ward were capable of treating only one or the other of the two groups. This made it necessary to give at least two antibiotics to cover the majority of bacteria if the source of infection was unknown. 'Ampicillin is for Gram positives,' I said. 'Gentamicin works on the Gram negatives.'

The two nurses looked at me warily – this was clearly a new concept. 'What's a "Gram"?' Bryan asked. It was a microscopy stain used to see bacteria, I answered.

'Just remember . . . two groups,' I said. 'Negative and positive.' Zuri happily smiled and nodded his head, but I was not sure if he got it.

Another bout of coughing from Sia's quarters drew the three of us back into the room. The child, hacking violently, looked to his mother for help, and then to us.

'Should we start both amp and gent then?' Bryan asked hesitantly.

'Yes,' I said. 'Perfect.' It was exactly what we needed to do. I felt waterlogged mud squish between my toes as I pushed off reflexively, on my way back toward the surface. We were in deep, but at least heading in the right direction.

21

FIRST, DO NO HARM

July 31, 2003

When I woke the next morning, the house was too quiet. Sela, the cook, was absent from her usual spot in the kitchen, so I made myself a simple breakfast of African baguette and jam. When I eventually left for the Lassa ward, I found her outside in the courtyard, huddled along with Chris and another guard. They stood just inside the gate, all ears turned to a beat-up radio held between them.

'What's going on?' I asked, straining to make out a few syllables amidst the static. Chris turned to me like a conspirator in a coup.

'Foday Sankoh be dead,' he whispered.

'Really?' I responded.

It was impossible to enter Sierra Leone without hearing of Foday Sankoh, a now captured RUF warlord. Similar to Charles Taylor, the man was a veritable poster child for crimes against humanity. I had heard that treatment for some sort of ailment was delaying his trial by the Sierra Leone special court. But, like any evil monster in a horror movie, his apparent death was still a surprise to everyone. There was somehow the unspoken expectation that he would suddenly rise back from the dead.

I let myself out through the gate and walked into town. The journey was eerily silent. Parked motorcycles lined both sides of the road, their normally frantic motors dormant. Quiet congregations clustered around available radios, with subdued children clinging on to parental limbs. I passed by for the first time without notice, unsure if I should miss my lost celebrity.

Bryan, Zuri, Amie, and our guard were all at the ward when I arrived. They huddled around the CB radio, where, in crisp English, a reporter was relating a croquet match between two Commonwealth countries. I listened with the staff for a few minutes, doubting any of us could comprehend the foreign statistics of the far-off game.

The program eventually arrived at the world news, to discuss a recent UN resolution approving the use of force in Liberia. However, the US was still refusing to commit its nearby forces, and the fighting continued in the rebels' attempt to oust Taylor from Monrovia. There was no mention of Mikhail, and I wondered how the aid worker fared, along with the city's battered populace.

As the broadcast moved on to the weather, the group around me appeared visibly disappointed. 'How about Foday?' Amie asked.

'Yeah,' Bryan said, while Zuri simply shrugged.

They had been hoping for confirmation of Foday's death by a reputable source, the only news, thus far, limited to word of mouth from Freetown. 'I'm sure they'll get to it later,' I said. 'Come on, guys,' I continued, ushering them out of the alcove. 'We need to start rounds.'

The three nurses and I began with Mariama, who lay limp on her creaky cot. As we entered, Amie yelled at the young teenager in Mende, and our patient struggled to sit up. 'So lazy,' Amie complained, punctuating each word with stabs of her finger in the air. 'She be lying here all day,' Amie said, before continuing with more Mende that did not sound much kinder.

'How is she doing?' I asked, when our young patient finally got sitting upright.

'Too young to be pregnant,' Amie griped, shaking her head disapprovingly. Although I certainly agreed with Amie, I was surprised that Mariama's young age was a point of concern, given the youthful ages of so many of the local mothers.

'Her boyfriend be young and lazy too,' Amie added with a knowing shake of the head. I remembered that Mariama came from a local family, not from one of the refugee camps, and wondered if that accounted for Amie's seemingly higher standard.

I had never seen Amie so upset before, and I could barely suppress an amused smile. It seemed to me that Mariama had every right to be 'lazy' – she was both seriously ill and pregnant. But while people pampered expectant women in the US, they seemed to take the opposite tack in Sierra Leone.

In the interactions I had witnessed while visiting the maternity ward, it appeared that the closer the laboring women came to delivery, the more likely it was that the African nurses would yell at them. I was unclear about the reason behind this marked cultural difference, but it seemed that, in an odd way, it was how Amie and her colleagues showed they cared.

'Any *medical* updates?' I asked.

'Her fever be gone,' Bryan answered helpfully while Amie continued to shake her head. The heart rate of Mariama's fetus also continued to be good. I thought our adolescent mother-to-be was doing remarkably well, despite her continued lethargy, and wondered to myself if she actually had Lassa. If Mariama's symptoms were from some other problem, then I was giving her ribavirin for no reason, with possible detriment to the fetus. Conversely, if she did have the disease, then the drug was potentially saving them both.

In the end, I decided to keep her on all the medications, while sighing with the realization that there was no way to know the best course. 'First, do no harm,' a fundamental principle of medicine, was good in theory. But it helped little when both choices could cause potential injury. I was unsure what Dr Conteh would do in my stead.

The absent Lassa physician was supposed to be back sometime within the next twenty-four hours, and I mentally urged him a swift return to the abandoned ward. Every moment he was gone was another opportunity for me to make a deadly mistake. I found myself bargaining with higher powers, ready to trade almost anything for a few insightful words from the experienced physician into Mariama's ambiguous situation.

'Complaining, complaining. No stop,' Amie said, referring to Mariama, just before we were about to leave the girl's room.

'About what?' I said.

'Abdominal pain,' Amie said with roll of her eyes.

'We gave her steroids,' Bryan added, referring to gluco-corticoids, a class of medications that imitated a hormone naturally produced during stress on the body and unrelated to the anabolic steroids used by weight lifters.

'Oh,' I responded, and a now familiar sinking feeling started to grow again in my stomach. Why had I not thought of it myself? When given in pregnancy, steroids cause the fetal lungs to mature earlier than normal, thus increasing the chances of survival if a baby arrives prematurely. Mariama's unborn child was close to that critical cutoff.

As I thought about the nurses' decision, I realized that it was a bit daring given Mariama's current situation. It was a substantial dose of the medication, which would help the fetus if delivered early. But its side effect, in the long run, was to decrease the ability of the mother's immune system to ward off infection. Since we were unsure if Mariama had Lassa or some other kind of illness, it was hard to predict what the actual effect of the drug would be.

I wondered how much of this dilemma my three nurses had thought about before giving Mariama the drug. Teaching, I was starting to realize, was the only way I could make any kind of lasting impact in the health of those around me.

'Good thought,' I said to the nurses, doing my best

impression of a medical school professor. 'Now what things do you normally give steroids for?' I continued.

'Stomach pains,' Zuri said without hesitation. Amie nodded in agreement.

'Yes,' Bryan concurred.

I was a bit thrown off by their unanimous answer. Certainly, there is no reason to give all pregnant women steroids. The medication requires cautious use. There is little benefit in giving it too early, when the fetus has no chance of surviving, or too late, when the infant's lungs have already matured.

'Which pregnant women with abdominal pain do you give them to?' I asked. I could see that it would be hard to guess when to use them in rural Africa, since exact pregnancy dates were mostly suspect.

'All of them,' Bryan replied with a knowing expression, as if he had caught a trick question. 'We give it to *anyone* with stomach pain.'

'Yes, we do,' Amie said. Zuri smiled his big grin. But I was only more confused.

'You give them to anyone with abdominal pain,' I muttered, looking from face to confident face. 'Even if they're not pregnant?'

'Of course,' Bryan answered self-assuredly.

'Really?'

Their unwavering consensus made me doubt myself. What was the hidden rationale? My last clinical rotation in the States had been over a year prior, but I tried to think back to the situations in which we gave steroids. Asthma came to mind, as did lupus, and there were some controversial studies on spine trauma. But no one had ever touted steroids as a universal cure for stomach pain. I couldn't figure out what the three nurses were talking about.

'Well . . .' I wasn't exactly sure what to say. What was evidently common practice for my nurses was far from what I remembered in the States. But I wasn't entirely certain why that might be.

The sound of static and intermittent beeping suddenly filled the ward while my expectant students waited for me to continue. Zuri tuned in the radio and spoke briefly into the attached handset. 'Jimmy Bagbo Camp,' he finally said to us. 'Ten-year-old boy.' The camp was calling for the ambulance.

'We can talk about steroids when you get back,' I told Zuri, thankful for a chance to gather my thoughts. Lightly humming to himself, the tech gathered his stuff and strolled out to the ambulance.

Bryan, Amie, and I continued on to see Little Sia, who had again pulled out his NG tube. His mother had refrained from feeding him this time, which had prevented any more episodes of choking. I decided that pulling out the tube was a sign of improving strength. The child's rash and lungs also seemed to be slightly better.

Fortuna, the presumed Lassa victim who had arrived from camp the day before, was chatting away with Nini in their shared room. Both women were doing well. Nini had almost completely recovered from the Lassa-induced bleeding, and the ribavirin had presumably prevented Fortuna from developing any further symptoms.

* * *

After finishing rounds, I left Bryan and Amie to do their work and snuck off to visit Dr Nassan while struggling to remember more indications for steroid use. I found the pediatrician sitting at his usual table in the pediatric ward. He greeted me with a professional nod of the head. 'How goes the battle?' he said.

'Uphill,' I answered.

The professor chuckled.

'I have a question for you,' I continued.

'Sure,' he said.

'Can you remember the indications for steroid use?'

'Well,' the professor said, speaking loudly to the milling patients and me as if used to addressing a much larger audience, 'we have asthma, autoimmune diseases, premature delivery . . .' He continued on to list eight or more. I had forgotten a couple, but none relevant to stomach pain or the confusing treatment at the Lassa ward.

'Thanks, that's very helpful,' I said. 'But I just can't figure out why the nurses at the Lassa ward seem to be giving steroids as a general aid for stomach pain.'

'Oh, that seems to be the local belief around here,' Dr Nassan said knowingly.

'Really?'

'Yeah, I can't figure out why either. But I don't think there is any evidence for it.' Disconnected from the world for over a decade, the isolated medical community had developed a dangerous tradition based on custom instead of science.

Discussing the situation with Dr Nassan helped me make sense of everything. 'You're the best,' I told him as I stood to leave. Of course steroids were not a cure for general stomach pain! I felt a little sheepish that I had even asked.

'Don't worry,' the gentle professor told me as I turned to depart. 'You have the knowledge you need . . . Only time will bring the confidence.'

'I hope that's true,' I told him. But I left worrying what would happen in the interim.

Zuri was in the courtyard with the ambulance when I returned to the Lassa ward. 'Recently rat hunting,' he told me.

'Oh?'

'No good.'

The ten-year-old boy Zuri had been transporting had not survived the ride. The tech opened up the back of the ambulance and bodily fluids spilled out the bottom of the door, to soak into the sandy street. Blood had poured from mouth, nose, and rectum during the one-and-a-half-hour journey, until the swollen child could spare no more.

As I peered into the back of the vehicle, I found myself surprised at how little I felt at the tragic death of the pre-pubescent boy. Prior to my time in Kenema, I knew that the heartbreak of his death would have struck me acutely. He was a child, after all, innocent to his fate. But I had been through so much since my arrival that the boy's untimely demise could not surmount my growing emotional defenses. For some reason, that the child had died beyond the high walls of the Lassa ward mitigated my sorrow. It seemed somehow outside my self-imposed jurisdiction.

I worried, almost detached from the situation around me, if the ward's dark recesses were stealing my humanity. I had already changed, in ways I was only beginning to recognize, and I was unsure if it was for better or worse.

As Amie and Bryan joined Zuri to put on PPEs and disinfect the area, I turned my back on the growing pool of infectious liquid that was gathering beneath the rig. I lacked the energy necessary to mourn another death – a sense of responsibility for those in my charge was all I could manage.

After the trio finished burying the body, the four of us congregated next to the CB in the ward. The radio program had failed to mention Foday all day. It seemed no one in the outside world cared any longer about Sierra Leone. The country was old news, and international attention focused elsewhere.

'About the steroids . . .' I said to the nurses before leaving for the night. 'Although it's okay for Mariama, we shouldn't be giving them to everyone with stomach pain.'

'Really?' Bryan said. Amie and Zuri also paid close attention. The nurses had become very receptive to instruction, as only those who had survived with so little training could be.

'Really,' I said. 'In fact, steroids can be potentially very dangerous because they suppress the immune system. So, for a while, why don't you ask me before giving them to anyone?' The three nodded their heads in solemn agreement.

'I know all of us are trying to help, but sometimes doing something can be worse than doing nothing at all,' I finished. 'Of course, the difficult part is deciding when that is.'

22

A VISITOR

August 1, 2003

I stumbled to the ward the next morning, longing to see Dr Conteh's calm face. It had been only five days since my teacher had left, but seemed like an eternity. I wondered if the physician would regret having left me in charge. Without him, the ward felt like a ship adrift without a captain.

No one was guarding the front gate when I got to the Lassa ward, and I entered to find it strangely absent of its staff members. Suddenly, the horrifying thought that the nurses were away burying one of our patients struck me, and I rushed into Little Sia's room, only to find the child lying comfortably on his cot. The boy made eye contact with me – he was well and, I hoped, possibly even getting better.

I quickly checked the other rooms. All the patients that I saw appeared fine, but in the last room I found Fortuna hooked up to the oxygen machine and panting heavily. Sweat dripped down the smooth indentation between her uncovered breasts as her chest rose with each rapid inhalation.

'It's okay. It's going to be okay,' I told her. I wasn't sure if she understood my words, but she clearly didn't have enough breath to speak. Fortuna communicated to me only through eyes white with fear, while her roommate, Nini, watched mesmerized with concern from the corner.

Fortuna's abrupt about-face shocked me — she had been doing so well since arriving from the refugee camps and receiving treatment for Lassa. I listened to her lungs to find them perfectly clear. There was no sign of inappropriate fluids or infection.

It was not until I pulled back her lower eyelid and saw the familiar ash gray color of anemia on its inner surface that things started to make sense. I could hear Dr Conteh's steady voice in my ears. Just as he had told me, ribavirin was both savior and curse. The drug had caused Fortuna to become severely anemic.

Although the oxygen machine was helpfully working at its maximum, it could not make up for the abrupt decline in her red blood cells, which normally function like boxcars, shuttling the needed gas from the lungs out to the tissues. Fortuna urgently required blood, before she tired out from her labored breathing.

Without identifying Fortuna's blood type, I could do little to help her. I knew Zuri kept an archaic set of transfusion equipment in the back of the ward for just such a task, but I had little idea how to use it. In the States, medicine is so specialized that a vast array of people perform the many necessary duties. Normally, technicians in the hospital blood bank are in charge of preparing blood, and I knew only the general theory of doing so, not the actual details. Even worse, the Lassa ward had no stored blood reserves. Fortuna required an appropriate donor.

I had no idea where the nursing crew had gotten off to, and I willed them to return swiftly. There was little I could do until they returned. Trying to keep my growing panic at bay, I started to play a game of Minesweeper on the ward's computer. It was all I could think to do to keep myself from staring unhelpfully at my sick patient. I clicked on one square, then another. No mine yet. Then I returned to Fortuna's room and watched her panting chest. She was still breathing, albeit much too quickly.

I went back and forth between the computer and Fortuna. Click, click, click. Breath, breath, breath. The ward's crumbling walls pressed inward, and I felt so utterly foolish. A woman was slowly dying while I played a video game. Some doctor I made. I simply waited to see which bomb, the one on the computer screen or in Fortuna's ticking respirations, would explode first.

A half-hour later, Amie and Zuri returned to the ward. 'Where have you guys been?' I said.

'We be checking for a blood donor,' Zuri told me.

'No good,' Amie continued, shaking her head.

I was suddenly impressed with the nurses' swift response. They were already several steps ahead of me, although unfortunately they hadn't yet found anyone to donate blood.

'She is at fifteen percent,' Zuri said, referring to Fortuna's hematocrit, proud he had already performed the ward's single diagnostic test.

'Wow!' I said. It was only slightly better than Amber's previous record. 'We really need to get her some blood.'

'We check all around,' Zuri said. 'But nobody be interested.'

'Even for money,' Amie said. 'And me and Zuri gave last month.'

Since both nurses had donated blood recently, they had to wait before they could do so again. 'You already typed Fortuna's blood?' I asked Zuri.

'Yes,' he said happily. Transfusing the wrong type of blood can quickly be fatal, since the immune system attacks anything that it identifies as non-self.

I hesitated before asking for the result, picturing myself hooked up to his pitiable equipment. 'What is it?' I finally said.

'B plus.' I breathed a guilty sigh of relief. I was A plus and unable to donate.

The body's immune system makes antibodies to destroy every kind of structure that it does not naturally contain before birth, as a defense against foreign diseases. The body recognizes three main features on red blood cells: A, B, and the Rh factor (commonly labeled as positive or negative).

People who have none of these features (type O negative) can thus accept only from their same type but can donate to everyone, since there are no structures in their blood that are unfamiliar to the recipients' immune systems. Those who have all three structures (AB positive) can conversely accept from every blood type, as their immune system is used to all three, but they can donate only to others that are AB positive. Since Fortuna was B positive, we needed to find someone with B positive, B negative, O positive, or O negative blood to help her.

'Someone ask for you outside,' the Lassa guard said to me, entering to interrupt our deliberations.

'Really?' I said. Immediately overwhelmed with excitement that Dr Conteh had finally returned, I forgot that we were in the middle of a discussion and ran out to find my missing mentor. My ordeal was finally over – the lost Lassa physician had at last returned to put everything right.

I bolted through the front gate to find a parked Merlin vehicle. But Dr Conteh was not there. Instead, Daren, the Merlin medical coordinator from Freetown, stood casually next to the car, along with a driver.

'Hi,' Daren said.

'Oh . . . Daren?' I answered, almost physically taken aback at not finding Dr Conteh, my presumed savior.

'Good to see you,' the medical coordinator said cheerfully. 'I'm just stopping by to check on the Kenema field programs.'

'Glad to see you,' I told him as the disappointment slowly sunk. But it was still nice to see a familiar face.

I suddenly remembered Fortuna and her grave anemia. 'Want to look at a patient with me?' I asked Daren.

He chuckled. 'No, I don't think I want to go in there,' he said, eyeing the formidable fence that surrounded the ward.

'I'll let you cowboys do that, and stay out here, far away from that nasty virus.'

'If you say so,' I said, shrugging. I was still glad to have a visitor and no longer surprised at the consistent reaction to the Lassa ward.

'You know,' Daren explained with a dry wink, 'my wife, who lives with our children in the Gambia, has already warned me against bringing home any communicable infections.'

I laughed. It was clear to me that I would get no outside help until Dr Conteh's return, and it abruptly struck me how amazing the missing Lassa physician's dedication had been to his neglected patients. His lifelong perseverance was even more impressive when compared to the many who feared even to enter the Lassa ward.

I felt my pent-up anger at Dr Conteh begin to dissipate. The elderly physician had mentioned that he had unsuccessfully been trying to retire for several years, but he had been unable to find anyone to train as a replacement. My visit had likely provided one of the few opportunities in decades for him to leave the Lassa ward for more than a day.

Especially after the death of the Freetown doctor, no one would take Dr Conteh's job – Lassa fever was a forgotten disease, just as he had first told me. Well past his prime, Dr Conteh unwaveringly continued with his life's work in isolation, because there was simply no one else who would. Few doctors anywhere could identify with such devotion.

Still worried about Fortuna, I asked Daren for his blood type. He was not a potential donor but said to check with his driver. 'I drive him,' the man from Freetown protested, pointing at Daren. With a mischievous grin on his face, the medical coordinator offered to walk for the day, and a quick test proved the driver to be a reluctant match.

Zuri set up for a transfusion from the defeated-looking driver while Daren asked Amie and me about priorities for the ward. 'I mean, don't get me wrong, money is tight,' Daren said. 'But is there anything in particular that you need?' Merlin did have a small budget from donated funds.

'What don't we need?' I asked wryly. 'First, I would love a bag valve mask and some emergency drugs.'

'And some more quinine pills too,' Amie added thoughtfully.

'If we're cowboys,' I said, 'then someone forgot to load our pistols.'

I discussed with Daren the oxacillin situation and told him I had had to charge one of the patients for the drug. The medical coordinator shook his head. 'We sent a whole case down just before you got here,' he said.

'Really?' I said.

'Yeah. Didn't Dr Nassan tell you?'

I looked at Daren in confusion.

'The meds disappeared when they got to the pediatric ward, before Dr Nassan had the chance to lock them up.'

'Disappeared?'

'I guess some of the nurses there stole it.'

'No.'

'Why do you think you could find it in the market?' Daren asked. 'Did you look at the vial? It was probably ours.' Foul play had not even occurred to me, but theft was a constant problem in any crisis setting – desperate people doing almost anything to survive.

Daren had to check on Dr Nassan, so I walked him over to the pediatric ward. 'Oh,' he said along the way, 'I almost forgot to tell you. They radioed us from Kono.'

'Yes?'

'Dr Conteh is sick with some kind of stomach flu,' Daren reported. 'The outreach team is going to give him a few days to recover before making the ride back.'

'What!' I stopped midstride upon hearing the news. I felt as if someone had hit me in the gut.

'He should be okay,' Daren said, misreading my reaction. 'I just told them not to push it.'

'Yeah,' I replied, putting on the best face I could. But I could think only of my continued responsibility for the patients at the ward. I would have given anything to have Dr Conteh back, but it seemed I would be alone for at least a few more days – there was little I could do.

After dropping off Daren to see Dr Nassan, I returned to the Lassa ward to find the driver fastened to the medieval transfusion equipment. A hose extended from the man's arm to Fortuna, who lay on a cot across the room. I was happy to find that Zuri was using disposable needles and that the driver was doing fine, although he feigned a pained expression.

With almost a pint of blood in, Fortuna was already breathing much more slowly. She appeared past her acute emergency, with the added red blood cells bringing additional oxygen to her tissues. I hoped they would be sufficient to maintain her through the rest of her ribavirin treatment.

Fortuna had made it past another obstacle on the road to recovery, but I knew only time would tell if she would be one of the lucky few to escape the Lassa ward's dim corridors. For the moment, there would be only me to help her, and I silently wished Dr Conteh a swift recovery. His continued absence felt like an almost palpable void.

23

ANOTHER DROP

August 1, 2003 (continued)

Later in the evening, after I finished work at the ward, Daren and I defied a light drizzle to find a late dinner at Kenema's sole restaurant. We sat down beneath a pair of naked light-bulbs, which flickered with the rhythmic rumbling of a gas generator. The simple room consisted of three wooden tables and a handful of chairs below an awning fashioned from a discarded UN tarp. It was my first break from the daily cycle of sleep and tending to the Lassa ward since Dr Conteh had left, and I was glad to have a moment's respite.

Daren and I ordered two beers from the indifferent waitress, who also turned out to be the cook and owner. 'Chop-chop?' she asked.

'Fried rice,' I said, pointing at the menu.

'No,' she said, shaking her head.

'Chicken and rice?' I asked, indicating a different item.

'No,' she said again.

'Cassava leaves?'

She shook her head again.

I went sequentially down the menu, but it was not until the last dish, palm oil stew, that the waitress nodded her head in affirmation.

'Hmm, that stew sounds like a good choice,' Daren said with a smile after I finished ordering. 'I think I'll have it as well.'

Two Englishmen walked in while we were waiting for our food. They were some of the first foreigners I had seen in Kenema. Daren knew one of them, Mark, a logistician for one of the other NGOs, and invited the pair to join us.

'So, what are you being punished for?' Mark asked me as he and his friend, Cole, sat down.

I gave him a questioning look.

'How'd you get stuck with *him* in this hellhole?' Mark said, pointing to Daren. Daren laughed.

'Working on Lassa fever,' I said.

'Yeah, he's a cowboy,' Daren interjected.

Mark raised his eyebrows. 'They had an outbreak of that among the refugees, right?'

'We've seen more than a few,' I answered. 'And Taylor seems to have some staying power.'

'I heard that ten soldiers from ECOWAS entered Monrovia today,' Daren said. 'Supposedly the fighting has stopped, for the moment.'

'The Nigerians aren't even armed!' Mark said, exasperated. 'I mean, they're only on a friggin fact-finding mission.

And here all these gigantic American warships have been floating aimlessly off the Liberian coast for weeks. I mean, how do they live with themselves?'

I noticed that Mark was slurring his words a little and realized that our guest might have had a few drinks before dinner. Belatedly, the Brit looked up from his beer at me. 'Oh, sorry,' he finished after realizing my nationality.

I shrugged, unsure if I should take offense. At home, it was easy to disassociate my personal views from those of my government. I had not made any of those decisions; politicians in Washington had. But abroad, it was harder to distance myself from the actions of my homeland. They reflected on me, whether I agreed with them or not.

'It's not America's fault,' Daren said, feeling a need to protect me. 'Why should they go in? It's not their country.'

'We came to Sierra Leone when they had problems,' Mark answered, referring to Britain. 'At least we don't leave our old colonies out to dry.'

'America didn't have colonies,' I couldn't help interjecting.

'Semantics,' Mark retorted. 'Anyways, America pushes crap all the time about how they're just out to help all the un-fortunate people – that's what they're saying in Iraq. But here you have women and children dying in Monrovia every day, yet they're afraid to get off their big aircraft carrier. My god, ten unarmed, untrained Nigerians have stopped the fighting for now!'

'Mark, we all know America went into Iraq because there's oil there,' Daren said, continuing his defense on my behalf.

'Of course they only act in their best interest. . . . That's just natural.'

The Brit and the Nigerian continued the argument, but I barely listened after that. I could only think of Daren's words – his support stung much more than Mark's attack. I doubted people back home saw things in the same light. But abroad, the impression was unavoidable.

Mark eventually headed off to use the bathroom, which left his friend Cole to apologize for him. 'Sorry about that,' he said. 'He just gets a little upset sometimes.' After a few easy-going jokes, Cole quickly had us back to normal conversation.

'So what do you do out here?' I asked.

'Oh,' he said. 'I'm only a businessman. Not doing all the good work you gents is.'

'What kind?' I was unable to think of any productive commerce in the country.

Cole paused for a moment before gazing around the room surreptitiously. He did it for so long that I started to think that he was putting me on.

'Diamonds,' Cole finally whispered. 'Don't say anything though, okay? I have a license now. . . . It's just that the locals think we have loads of cash. It can get a bit dangerous.'

'Oh,' I said, trying to hide my surprise. I took a second look at the friendly Brit next to me. He was one of the infamous diamond merchants who were in part responsible for the long conflict in the region. Cole was not what

I had expected, lacking an ugly scar or an oily complexion.

Helplessly fascinated, I probed further. 'How exactly does that work?' I said.

'I fly down from London every couple of months to buy some diamonds.'

'From the miners?'

'No, mostly from the Lebanese dealers. They buy them from the local miners.'

'Aren't they more expensive then?'

'Still cheap enough. A few trips a year is all it takes to earn a pretty good lifestyle back in Britain.'

Cole told me how he had first entered the industry while traveling through Eastern Europe just after the fall of the Soviet Union. He had bumped into another expat who explained the trade of buying cheap diamonds in areas where conflict had deflated prices, and then selling the gems at market value in Brussels. Cole had seized upon that local opportunity and eventually continued traveling from country to war-struck country.

The diamond industry had instituted a program over the last few years, called the Kimberly Accord, after receiving negative press about being a stimulus for global conflict. The idea was that the pact prevented such abuses by certifying the country of origin for every diamond and banning the sale of gems from conflict areas. But it is impossible to tell where a diamond has been mined after it has been cut. 'The thing's just a joke,' Cole told us.

Over the previous decade, the rebels of Sierra Leone, with the help of their neighbor Charles Taylor, had sold their illegally mined diamonds through Liberia, thus subverting the accord process. With the recent reversal of fortune next door, this illicit flow had now switched. The diamonds mined in Liberia were beginning to receive their certificates, and enter the world market, through Sierra Leone.

When Mark returned from the bathroom, the conversation returned to less controversial topics, but I could not help wondering about Cole's role in the local crisis. The Brit seemed like a nice guy, and I was unsure how much blame he personally deserved. Taken in isolation, his actions were perhaps too trivial to make any difference – they accounted for only a few more guns and a couple additional rockets added to the local fighting. Certainly others would fill his shoes if he gave up his trade.

Cole was a small but real part of a violent deluge that ultimately led to incredible suffering. He was merely the beginning of a chain of buyers who put weapons in the hands of dangerous men in order to place a ring on a loved one's finger. In many ways, he was little different from those final lovestruck consumers. From my vantage point in the remote West Africa jungle, I could see he was only a tiny drop in the overall process. But one of the many making up a brutal downpour that, for over a decade, had laid waste to a land of perilous slopes and vulnerable children.

IV

FINALLY A DOCTOR

24

MORE THAN MEDICINE

August 2, 2003

'That Taylor's a slippery one,' Daren said to me while we ate breakfast in the common room.

'Yeah,' I said. 'What a piece of work.'

'I don't think they'll ever get him out,' the medical coordinator continued.

The radio was reporting that West African diplomats had arrived in Liberia but had been unable to secure an audience with the elusive dictator. Without the backing of any real troop presence and only the verbal support of the US, it appeared that the delegation would leave empty-handed. The devastating fighting seemed likely to resume yet again.

'He's even better than that Clinton guy,' Daren said. I laughed, finding it an unexpected analogy. The Western media focused on the Liberian president only as a modern-day dictator, but the West Africans seemed to have more mixed feelings. They demonstrated a grudging respect for the man who had withstood Western pressure for so long. Closer to the action, the political landscape was less black–and–white.

After making plans with Daren for lunch, I made my way over to the ward. When I arrived, I found Amie sitting securely on her traditional stool in the front alcove. With a relief that did not seem to lessen with the passing of time, I learned from her that everyone had successfully survived the night. 'And Fortuna be breathing much better since the transfusion,' the nurse also informed me.

Zuri showed up a little later, and the three of us began rounds, starting with Mariama. 'She doesn't look good, does she?' I said. Our pregnant patient had worsened noticeably.

'Such a problem,' Amie said, shaking her head as if Mariama's decline was somehow our patient's own fault.

Zuri handed me Mariama's chart and pointed to her temperature. 'Really?' I said. 'A hundred and four?'

'Yep,' he said. I was surprised. Mariama had been fine when I left the previous night.

'Check it again,' I told him.

We waited while Zuri rechecked the temperature. The thermometer rolled about lazily in the pregnant woman-child's mouth, but the result still remained too high.

'Hmm . . .' I said. 'How does she feel?'

'Achy,' Zuri translated.

Amie rolled her eyes. 'She be pregnant,' the nurse said.

'Yes, yes,' I said. 'But why does she have a fever?'

I looked at the medications written on Mariama's simple chart. She was still receiving everything the ward had to offer: ribavirin, ampicillin, gentamicin, and quinine. The combination should have covered most types of infection.

I examined Mariama thoroughly and found that the heart rate of her unborn baby was still fairly normal, but I failed to find anything that would pinpoint the source of her fever. I stood next to her bedside for some time without speaking, trying to will an answer out of my lethargic patient.

Zuri happily hummed to himself while Amie continued to roll her eyes. Puzzled as to the cause of Mariama's symptoms, I wished yet again that Dr Conteh was there to help. 'I guess we should just keep her on everything,' I finally said, unable to think of anything else to do.

'Everybody have fever,' Zuri informed me when we got to the next room.

'You've got to be kidding,' I said, looking at Zuri to see if he was joking. 'All three of them?'

'Yep,' he said.

I surveyed the room suspiciously as we entered. Fortuna lay on the closest bed. Her breathing had clearly improved with the blood transfusion, but she sprawled across her cot with a damp rag across her forehead. 'Let me see the chart,' I told Zuri. I confirmed that Fortuna was also on the four standard medications. 'That just doesn't make any sense,' I said.

Baffled, I moved on to Nini, who lay ill in the far corner. 'Her too?' I asked Zuri. He nodded. Nini had been improving since her miscarriage. She was only on ribavirin and quinine. 'I guess you should start amp and gent as well,' I told the nurses.

When we got to the third roommate, a previously

recovering woman on quinine therapy for malaria (Dr Conteh had admitted her before he left), I started to wonder if I was going crazy. 'I just don't get it,' I told the two nurses. I had never heard of malaria returning while on such treatment and was clueless as to the source of her new infection.

'Are you sure that thing is working?' I asked Zuri, pointing to his battered thermometer.

'Little Sia have no fever,' he responded, proving that the device was still functioning properly.

'I guess . . .' I said.

We went over to Sia's room, where the child lay in his mother's lap, the NG tube again sticking out from his nose like a miniature elephant trunk. 'Check it again,' I urged Zuri.

'Ninety-eight point six,' he eventually told me. The child didn't have a fever – his temperature was the epitome of normal.

After rounds, I paced up and down the halls, trying to come up with some theory to explain the rash of fevers in the ward. Was it all coincidence, or was there some unknown outbreak at work? I wondered if the Lassa virus was spreading through the ward despite our infection-control precautions, or if some kind of mutant strain had become resistant to our treatment. How could I help my patients if I didn't even understand the new threat?

After a morning without answer to the Lassa ward's feverish puzzle, I briefly headed back to the guesthouse to say good-bye to Daren before he headed back to Freetown.

Mohammad and Lila were also there when I arrived. The fevers were still on my mind as we shared a lunch of un-identifiable meat mixed with rice and oily sauce.

'You don't by any chance have a bunch of patients with fevers today, do you?' I asked Mohammad, wondering if the maternity ward shared my mysterious outbreak.

'No,' he said, suddenly throwing his hands in the air. 'Not that anyone would tell me!'

'People can be so rude!' Lila interjected. Daren looked at my two roommates and chuckled.

'I want to talk to you about what I just heard on the news,' Mohammad said, eager to ask me a question.

'Yes?' I said.

'I heard today that, in America, a man in a coma for ten years is now starting to move.'

'Okay . . .'

'This is true?' the obstetrician asked intently.

I laughed, but Mohammad remained very serious. Somehow, as the sole American, I was the expert on the situation, despite being as far off in remote Africa as my fellow colleagues.

'This is true?' Mohammad repeated.

'Sure, I guess it's probably true,' I said, obviously not quite as impressed as the obstetrician. I had listened to the same story earlier on the radio. Supposedly the man had briefly moved his eyes, as well as a finger. But he was still pretty much a vegetable.

'What I want to know,' Mohammad said with great animation, 'is who kept him alive?'

'What do you mean?' I asked him.

'Who was taking care of this man for all this time?' Mohammad continued, as if that were the most unbelievable part of the story.

'I don't know. I guess he was probably in a nursing home somewhere,' I said.

'What is this?' Mohammad asked.

'A nursing home? It's a place for people that can't take care of themselves. They have nurses and caregivers and such . . .'

It took me a few minutes to describe the foreign concept to Mohammad. Lila and Daren had at least heard of nursing homes, although they weren't much clearer on the details. In the third world, with limited funds and facilities, the family unit was responsible for caring for the daily needs of the ill and disabled. Not even the richest would use such a facility.

'In this nursing home, they have many of these people in comas?' Mohammad finally asked, perplexed.

'I suppose so,' I said. 'I'm sure there are hundreds of people, probably thousands, spread out across America.'

Mohammad, Daren, and Lila all shook their heads in awe. 'Your country is truly amazing,' Mohammad said. 'That you can take care of all these people, even those with ruined brains.'

'Yes, amazing,' I said, uncomfortably aware that a large portion of my fellow citizens paradoxically had little access to the most basic medical services. There was no point in even attempting to explain to my foreign colleagues the partitioning of medical resources in my country. With our great means, they clearly assumed that we cared for the needs of everyone in my homeland. Health care in America was truly more remarkable than they imagined.

After wishing Daren swift travels, I headed back to the Lassa ward to find Amie out front. 'Would you look at my youngest?' she asked me. 'He be a bit sick.'

'Of course,' I said, surprised and flattered by the request. Amie had seen my awkward struggles to manage the ward in Dr Conteh's absence. I was more than a little shocked that she trusted my judgment.

We found Amie's son sitting on the wooden bench in the anteroom. He was very well behaved and stood up politely to introduce himself. His budding adolescent muscles peeked out from under a clean Polo-type shirt. 'How old are you?' I asked him.

'Thirteen,' he said shyly.

'Well,' I said, taken aback a bit. 'Aren't you a big one.' Both Amie and her son smiled. Despite his present illness, I was amazed at the teenager's healthy physique. Compared to other children his age, I thought, he must be a giant.

However, it took me a few moments before I realized that the boy was large only in comparison to his local compatriots and would have been of normal height in the States. I had grown accustomed to the ubiquitous stunting. Amie had taken excellent care of her son. A good diet, along with easy access to health care, had allowed him to grow up healthy and strong, as all children should.

'He be sick with fever since yesterday,' Amie informed

me, and all I could think of was the Lassa ward's mysteriously feverish patients.

'Has he been around the ward lately,' I asked Amie, 'when I wasn't around?' Amie shook her head. There was no way his symptoms could be connected, I told myself repeatedly.

The boy had only a minor temperature, in addition to muscle aches. 'You think malaria?' his mother asked.

'Sounds reasonable,' I told her, ignoring my more exotic speculations. We checked his weight and I did some math. 'Give him one and a half pills of quinine every eight hours,' I told her.

Severe cases of malaria require an IV to get the first dose in quickly, followed with six days of oral quinine to clear the parasite completely from the body. However, Amie's son did not look particularly ill. He was well nourished and presumably had continuous exposure to repeated malaria infections throughout his young life. With such mild symptoms, I figured we could keep from poking him with a needle.

'If he doesn't look better tomorrow,' I continued, 'we'll start looking for other things.'

'Tell the doctor tanks,' Amie said to her son. He politely did as instructed. Amie thanked me as well. 'I be back after the market,' she said.

'Don't worry,' I replied. 'You can take some pills from the ward.' Quinine was an inexpensive drug. It seemed a little silly to make her go buy it.

Amie gave me a funny look. 'But we be out,' the nurse replied, looking at me as if I should already know.

'What do you mean we're out?'

'Remember, I tell Daren to get more.'

'You told him we *needed* more.'

'Yes, because we be out,' Amie matter-of-factly told me.

Dumbfounded, I quickly learned that although all the charts had orders for quinine written on them, the patients had not been receiving any medication for malaria coverage. I had spent all day searching for some bizarre cause, but the solution couldn't have been more mundane. The answer to the mysterious outbreak of fevers was so simple: no one was being treated for malaria.

Several of our charges had received blood transfusions, which was the likely source of their recent malaria infections and new fevers. Almost all local inhabitants had malaria chronically in their serum. The procedure invariably introduced a new strain of parasite to the recipient and resulted in a symptomatic malaria episode.

I went about restarting the feverish patients on IV quinine and arranged to buy more oral tablets from the market, all the while wishing Amie and I had communicated more effectively. The current mistake had not cost lives, but it easily could have.

Ironically, although management and administration skills are essential to treating patients, such topics had been conspicuously absent from the many books I had memorized for medical school. My training had focused only on what was the proper thing to do, not how to make sure it was actually done. I left that night quite sure that I had learned a new lesson: healing the sick requires more than just medicine.

25

BORROWED CHIPS

August 3, 2003

Little Sia's emaciated body lay facedown on the rotted bed. A flaming swath extended across his back, causing his dark skin to flake off at the edges. Overtaking the fading ink line like a forest fire, the blaze consumed virgin flesh. 'No!' I said, unable to help myself. It had spread just as I had feared.

'Boom . . . boom . . . boom.' Marching to the beat of a drum, the inflammation continued over his body: up the shoulders and neck to wispy hair, down the calves and feet to petite toes.

'Hah!'

'Yah!'

'Ahh!'

Unseen patients down the hall shouted short exclamations, leading to screams. I wondered if they somehow knew what was happening.

The inferno enveloped Sia whole, leaving behind only exposed muscle, similar to a cadaveric dissection. I could trace the fine detail of the structures: the graceful arc of the trapezius inserting into the spine, the round bulges of the immature deltoids covering his tiny shoulders, and the body of the triceps grasping tightly to the elbow.

The blaze spilled out around him – it ate away at his bed and crept toward me across the floor. As it painlessly climbed my paralyzed legs, Sia pushed himself up with one hand and turned his denuded face to stare directly into mine. In a voice many times too deep for his young age, he bellowed, 'God has put us here for a reason!'

'Amen!'

'Hallelujah!' answered the choir of hidden patients.

'Do you know why you are here?' Sia demanded, his eyes, opaque from scarring infection, reflecting back my frozen image. But before I could fashion an answer, crashing cymbals woke me. Soothing Sunday music poured in through my open bedroom window to calm the pounding of my heart.

When I arrived at the ward, unscathed walls proved there had been no supernatural proceedings, and Amie assured me all of the patients were fine. Her son's fever had also abated, I was happy to hear, although her child still felt a little discombobulated from the quinine.

Zuri was off with the ambulance, which left only Amie and me to do the rounds. With images of flames still in my head, I felt obligated to check first on Little Sia. His rash had receded a few more inches down his back, although it still covered his buttocks and groin. It was a slight improvement, but not quite enough to arrest my troubled dreams.

Except for Nini, the other patients had all broken their fevers and returned to normal temperatures. 'Are you sure she got her quinine?' I asked Amie as I suspiciously eyed our patient. My personal pendulum of trust had swung to the other side, and I found myself doubting everything I heard.

'Yes,' Amie answered. 'You say they must get the quinine, so she must get it.'

'Yes. She must,' I agreed, still unconvinced.

'See, look here,' Amie said, showing me the part of the chart where she had personally recorded the dispensing of the medication.

'Ask her if she took it,' I continued, undeterred. Amie translated and Nini nodded her head in affirmation.

'Hmm,' I said, still slightly skeptical.

When I asked about other complaints, Nini pointed, wincing, to where her IV was located in her forearm. I held her hand up to an errant beam of light that had managed to slip its way through the heavy cement window. Nini's limb was hot and swollen, with puffiness extending from fingertips to midforearm.

My uncomfortable patient would barely let me touch around the IV site itself. Doing my best to be gentle, I felt a solid rope that extended up toward her shoulder in the exact distribution of one of the major veins of the arm. I had had a patient with the exact same problem during one of my rotations in medical school: thrombophlebitis, a bacterial infection of the blood vessel.

Having an IV in for extended periods of time was the most frequent cause. Given the unsanitary surroundings and the length of ribavirin treatment, I was surprised in retrospect that more of the patients in the ward had not come down with the same thing.

Staph was again the most likely causative agent, since the organism covers the skin of even healthy people. It becomes a problem only after a prolonged break in our foremost protective barrier. 'What do you normally do for this?' I asked Amie, who was looking over my shoulder. I was certain she had seen the problem before.

'Take out the IV and use hot packs,' she told me, looking for confirmation.

'That's good,' I said. 'And keep it elevated.'

Removing the IV eliminates the 'focus' of infection and is the main treatment. Staph forms a film around foreign objects in the body, to keep the immune system at bay. In the States, we also give antibiotics.

'Can she afford oxacillin?' I asked.

'No,' Amie said, shaking her head.

It took me a moment to control a fit of anger at the injustice and corruption that prevented me from providing Nini with the proper treatment. The practice of medicine requires an acceptance of many things: pain, suffering, and even death. But knowing there was an easy cure and not having the resources to give it was not normally one of them.

In Nini's case, I was tempted simply to buy the medication myself. But I wanted the nurses to have a lasting plan for treating the frequent infection – they could not afford to give oxacillin to everyone. 'Sustainability' is a concept frequently discussed in public health circles, much of it in response to short humanitarian trips by clinicians who end up treating elevated cholesterol or high blood pressure for only a few weeks, doing little to help the targeted populace.

The doctor part of me just wanted to fix the problem, while the public health side sought an ongoing solution. But both could be taken too far. A lack of perceived sustainability was one of the main reasons for the long delay in attempting HIV/AIDS treatment in the third world. Neither side offered any easy answers.

With good supportive care, I hoped we could find a way to do without extra medication, leaving an affordable remedy behind for the nurses when I eventually moved on. Luckily, thrombophlebitis is a slow-moving disease, and I doubted there was much risk in waiting.

A little later, the guard entered the office to find me working on my paper. I had found little time to write over the last few weeks but was doing my best to keep on schedule. My time in the ward had made the topic of my paper resonate all the stronger. The ravages of Lassa fever, which had started as an exciting, although esoteric, subject, had become all too real.

'Visitors for Dr Conteh,' the guard told me.

'What?' I said. 'Where?'

'There,' the guard answered, gesturing toward the entrance. 'For Dr Conteh.'

'Really?' I said, a little surprised. I had never before seen any visitors for the Lassa physician at the ward. 'I guess you should bring them in then.'

The guard returned with seven tanned men in full military camouflage, complete with caps angled sharply to the right. Although not exactly sure what I was expecting, it wasn't the group that entered. I scanned the patches on their uniforms, which confirmed they were all from the Pakistani battalion. The rest of their copious insignia was undecipherable to me, except for depictions of a staff with curled snake, the universal sign for medicine, on almost all of their shoulders.

'Please come in,' I said, moving the chairs so that the group could fit into the small quarters. The delegation squeezed in around me, the tufts of their trimmed black hair coming up to about my chin. It made me nervous to have visitors in the halls, so close to the infectious patients.

A man in front with a neatly groomed mustache took a half step forward. 'I am Major Raza, medical director for UNAMSIL,' he said in an official tone. 'Is Dr Conteh available?'

'Sorry,' I said, again wishing more than anyone that Dr Conteh had returned to the ward. 'He's in Kono at the moment,' I continued. 'Should be back in a day or so.'

'Oh. I was told he would be here,' the major said, clearly upset at my response. He looked for help among his compatriots on either side before turning back to me. 'You are?' he asked hesitantly.

'Ross,' I answered. 'I'm a . . . um . . .' I hesitated, almost saying I was a medical student but then realizing it might be a bit difficult to explain why I was running the facility. I didn't really know who these people were and didn't want to get anyone in trouble, Dr Conteh and me included.

'I'm . . . ahh . . . taking care of the ward while he is gone,' I finally finished.

Major Raza's face lit up. 'It is an honor to meet you,' he said, before proceeding to introduce me to his countrymen. There were six physicians in total, three having just arrived to replace Major Raza and his two assistants, who all appeared quite happy to be leaving.

The lone man in the back was the driver, who had slipped out of the room before he could be introduced. 'Uh . . . could you get him back in here,' I said. 'We can't have people walking around.' Major Raza gave a command in incomprehensible but obviously stern words, and the driver scurried back into the room to stand painfully straight at attention.

'My apologies,' the major said. 'I was just telling my new colleagues about the contagious nature of the disease.'

At the group's request, I gave a short talk on Lassa, with a focus on symptom recognition and proper referral. Despite having their own medical facilities, UNAMSIL had decided to transfer all suspected Lassa cases to the Lassa ward, due to the specialized treatment and infection-control procedures needed. The UN had determined that its soldiers, such as the Nepalese private we had taken care of, would be best served in Dr Conteh's experienced hands. Since they did not currently have any active cases, I didn't point out that, for the moment, they had only mine.

UNAMSIL had previously contemplated evacuating soldiers who became ill with presumed Lassa, but deemed the necessary logistics impractical. Transferring highly infectious patients across international borders necessitated too difficult a coordination, even for that UN body. Other countries, even the ailing soldiers' homelands, had proven particularly hesitant to admit people in the throes of the deadly illness. Sick expatriates frequently became stranded in Sierra Leone, just at the time when they most needed out.

'You have been very helpful,' Major Raza told me after I finished. 'Thank you for your time.'

'You're most welcome,' I told him as I proceeded to escort the group out the door before Major Raza could change his opinion of me. I was still waiting for one of them to look at me and ask me if I wasn't really just a medical student. I felt sure that they somehow must know – any extra word might give me away.

'Best of luck,' I told the three new doctors, quickly usher-ing them out the front gate. 'If your stay here is anything like mine, I'm sure it'll be quite the unique experience.'

I was still recovering from my close call with the UNAMSIL group when Zuri returned to the ward with the ambulance. He brought with him two refugees, a mother–daughter pair who both had fevers and flulike symptoms. The mother carried her sleeping daughter, who, in turn, clutched a ragged doll in weary arms. 'They be treated for malaria but still have fever,' Zuri told me.

'What did they use?' I asked.

'Chloroquine,' the tech answered.

I shook my head in disappointment. 'Is that all?'

'Yes,' he answered cheerfully.

Chloroquine is the classic medication for malaria treatment. It has few side effects and is cheaper and easier to use than quinine. But although it was remarkably useful upon its first worldwide introduction in the 1940s, over 70 percent of the malaria parasites in Sierra Leone had now developed resistance to the drug.

The few newer antimalarial medications cost too much for the battered Sierra Leonean government to afford. Quinine, which was also relatively cheap and which we were using in the ward, was difficult to administer intravenously in the outreach clinics. Thus, the Ministry of Health continued to recommend chloroquine as the first-line treatment.

'Well, that makes it kind of difficult, doesn't it?' I told Zuri.

'Life never be easy,' he replied with a pearly grin.

The unfortunate practice of using chloroquine in the country added additional uncertainty to Lassa diagnosis. Early identification became even more difficult, since the normal alerting symptom of a fever that failed to respond to antimalarial and antibiotic treatment was not specific to Lassa. When a patient did not get better on chloroquine therapy, it was impossible to know early on if the cause was the deadly virus or drug-resistant malaria.

If the symptoms in the mother–daughter pair were due to Lassa, then the two were close to crossing the dangerous line into stage three, when the efficacy of treatment became severely limited. On the other hand, if they had drug-resistant malaria, then there was no reason to risk the side effects of ribavirin.

I looked at the mother again. She appeared sick but was doing her best to comfort her equally ill daughter. The woman's dark eyes reflected back my own face, by the filtered light of the setting sun. Choosing which medications to give the pair could potentially be the difference between life and death. Some people accuse doctors of 'playing God' in such situations, but in truth it felt far from a game, and I had little choice in the matter.

For the millionth time, I wondered why I was there. Why had I decided to get on a plane for Sierra Leone to research some obscure virus? Was it to make such judgments, or did I overreach? There would be more flames to haunt my tired dreams that night, I knew. At that point, the fuel seemed inexhaustible.

'Start them on quinine and we'll see how they're doing tomorrow,' I finally said, deciding to withhold ribavirin for the time being. Zuri nodded his head. With those simple words, I determined both the care and fate of the two lives before me. Response to therapy, or lack thereof, would establish their status – I was betting with borrowed chips that they had at least one more day.

26

HEAL THYSELF

August 4, 2003

Blaa! Blaa! my alarm rang. I rolled over on a bedsheet damp with sweat and attempted to raise myself from lagging slumber. Drowsy with heat, I swallowed to clear the saliva that clung to the back of my throat. Pain lanced across enlarged tonsils, lingering afterward as if in anger. 'Uhh,' I mumbled.

Grabbing a towel, I plodded to the bathroom, where a mirror presented a ragged and unshaven image, my blond hair all askew. Underneath exhausted eyes lay puffy bags that looked like miniature pillows. My reflection rubbed a swollen face, but my features did not return to normal, and then it hit me. Had I contracted Lassa? Daily work at the ward had lulled me into nonchalance, but suddenly each questionable practice seemed just another way to have caught the deadly illness.

As soon as the thought entered my mind, I ran back to my room and rummaged through my backpack. Throwing a medical kit on the bed, I dug through its pockets, launching gauze and pills across the unmade sheet. At the bottom, among Scooby-Doo Band-Aids and aspirin tablets, I found my beat-up thermometer.

Pushing the button, I stuck it under my tongue and paced from one side of the room to the other. After belatedly remembering that exercise would give me a falsely high reading, I sat down among the strewn medical equipment, shifting only to remove an errant pill bottle from underneath me.

My heart was pounding in my chest, and I told myself to calm down. I had taken my malaria meds, hadn't I? It was probably just the flu or a sore throat, I hoped, but the image of a puffy face remained seared into my memory. It was abnormal – I had never experienced anything similar before.

With eyes crossed, I strained to see the increasing numbers on the thermometer while imagining what would happen if I had contracted the virus. Would I check myself into the Lassa ward? Dr Conteh was not even there to help. Could I treat myself? My fate would be in the hands of the nurses.

Should I try to get out of Sierra Leone? The UNAMSIL medics had declared it impossible, and they had much better resources. I wondered if there was any other choice. It seemed there was a dearth of practical options.

I knew Merlin had tried to evacuate a past Lassa case, a female pediatrician who came down with a high fever while visiting the pediatric ward. She became severely ill, and treatment with both antimalarials and antibiotics were unable to break her fever. Although Dr Conteh started ribavirin treatment in the ward, the woman's blood pressure became increasingly volatile.

I had heard rumor of the heated negotiations needed to convince a Red Cross helicopter to fly the contagious woman to Freetown. Once there, Merlin personnel attempted to transfer the sick patient to a plane that they had chartered. However, a horde of people wearing full PPEs on the tarmac frightened the surprised pilot, and it took several days to find someone who would agree to man the flight.

A diplomatic row had then ensued over which country would accept the highly infectious patient. Her native country refused her entry, and Britain, where she had been studying in a program similar to my own, also denied her permission. After considerable delay, Germany offered to treat the ailing woman in a special containment facility.

The whole transport process took multiple days, likely worsening the pediatrician's illness. The UNAMSIL medics were right: it was almost impossible to evacuate. Treatment in the Lassa ward was probably the best choice. At least there was a ready supply of ribavirin.

The thermometer beeped in the middle of my fretful calculations, cutting short my racing thoughts. It read 98.6 degrees, exactly normal. Could that be right? I felt hot and started to notice a headache. After repeating the process again, I received the same result. *You're just stressing yourself out,* I told myself.

I went into the bathroom again and stared at my swollen eyes. They just did not seem natural. Water from the unheated shower cooled my forehead, but each painful swallow reminded me that something was wrong. After dressing, I checked my temperature again. It had not changed even one-tenth of a degree.

I was tired and felt an amazingly strong desire to sleep, but there was no one to replace me at the ward. I couldn't take the day off. 'Please radio the car for me,' I told Chris, who was stationed at the guesthouse exit. I didn't feel like walking.

'No problem,' the security guard said, clearly happy that he could help and that, after all this time, I had finally come to my senses about walking.

Amie, Zuri, and a few of the recovered patients were mingling around the radio when I arrived. The rebels were shelling Monrovia again and demanding Taylor's immediate removal. The crew listened attentively to the radio's description of the devastation from the nearby fighting while I sought refuge in the office, shutting the door behind me.

My temperature was the same when I checked it again, and I stared suspiciously at the thermometer while a familiar voice lofted over the flimsy office partition. 'There is heavy gunfire . . . We are seeing casualties but are unable to leave our compound,' Mikhail said over the broadcast. 'Rounds are dropping everywhere . . .' he continued, his line crackling out prematurely. It was clear that it had the makings of a horrible day all around.

After resting for a bit, I attempted to see patients through a foggy daze. Luckily, the mother–daughter pair from the day before had responded to quinine therapy. They must have had chloroquine-resistant malaria, not Lassa. My precarious gamble had paid off, but I barely had the strength to enjoy the small victory.

In the other rooms, my patients persisted with what had seemingly become their status quo. Mariama had several minor complaints but no longer a fever. Fortuna's breathing continued to improve and her roommate, Nini, still had a swollen hand. Sia's rash was unchanged.

After wearily finishing with my minimal labors, I secluded myself in the office and rechecked my temperature obsessively. I didn't want Amie or Zuri to know how I felt — vocalizing my fears would have made them too real.

Don't overreact, I told myself, trying to postulate other reasons for my concerning symptoms. *There is no need for alarm.* But all I could think of was the terrible deaths I had witnessed within the ward's dark walls — the copious blood, the sudden leak of fluids, and the slow but inescapable decline.

I rested a drowsy head on the wooden desk and nodded between unconsciousness and an uncertain reality. Around noon, I informed Amie that I was heading back early to the guesthouse. 'Send someone if you need me,' I told her.

'You all right?' she asked me with concern.

'I'll be fine. Don't you worry,' I mumbled.

Outside, rain poured steadily down, encasing the deserted street in a liquid cocoon. I traipsed back to the guesthouse under an overwhelmed umbrella and belatedly wished I had radioed for the car. Lacking sufficient energy to avoid the puddles, I walked uncaringly through them.

Heal Thyself

As I passed through town, a flash of colorless skin within one of the dilapidated porches briefly caught my eye. Inside, I glimpsed the freckled face of a prepubescent albino boy, framed by tufts of curly orange hair. He was the first of his kind that I had encountered in Africa, and his ghostly eyes watched me intently as I walked by through the falling showers.

When I finally stumbled into my room at the guesthouse, I collapsed into the unmade bed, my thoughts too groggy to fully consider my own predicament. As soon as my cheek touched the makeshift pillow, I dropped immediately into bottomless slumber, the child's pale visage haunting my swollen lids.

27

DOTS OF HOPE

August 5, 2003

I woke peacefully in bed and stretched out my arms, brushing them casually against the surrounding mosquito net. It was only when I sat up that I abruptly recalled the reason for my early slumber. As the nightmare of being sick suddenly flooded back, I swallowed reflexively. My throat was mildly sore, but the lancing pain was gone.

In the bathroom I found a disheveled face; however, the swelling had receded into memory. A quick reading from the thermometer confirmed my good fortune, and I sighed with great relief when I realized that I had not actually contracted Lassa. My brief symptoms, likely some harmless illness, had come and passed too quickly.

Birds chirped outside the window, and clouds lightly draped a midday sun. It's impossible to describe how ecstatic I felt to have escaped my latest brush with the deadly Lassa virus, even if this one was mostly in my head. Having had to confront my own mortality, I felt momentarily freed from the mundane constructs of daily existence. Each minute of my new life seemed like stolen treasure – it was as if I were physically trying to suck in every sensation around me, through every sense and pore.

Overjoyed not to be lying on one of the rotted Lassa ward beds or encased in a hermetically sealed plastic bubble, I finally checked the time. My watch read 11:00 A.M., meaning I had slept for almost twenty-four hours. I laughed out loud, for some reason finding my long slumber immensely funny. With a grin bigger than Zuri's, I raced to dress and throw down a belated breakfast. My deep sleep must have proved a cure for whatever ailed me.

While I ate, the radio in the dining room reported on progress in Liberia. Even as U.S. forces remained floating offshore, two hundred Nigerian soldiers had landed at the Monrovian airport. They had not yet left the tarmac, but I was happy to hear that the mere presence of troops on Liberian soil had again restrained the fighting. I suddenly felt optimistic that they might bring an end to Taylor's long reign.

I wondered if the old men who started such wars ever contemplated their own mortality. They always seem to be safely hidden away from the fighting, huddled under some secure bunker. It would be better if the foot soldiers decided when to go to war – how many fewer battles we might then have. Peace might be much easier to find if those negotiating for it had just experienced their own brushes with death. If Taylor had to put his own life on the line to shoot each additional bullet, the fighting would surely end.

I cheerfully whistled on my walk to work, every color

seeming all the more vibrant. I paused to chuckle at a passing van that had a live goat strapped awkwardly to its roof. The braying animal, straddling piled-up gear, led me down the puddle-filled road. I could not have felt any happier.

Upon my arrival at the ward, Amie reported an incident-free night. 'That's wonderful!' I said.

'You be feeling better?' she asked me.

'Much better,' I assured her.

'We also get a message from Kono. Dr Conteh be much better too, but they have to wait on the roads to dry before coming home.'

'I'm glad he's improved,' I told her. Although previously the news of Dr Conteh's further delay would have given me a panic attack, today not even that could penetrate my cheerful demeanor.

Zuri was off with the ambulance, leaving Amie and me to do the rounds. We started in the back room, where an adolescent boy slept on the empty cot across from Mariama.

'Who's he?' I asked.

'Her boyfriend,' Amie said, clucking in disapproval.

'I think it's nice that he came to visit,' I told her, and Amie rolled her eyes. I enjoyed egging her on a bit. The two of us had established a close bond somewhere amid the trials of the previous week.

'That girl always be complaining,' Amie said, wagging her finger as if she had seen enough.

'What's she "complaining" of now?' I asked.

'She say her stomach hurt very bad.'

I dutifully examined Mariama's gravid abdomen, but it felt reassuringly soft, and the fetal heart rate was still strong. I also thought little of the matter.

Amie and I moved on to the next room, where we found Little Sia's rash completely scabbed over. He looked much better and squirmed under his mother's restraining hands while he tried to remove his NG tube. 'He seems to be improving,' I told Amie, elbowing her a bit for emphasis.

'True,' she said, laughing at my enthusiasm.

'If he pulls it out, just leave it and we'll see if he can start eating on his own.'

Next door, Nini lay in bed with her hand clutched tenderly to her side, her infection appearing unchanged. I became frustrated that it would not heal and scrounged around the ward for supplies while Amie looked on, perplexed. After bringing a pile of items back to the bedside, I made an overhead sling out of old bandages and an IV pole, to improve the venous drainage from her limb. 'Keep it up until tomorrow,' I insisted. It was my last attempt. If it failed to improve, I was going to buy the needed antibiotics myself.

The rest of the rounds were uneventful, and we finished by readying the mother–daughter pair to return to their refugee camp. They needed only some oral quinine to complete their malaria treatment. The two looked much better, with the young girl playing quietly with her doll while her mother watched attentively. I was content that I had had at least one quick success.

* * *

Shortly afterward, Zuri returned with the ambulance. He grinned at me and I grinned back, feeling as if maybe I finally understood the secret to his happiness. 'Before I be taking them to the refugee camp,' he said, motioning to the healing mother–daughter pair, 'could you look at a friend?'

'They're sick?'

'Think so,' he said.

'Of course.'

Zuri went outside to retrieve the new consult, and it was hard to maintain my doctor face when the starkly emaciated figure entered. The man paused for a fit of rumbling coughs before sitting down on the examination bed. The ragged African's body was so wasted that his sunken eyes appeared only as overlarge shadows above sharply protruding cheekbones.

A younger woman accompanied our new patient and patted his back as he recovered from the coughing. Zuri happily chatted away with her while I waited for the tech to translate.

'Zuri,' I finally said, to get the tech's attention.

He kept blissfully talking away.

'Zuri, the patient,' I said again, a little louder.

'Sorry,' he finally said, a little sheepishly. 'He be her older brother,' he continued, nodding from the girl to the thin man. 'I know his sister better.'

'I'm sure you do,' I replied.

Zuri translated our new patient's story of developing a

cough over the last year. Unable to work, the man had left a job at a mine in Tongo to return to his family in Kenema. The sister described how her brother had become progressively fatigued and eventually lost the desire to eat. He suffered from fevers and night sweats, she told us, with concern written across her face.

As the man's story unraveled in front of me, with my new patient continuing to cough violently, I slowly backed away from the table and attempted to put on a mask as subtly as possible, a clearly impossible task. After a particularly large bout, I had the exhausted man do the same. Her brother coughed up blood sometimes, his sister reported.

The man's presentation was classic for tuberculosis (TB), an ancient bacterial disease that has plagued mankind for ages. The causative bacterium spreads from person to person in airborne droplets, launched from one person's lungs and inhaled by another's. It gives a classic appearance in the afflicted, who look as if they have been 'eaten' by the disease, the reason for one of its oldest names: consumption.

In the nineteenth century, TB was the leading cause of death in America, where the authorities of the time locked away the afflicted in isolated asylums. Environmental improvements, mostly in housing and nutrition, have greatly reduced the burden of the disease in the developed world. But it is still a serious health problem in developing countries.

Mining is a known risk factor for TB; close quarters and an abundance of soot increase the chances that the disease will spread. A little further questioning revealed that the miners all lived crammed together, more than forty men per dilapidated house. One of the other occupants had a similar cough, the likely source of my patient's current infection.

'Sir, you need to be treated for tuberculosis,' I told him. His sister nodded her head in understanding while the brother had another fit of coughs. If left on its present course, with such a severe infection, the man's disease would undoubtedly be fatal. Most healthy people can fight off TB, at least partially, but it is particularly aggressive in those with poor nutrition or concurrent disease.

HIV figured most prominently in the latter group, with a noted resurgence of TB across the globe as the AIDS pandemic spread. Once a person is infected with HIV, even old TB infections that have been successfully walled off by the immune system can renew unchecked. It was very possible that Zuri's acquaintance had both HIV and TB infections.

I listened to the man's story further and learned about his family and kids, all the while wondering if I should mention the possibility of HIV. In the end, I decided not to. There was no treatment or testing available in the region. If the man had HIV, he was simply doomed to die. I thought it best to spare him and his family what was locally a terrible stigma. It was a choice inconsistent with Western ethics. But, as Dr Conteh had told me, medicine was different in Africa.

TB treatment is difficult even in the absence of HIV infection and requires daily medication over multiple months. Since patients often start feeling better shortly after beginning treatment, they frequently stop taking their pills prematurely. The disease invariably returns with bacilli more resistant to the medications, a pattern that has caused a worldwide increase in multidrug-resistant TB, an organism immune to normal treatment.

For that reason, the WHO has developed a special program: Directly Observed Therapy (DOT). It has been a massive success in curing patients with TB in the third world, a previously impossible task. The crux of the system is a mandate that infected persons have a third party, normally a nurse, watch them take their pills daily.

Although I lacked the TB medications and logistical support needed, I had heard that a DOT program was just opening in Kenema. Luckily, the emaciated man was in one of the few areas in the region with access to treatment. If he was free from HIV, then his prognosis was good.

Zuri and I were talking about getting our patient into the DOT program when a high-pitched scream pierced the ward. I instinctively ran to its source in Mariama's room to find her boyfriend leaning over the head of the bed. Mariama was panting, pure fear painted across her youthful face, as the boyfriend eyed me nervously.

'What's going on?' I demanded, staring at the boyfriend accusingly. I had a flashback to my arrival in Kenema and the violence I had seen that night.

Amie and Zuri arrived shortly afterward. They had not felt the need to hurry. Amie looked disgusted. 'She be doing that all night,' Amie said, rolling her eyes.

'Doing what?' I said.

'Screaming and screaming, keeping up the other patients.'

'Why?' I asked, confused. 'What's going on?'

'Stomach pain,' Amie said, shrugging. The adolescent boyfriend had nothing to do with it, I realized. I felt bad that I had given him such an evil look.

I put on the PPE and went over to feel Mariama's abdomen while the boyfriend scurried into the corner. 'Where does it hurt?' I asked. Mariama cupped her hands beneath her belly button.

I pushed down on her clenched abdomen, then let out a loud chuckle. 'What be funny?' Zuri said, looking in from the doorway.

'How long has she been having the pains?' I asked.

'Since yesterday,' Amie replied. Each had lasted for only a few minutes. Mariama's belly was already starting to relax beneath my hands, but fear still covered her face.

'Tell her not to worry,' I said as I redraped Mariama's exposed abdomen. 'She's going to have a baby.'

28

A TINY MIRACLE

August 6, 2003

'So?' I asked Amie, who sat at her normal perch in the ward.

'Mariama deliver after midnight,' the nurse replied. 'The—'

'A boy or a girl?' I interrupted excitedly.

'A boy,' Amie said. Eager to see the baby, I rushed off to Mariama's room, Amie trailing behind me.

The young mother slept on her bed, her boyfriend attentively hovering by her head. Although they looked more like prom dates than new parents, it was an endearing image. I snuck up from the doorway to stand next to them. 'Where's the baby?' I whispered to Amie, who still followed.

'There,' Amie answered, her voice flat as she pointed across the room to a small bundle on the other cot. 'Not going to make it.'

'What!' I said.

I put on gloves and gently unwrapped the swaddled blanket. Within, I found lifeless flesh that leached heat from my hand, just like the cadaver I had dissected during my first year of medical school. With horror, I scooped up the cold infant onto my forearm, cradling his head between my thumb and index finger while his limbs flopped loosely to both sides. Consistent with my previous estimate of now thirty-four weeks, the child was about twice as large as the palm of my hand. It should have been enough time to survive.

I inspected the baby with a growing sense of remorse. The wrinkled flesh that rested on my arm had no obvious deformities. His body, although minute, appeared properly formed. Had my use of ribavirin to treat his mother caused this awful tragedy? Full of self-doubt, I felt a desperate urge to undo what I might have done.

A tiny motion caught my eye – the abdomen of the small infant stirred faintly. I placed two fingers across the boy's belly to confirm his diminutive movement. My pulse quickened. Mariama's child hovered precipitously near the edge of death but had not yet crossed that fine line.

I stuck a latex-gloved pinkie finger into his petite mouth and gently curled it against his upper palate. A healthy infant would start sucking, one of the most basic reflexes. Mariama's newborn had no response.

'What happened?' I asked Amie urgently, unable to take my eyes off the listless baby.

'Too small to live,' she answered.

Previously a traditional birth attendant, Amie had delivered the child in the early morning. She reported matter-of-factly that labor had left Mariama exhausted, despite her child's small size.

'Did he cry?' I asked, still confused as to why the infant had done so poorly.

Amie shrugged. 'Yes,' she finally said.

The baby was still alive, and I could not understand why Amie wasn't doing anything to save him. It took me a few minutes to piece together the full story: convinced the child was going to die, Amie had apparently put him off to the side to keep the new mother from bonding with the fated infant. 'Be better this way,' the nurse said. I looked up from the tenuous life that I carried to Amie's impassive face. The ramifications of her decision sank in slowly.

My head nurse was likely right – most of the preemies in Sierra Leone probably died early deaths. Far from steroids and neonatal units in the West, they lacked even basic prenatal care. Having seen the infant with Dr Nassan in the pediatric ward, I knew improper treatment killed many of them. With the worst maternal and infant mortality rates in the world, even those born under the best of conditions in Sierra Leone had an uncertain future. What seemed to me cruel indifference was to Amie a compassionate gesture, sparing the mother what the nurse felt was the inevitable death of the baby.

Our recent arrival to the human race lay ever so lightly on my forearm. It appeared that his stay would be unduly short. Coming from the West, where such a newborn would most likely survive to lead a normal life, I found it impossible to countenance such an uncontested death. I felt a sudden surge of anger at a world that could contain such raw injustice.

I tucked the tiny boy back into his blanket and walked quietly to Mariama's bedside. Her boyfriend retreated again to the corner. 'Did she want it?' I asked Amie softly. The nurse did not answer but joined me to stand over our gently sleeping patient. 'Ask her,' I said more forcefully. 'Ask her if she wanted the baby.'

Amie watched me without overt expression, her deep eyes unblinking. I had no doubt that we both wanted the best for Mariama, but our worldviews were so incongruent. We came not only from different lands, but from disparate realities. Suddenly the chasm seemed so shockingly vast.

I gently shook Mariama's shoulder. The exhausted teenager woke slowly, groggily looking around the room before eventually focusing on Amie and me. 'Ask her if she wants it,' I said again, this time more softly.

The unmoving jungle air hung around us like a hushed pillow until Amie abruptly broke the silence with a short staccato of words in Mende. Mariama looked back and forth between her caregivers' mute faces. I was unsure if our patient understood the question at first, but then the young woman nodded her head in unambiguous affirmation.

'Tell her I don't know if he will survive,' I said. 'But if she wants, we can try to keep him.' Amie hesitated for a moment, then translated. Mariama nodded her head again, yes. Yes.

Time, which had seemingly slowed during our somber deliberations, suddenly jumped into fast-forward. 'We have to get him warm!' I urged, anxious with newfound purpose. Newborns have very little fat and are unable to maintain their own body heat. There was little I could do for this baby but to hope that the infant's decrease in body temperature was the cause of his unresponsiveness.

The ward had no warming cubicles or heated blankets, like those used in the States, so I had Amie assist me in stripping both Mariama and her baby naked. Then we placed the infant's freezing body between his mother's bare breasts, with Mariama shivering violently from both the cold and her exhaustion. We proceeded to wrap the pair in every available blanket and transformed them into an undistinguishable mass, heaped high upon the cot.

The catharsis of action over, there was nothing to do but wait. I paced the halls, looking at my watch every few minutes. *The covered pot boils quickest,* I told myself as I resisted the recurrent urge to take off the blankets and check on the progress of the hidden baby. At Amie's insistence, we saw the other patients, all of whom passed in a blur. Nini's hand was still up in a sling, possibly doing better. Fortuna was continuing with her ribavirin regimen. Little Sia's NG tube had come out, but he was eating properly. Although I made a perfunctory check on everyone in the ward, nothing could pull my thoughts away from the heavy bundle in the far room.

Immediately after finishing, I looked in again on Mariama but could assess little beneath the obstructing pile of blankets. Like an expectant father, I returned to pacing the halls, with pauses every few laps to check on the pair. Our infant would have to be born twice to live.

* * *

An hour later, I finally woke Mariama. She looked out from underneath the towering heap of blankets like a confused tortoise that had flipped within its shell. I gently peeled away her coverings, unsure if underneath I would find a living baby or a dead body. I finally reached the little infant, who lay flaccid on his mother's exposed chest. He was breathing softly, and I sighed in relief, observing that he was warmer than before. His color had improved from ashen gray to salmon pink, partway to the vibrant flush of a healthy newborn. But the sucking reflex again had no response.

Muttering encouraging words, I covered the pair back up. Before I passed out the doorway, Mariama was already asleep again. I busied myself around the ward, cleaning up the doctor's office and stacking spare cases of ribavirin, hoping I was doing the right thing. When I could find no more chores, I sat impatiently listening to the daily radio report: although the Nigerian troops had made it into Monrovia, the city siege continued. Taylor remained in power. There was so little I could do.

The news program interviewed Mikhail again, and my fellow Merlin worker described his unsuccessful attempts to enter the LURD-controlled territory, where many of the injured were located. The rebels' area had food but lacked medicine. Taylor's side had medicine, but no food. The refugees in the Lassa ward had family in both regions, although no one knew who was alive and who was dead.

★ ★ ★

I waited uneasily until noon before checking on my charges again. Unwrapping the layers as if I were handling a suspicious package, I found the little infant inside, warmed finally to body temperature. He lay with legs and arms curled close to his body, his hands clenched into tiny fists. I looked at his perfectly human figure and admired the faint wrinkles over each knuckle.

When I put my finger into his diminutive grasp, he pulled back, giving some resistance. I stuck my finger in his mouth and felt an uncoordinated but distinct lick. 'Better,' I said with my best reserve, trying to restrain myself from jumping with excitement.

Mariama held her child in an awkward but loving grasp. She was obviously starting to bond with the baby. After mold-ing her hands to make the pair more comfortable, I covered them both again. As I passed out of the room, I paused to look at the indistinct heap through the doorway. The more Mariama became attached to her baby, the worse it would be if he died. I doubted Amie would forgive me if that happened.

Around three in the afternoon, I checked again. The tiny boy was pink and warm. I laughed aloud, scaring the boyfriend, when I put my finger into the infant's mouth. The child tickled me with his tiny sucking, which seemed to be the most joyous sensation I had ever experienced.

The next step in my impromptu plan was to get the baby to breastfeed. I had never felt such pressure to start. Normally, newborns have excess nutritional stores to survive for several days while the process begins, but Mariama's infant had been both premature and traumatized. I was uncertain how long he would last without nourishment.

Together, Amie and I sat Mariama up. The new mother wobbled weakly, her movements grossly uncoordinated. I tried to get her to hold the baby properly to feed, but she kept squishing his head too firmly into her breast. After an unsuccessful half-hour, we finally gave up. 'We'll try again later,' I said, inwardly concerned about how much time we had before the infant tired completely.

Mariama had not eaten in over a day, so we got her some food. Amie wore an impassive face, shielding judgment. I wondered if she felt I was being a naïve Westerner, going to such lengths to save a baby that she was convinced would surely die.

The sun was setting when we tried again. Sustenance and additional sleep had soothed Mariama's shaking hands, and the young teenager stroked her baby's cheek gently with her nipple. The weak infant repeatedly reached out with his lips but failed to latch on. Another fruitless half-hour left me disillusioned and Mariama visibly frustrated.

We were about to give up when suddenly the infant's dainty mouth finally found the correct spot. Resounding smacks filled the room as the baby slurped vigorously. It was such a simple action, but I felt as if there could be nothing more wondrous, not even if the sun suddenly burned through our roof to shine down radiant light into the battered ward.

A Tiny Miracle

Struck in awe, Mariama and I gazed at the small bundle of determined motion. It was an intense world in which I found myself – one severe in its taking, but equally generous in its giving. The new mother fed her spirited child, encased by a hallowed glow, and I gave silent thanks for our tiny miracle of living.

29

THE GROWING DARKNESS

August 7, 2003

'Morning, Doc,' Amie said when I arrived at the ward the next morning.

'Morning,' I replied, continuing our well-worn ritual. 'So, how did we do?'

'Tanks God,' Amie answered.

'And the baby?' I asked.

'Eat three more times,' Amie answered impassively. Despite a rough beginning, it sounded to me as if the child was beginning to adjust appropriately.

I was eager to check on the baby, but the quiet purr of the oxygen machine stopped me in midstep. Zuri came out of the adjacent room. 'New patient,' he reported. 'From the refugee camp this morning.'

Amie joined Zuri and me to follow the foreboding hum of compressed gas through the dark doorway. Within, we found a woman with her back to us, bent over the far bed. As we entered, she turned to face us with tear-filled eyes. Behind her, a small girl with colored ribbons in her braided hair lay in the middle of the cot.

'Eve,' Zuri told me, naming our new patient.

'How old?' I asked.

'Four,' he said.

A nasal cannula filled the girl's petite nose with a gentle swish of oxygen, and an IV dripped clear fluid into a vein in the crease of her elbow. Eve's closed eyes remained unresponsive to my touch as I lightly placed a gloved hand on her abdomen. My arm shot up and down with the ill child's rapid breaths, and I wondered how long she could maintain the troubled pace.

According to Eve's mother, her daughter had developed a fever and a sore throat over a week prior. As Eve's symptoms worsened, her mother took the child to the refugee clinic, where a local medical worker had given antibiotics and quinine. But despite several days of therapy, the girl's symptoms had only worsened.

Eve had slowly withdrawn from the world around her, and her petite body had swollen with a steady leakage of fluids. The child had developed the classic bloodshot eyes of Lassa infection by the time she arrived at the ward, and my two nurses had wisely started her on ribavirin in the early morning.

I listened to Eve's lungs and could hear loud gurgling, as if someone had poured several cups of water down her windpipe. The fluid there was preventing proper oxygen exchange, and Eve was slowly drowning. I turned off the IV drip that the nurses had started – giving additional fluid would potentially aggravate that buildup.

Eve was gravely ill. In the States, she would have gone immediately to an intensive care unit (ICU). Doctors would have put a tube down her windpipe to secure her airway, hooked her up to a ventilator to regulate her breathing, and ordered a battery of tests to monitor her organs. But the ward had none of the required equipment.

I searched the storage room for anything helpful and sifted through the pitiable medicine cabinet. Eve was already getting ribavirin but was well into the third stage of Lassa infection. I was unsure how much benefit the medication would have, so far into the disease process.

The only additional drug I found of debatable utility was Lasix, a diuretic 'water pill.' It increases urine output, thus reducing the total amount of water in the body. Conceivably, I surmised, it could improve her lungs and breathing.

However, Eve's underlying problem was not an excess of body fluid, but a virus-induced shift of liquid from her blood vessels to her lungs. Her heart rate was high and blood pressure low, the classic findings of shock. While she had too much fluid in the respiratory tract, she conversely had too little pumping in her arteries.

In any halfway-developed country, there were additional drugs, such as adrenaline, that solved this problem by increasing the strength of heart contractions. But these medications were conspicuously absent from the storage room. Some unidentified Merlin manager had decided that the drugs were nonessential, when even basic antibiotics were in short supply. Although I desperately wanted the vials, it was hard to argue with that assumption.

In the absence of such medications, treatment had to be a balancing act, since focusing solely on one organ system would worsen the other. To help her blood pressure I needed to provide fluids – to help her lungs I needed to remove some.

Unable to decide whether to give Eve Lasix or, conversely, more fluids, I continued with rounds. Mariama's newborn was doing well and lay feeding in his mother's arms, the heap of blankets no longer necessary. The infant's adamant smacks induced contagious smiles, and I was overwhelmed with his marked improvement.

The other patients were recovering slowly, and we finished with Sia, who was also doing much better. His mother held him carefully to prevent choking as she fed him an unappetizing-looking mash of rice and yellow sauce. His eyes recognized me from my frequent visits and followed me without a pause in his determined chewing. I hoped Eve would have as miraculous a recovery.

Throughout the rest of the day, we listened to the radio broadcast the fortunes of others slightly farther away. Twenty US marines had finally landed in Monrovia, to the flocking crowds of an exuberant populace. The troops' true mandate was only to 'secure' the US embassy, but the fighting had momentarily ceased due to a handful of the sole superpower's soldiers on Liberian soil.

I continued to debate giving Lasix or fluids to Eve throughout the rest of the day and almost told Amie to give one or the other each time I listened to the child's wet lungs or checked her blood pressure. But I stopped on each occasion, not knowing what the effect would be. *Primum non nocere* (first, do no harm), I told myself repeatedly, but the ancient maxim provided little solace.

As the sun outside slowly set, I looked in on Eve one final time before leaving for the night. Standing side by side, her mother and I shared a quiet vigil. We watched the child's heavy breathing, both lost in our own thoughts. Eve's mother, perhaps, remembered her daughter's first steps or a special bedtime kiss. Limited merely to memories of Eve's earthly suffering, I saw only the darkness grow around her while hoping in the depths of my heart that I had made the right decision.

30

ONE LAST DAY

August 8, 2003

The next morning, anxious to get to the ward, I stuffed down a hurried breakfast. Thoughts of Eve had kept me up through the night as I debated if I should have given her Lasix or, instead, added additional IV fluids. There seemed to be no absolute answers – having left the narrow boundaries of medical science, I was adrift within an imperfect art.

A cough outside the screen window interrupted my continued deliberations. 'Ross . . . Ross,' Chris whispered to me.

'Morning,' I said.

'Turn on the radio,' Chris continued. 'Taylor, he resign!'

I switched on the news, which reported that the Nigerian peacekeepers had left the airport and pushed into the heart of Monrovia. Cheering hordes had welcomed the ECOWAS troops as they secured the starved and beaten city.

Taylor had subsequently stepped down as president but left an ally in control. Although the former president was promising to leave the country within the week, it was unclear if he was serious. The Nigerians had intercepted a last-minute shipment of ammunition on their way in from the airport. It was apparent that Taylor was desperately searching for a way out of his self-inflicted predicament.

Overall, it was still a positive development, and the good fortune continued when I arrived at the ward to find that everyone had survived the night. I immediately checked on my most critical patient and found Eve's mother standing next to the bed, exactly where I had left her. The heart-torn woman glanced at me once in acknowledgment before returning a loving gaze to her ill child.

Eve appeared to be sleeping peacefully. The child's breathing had slowed to a gentler pace. Listening to her lungs, I could hear only a faint whisper of fluid. It seemed that the girl had improved without the need for either fluids or Lasix. I left the room with a bounce in my step, happy with her progress.

The morning got even better when I spoke again to Amie. She had just gotten off the CB. 'Dr. Conteh be heading back now,' she reported.

'Are you sure?' After the protracted wait, the news seemed almost too good to be true.

'Yes. He be here tomorrow for sure,' she promised confidently.

All three nurses were present, and we quickly got together for rounds. We started with Little Sia, who was sitting up in bed under his own power, munching away hungrily at some mashed gruel. His mother turned him over for us and pulled down ragged shorts to demonstrate that the rash had completely scabbed over. 'That's looking pretty good,' I said. The nurses all agreed.

'Much better,' Bryan concurred. He had the added benefit of not having seen it for almost a week.

Trying to escape, the child mooned us with squirming buttocks. 'I think his strength is starting to return too,' I said happily. 'That's the most activity I've ever seen him do!'

In the next room, we found Nini without her makeshift sling. Her fever had vanished and her hand had returned to normal size. She was chatting with Fortuna, who had just finished her last day of ribavirin therapy. 'Lots of talking about Taylor's resignation,' Zuri told me, smiling. 'Everybody be happy.' If the ex-president left Liberia as promised, our refugees would finally be able to return home. It felt like an impromptu party.

Crying echoed down the hall, and we followed the spirited sounds to Mariama's room. Fully recovered from the delivery and her illness, the new mother gently rocked her young baby in content arms. Her child's fierce wails were a good sign he was doing well. I was confident that the pair could go home soon.

I gave instructions for strict breastfeeding, and Mariama promised to do so. I knew the baby's long-term prognosis, like that of all Sierra Leone's children, was far from certain. But he had at least survived his tumultuous beginning.

'What's she calling him?' I asked Amie as we walked back out the door.

'Momo,' Amie answered, with a tender smile. 'A good name, I think.'

When I realized that Mariama had named the child after me, tears welled in my eyes. I had never experienced, or expected, such an honor, and it took me a moment before I could speak.

'Thank her for me,' I finally answered.

'I will,' Amie said. Little had I known that I would find such precious riches in a land of ostensible poverty.

As the nurses went about their daily duties, I wandered around the ward, quietly surveying the familiar surroundings. I was pleased that Dr Conteh would find a well-functioning facility upon his return. Only two weeks had passed since his unexpected departure, but I had changed so much in that interim – it seemed like a lifetime ago.

Although it was hard to analyze my time running the ward from such close proximity, I was aware of feeling somehow different. In many ways, I hardly recognized the person I had become. I had learned a few medical tricks and seen some unusual patients but knew neither were the source of my inner transformation. There was something else, an acceptance of things, responsibility and more, that had changed in me as well. My shoulders were laden with new weight, but sturdier from carrying such a burden.

A little later in the day, I walked over to the pediatric ward. Little Sia had survived his infection, and I wanted to transfer him to Dr Nassan's therapeutic feeding center for a little extra nutrition to complete the boy's recovery. The child's care had been a continuous obsession for me, but I was now confident that Dr Nassan's capable hands would usher Sia quickly home.

I passed through patients and their families on the open walkway, smiling along the way, to find Dr Nassan eating lunch in a back room. He was happy to accept responsibility for Sia.

We discussed our plans for the future and agreed it would be good to eat some real food, although we had very different definitions of what that would be. Almost done with his year, Dr. Nassan was shortly returning with his girlfriend to an academic post in Ethiopia, where he would be closer to his teenage daughter. A new doctor would be replacing him at the pediatric ward and supervising a quick transition of that facility back to local management. War was over in Sierra Leone, and funds were quickly drying up for local aid work.

I was also thinking of the future. I had a paper to turn in and was excited about soon seeing my friends and family, as well as a special girl waiting back in London. I had a final year of medical school to finish and would need to apply for residency, the next step in my training.

On the way back to the ward, with an easy heart, I waved to the workers and patients I knew. It was amazing how at home I now felt among the previously foreign surroundings. The hospital was no longer strange or intimidating – the occasional stray chicken or bullet hole appeared exactly as they should.

I greeted the guard at the entrance of the Lassa ward and happily passed through its familiar gate. After jotting down a few notes in the office, I went to check on Eve again. I entered the room to find the girl's mother situated side by side with Amie. The two African women stood with their backs to the door, a comforting hand resting on each other's shoulders.

I walked up to join their silent vigil. Our small patient lay dwarfed by the adult bed – the serene girl looked completely at peace. Amie turned to me. 'Not breathing,' the nurse said in a hushed voice. It was then that I realized little Eve was dead – God had again had his way.

31

FINALLY A DOCTOR

August 9, 2003

'Dr Conteh get here last night,' Amie informed me when I arrived at the ward the next morning.

'Really?' I said.

'He be in a little later,' she said.

'Okay . . . well, we should probably round now.'

Although my solitary stint at the ward was finally at its end, I surprisingly felt as if Amie's news was only of minor consequence. I had changed sometime amid Dr Conteh's multiple holdups and come to accept my role within Lassa ward's dark walls. True, it was an imperfect one filled with both joy and suffering. But though there were many things I couldn't change, I had found solace in those I could.

The guard interrupted Amie and me at the end of rounds. 'Someone ask for "Dr Ross,"' he said. I went outside wondering who it could be and found two Caucasian men in front of the entrance. One of them was doubled over, holding his knees to his chest. 'Can I help you?' I asked.

When he looked up, I encountered a face drained of color but recognizable nonetheless. 'Cole?' I said. To my surprise, it was the diamond dealer I had met before, with Daren.

'Uh . . . hi,' he said with a pained expression.

I invited the pair into the ward and sequestered them in the doctor's office, away from the Lassa patients. Cole paused several times along the way to clutch at his stomach. 'Is there a WC?' he asked. I had a guard take him to the bathroom next door and hoped he wouldn't fall into the primitive dirt hole that functioned as the toilet.

'Thanks so much,' Cole said when he returned. 'I've had so much diarrhea and vomiting for the last two days that I don't know what is left to come out.'

'Sounds horrible,' I said. 'What happened?'

'When it first started, I thought I might have malaria, so I took some artusenate I had with me,' the Brit told me. Artusenate was a newer, more expensive antimalarial medication that was locally unaffordable. 'But things only got worse. There's been no end to the diarrhea and vomiting.'

'I found him the next day,' Cole's friend said, 'and took him straight to the Pakistani battalion, where they gave him an antibiotic called Bactrim, and quinine pills for malaria.'

'The physicians there said that if I didn't start to feel better, I should see an American doctor at the Lassa ward, who is a specialist in tropical diseases,' Cole finished.

'Oh?' I said.

'Yeah, they said that the guy had just given them a lecture,' Cole continued.

When I realized that I was the supposed expert, I had a

hard time keeping a straight face. Evidently, I had made a good impression on the Pakistani physicians. 'I see' was all I said.

Cole still had an upset stomach, although his projectile vomiting had transformed, without food, into the dry heaves. He clutched his head in his hands while rocking back and forth in the chair. 'The room keeps spinning,' he said. 'But even worse is the ringing in my ears.' Picturing Dr Conteh returning from his long trip to find vomit all over his office, I had Amie quickly procure a bucket.

'I've been trying to take this pill,' Cole said, weakly holding up a white quinine tablet in his hand, 'for the last hour. But I just can't work up the courage to swallow it.'

Quinine was a bitter pill to take even when one was not nauseated, and I thought it was particularly cruel to make anyone take it while in the midst of the violent heaves. Since there was not yet any reported malarial resistance to Cole's first antimalarial, artusenate, I was confident the sick Brit did not have malaria.

'You don't have to take it,' I told him, thinking the majority of his continuing symptoms were probably due to quinine's infamous side effects.

'Really?' he said. 'Are you sure?'

'Yeah. We'll get you feeling better.' Cole proved particularly easy to convince.

Cole most likely had travelers' diarrhea, a term denoting a group of bacterial infections that in adults cause distressing but rarely life-threatening symptoms. Bactrim was the traditional remedy, covering the most frequent bacterial causes. Although probably adequate treatment, there was increasing resistance to this drug. A different one, Cipro, had become the standard of care in the US.

Cole's companion needed to leave, but I assured him I would take care of his friend. Since the diamond dealer could readily afford whatever he needed, I had the guard purchase several Cipro tablets of dubious origin from the market. After giving Cole a Tylenol for fever and an IV line for de-hydration, I propped a chair up safely within the office's walls and let him fall asleep with the fluids dripping in.

Afterward, Amie and I listened to the radio while waiting for Dr Conteh to arrive. President Bush and the former president Taylor were continuing their standoff: Taylor was demanding that America bring forces to stabilize Liberia as a precondition for his departure, and Bush was repeating his calls for Taylor to leave but was refusing to discuss com-mitting US troops. Although the consequences were dire, the exchange made the two rulers seem like siblings having a childish argument. 'You are . . . am not . . . are too,' they seemed to say.

Dr Conteh returned a little later in the day, dusty from the road and worn from his own bout of illness. His face seemed to carry a few more wrinkles than I remembered. The trip and his sickness had heaped more punishment upon a body already worn from decades of caregiving.

'It's great to see you,' I told the Lassa physician. Upon finally seeing him back at the ward, I realized how much my lost mentor had taught me, both through his presence and during his absence. My two besieged weeks of running the ward had only cemented my admiration for the man, who had run it single-handedly for so long. The lessons I had learned, of medicine and more, were a debt too great to repay.

'Actually, it is good to see you too,' he replied. 'Sorry it took so long to get back.' I took my weary mentor on a short tour of the patients and impassively reported the numerous deaths that had occurred while he had been gone. The Lassa physician nodded his tired head in approval. I had done slightly better than the usual average for the ward.

'Surprised it's still standing?' I asked, looking around at the crumbling walls of the flimsy building. I wondered then if my mentor had doubted me as much as I had questioned myself.

'Not at all,' Dr Conteh said, placing a hand on my shoulder.

'Are you sure?' I said.

'You know, they have a funny saying in Kono,' the Lassa physician continued, his eyes briefly twinkling with a hint of his past vigor. 'Although a fat woman can't fit through the door, when there is war she can pass through the window.'

'I'm a fat woman now, am I?' I said with a half-smile.

'It seems that maybe you were,' he simply said.

Dr Conteh headed home early to recover from his trip, and I spent the remaining time tidying up the quiet ward. My bonds with the patients were slowly dissolving. I could feel that a chapter of my life was ending. Although I was thankful that Dr Conteh had returned, I was surprisingly sad to let go of my responsibilities.

Eventually, I drifted to the empty room where Eve had died, my thoughts turning to the small life that had so recently passed. Her former cot was empty, cement-covered windows keeping the afternoon light at bay. Only the smell of bleach and the familiar hint of blood occupied the dark shadows. In silent reflection, I listened to Momo's gentle wails from down the hall. They were a fitting dirge for the dead.

I stopped lastly in the office to wake Cole from his awkward slumber. 'How're you feeling?' I asked.

'So much better,' he said. The Tylenol had broken his fever, and the side effects of the quinine had worn off. Refreshed from the IV and a little sleep, he was past the worst of his illness.

'You'll need to take the rest of these Cipro pills twice a day for the next seven days,' I told him. 'And make sure you drink lots of fluids.'

'I will . . . I definitely will,' Cole assured me. 'Thank you so much for your help.'

We walked together out to the front entrance, past the ominous sign warning about the dangers of Lassa fever, which had stood out so clearly upon my arrival. There, Cole paused to again express his gratitude for his brief treatment.

'I don't know how to thank you,' he said. 'I feel like a new man.'

'That's thanks enough,' I said.

'I hope it doesn't offend you,' Cole said, 'but when we first met, I didn't know you were a doctor.'

I shook his hand with a bittersweet smile, deepened by the events of the last few months – a period for me steeped in death, but also rich in life. For a moment, I gazed out in the distance, where a setting sun outlined jungle-covered mountains. There was not a cloud in the sky.

'That's okay,' I finally told him. 'The truth is, neither did I.'

V

LAST RITES

32

SEEDS OF SUFFERING

August 11, 2003

Stagnant pools of water from the night rains reflected back the clear morning skies, and I stepped carefully along the side of the road in an attempt to avoid the largest puddles. Ossay waited for me in the driveway of the Lassa outreach compound. 'Morning!' he said upon seeing me, before enthusiastically shaking my hand in the local manner. 'It be so wonderful to see you!'

'Morning,' I said back to him with a big smile. 'It's good to see you too.'

While holding on to my fingers with a casual grasp, Ossay proceeded to take me into the complex to introduce me to the rest of his team. Five attractive women in their early twenties made up the group, all with matching green-checkered bandannas, shirts, and skirts.

'Nice to meet you,' I told them, and they all giggled bashfully in unison.

'Don't be fooled,' Ossay told me. 'They all be married.'

'And you would be too, if you were not so rude!' one of them told Ossay, wagging a finger jokingly.

Although at first shy from my foreign presence, the women quickly warmed up as I asked questions about the outreach work. They seemed to love joking with Ossay, as if he were their little brother. He kept issuing official-sounding instructions, which, with lightly veiled amusement and abundant commentary, they eventually ended up following.

After Dr Conteh's return, I had placed the Lassa ward patients back into his capable hands. Freed from responsibility for those dark halls, I was finally taking up Ossay on his offer to observe the Lassa outreach team at work. I had only a short time remaining in Kenema and wanted to see all I could.

The car for our day trip arrived a few minutes later, and the driver, a muscular man with a shaved head, strutted out of the vehicle wearing a leisure suit of velvet leopard print. 'How dee body?' he said in a deep voice. Doing my best to keep a straight face, I shook our chauffeur's hand.

'Dee body fine,' I told him, imagining the revelry his secondhand outfit had seen during a previous incarnation in much different surroundings.

Honored with sharing the front seat, I squeezed between Ossay and the driver's fuzzy attire. 'So what are we going to do today?' I asked Ossay as we started to bounce down the dirt road.

'You will see!' he said with youthful glee. 'I show you the outreach program. How we teach the villagers about Lassa.'

'You give classes?' I asked him.

'Yes, and much more!' Ossay said. 'We educate by talking and making plays and even dancing.'

'He no be much of a dancer,' one of the female team members said from the back. I laughed. Ossay was such a natural entertainer – I was sure he was great at his job.

We splashed down the muddy road, with Ossay, like a proud parent, pointing out the signs his team had posted among the tall foliage to either side. The colorful drawings described Lassa symptoms, gave instructions for suspected cases, and implored the populace not to eat the *Mastomys natalensis* rats. It was amazing to think that the local masses knew so little about a disease that so frequently afflicted them, but health literacy rates were very low, and rumor was the main source of information in the villages.

A few of the posters showed the familiar picture of a cat eating a rat, the same one I had seen on one of Bryan's T-shirts back in the ward. 'See that one!' Ossay said. 'Also from one of our programs.'

'Why the cat?' I asked.

'We gave out kittens to all the villagers,' Ossay said. 'So they could eat the rats.'

'That sounds clever.'

'At first, it be very clever. We all be so excited! Maybe no more Lassa . . .'

'Then?'

'Then, suddenly, all the cats be gone.'

'Gone?'

'Yes, after about three months . . . no more cats.'

'Where did they all go?' I asked him

'We check around,' Ossay said. 'To find out where they went.'

'And?'

'You foreigners never believe it. . . .'

'Where?'

'Into the villagers' bellies,' Ossay said, with a disappointed shake of his head. I looked at him in surprise. 'No much food out here,' he continued. 'The villagers just be waiting for them to fatten.'

As we came around a curve about an hour into the journey, our driver abruptly slammed on his brakes, causing us to slide sideways on the slick soil. We came to a gentle halt only a few inches away from the bumper of a dilapidated pickup truck that had stopped in the middle of the road in front of us.

Stretching out in front of the parked vehicle were a dozen cars lined up below a large hill, a veritable traffic jam in the middle of the African jungle. At the top, the wheels of a run-down station wagon spun furiously without traction. Dirt arced high into the clear blue sky, to land on top of a group of mud-covered men who were trying to shove the vehicle forward.

'Always happening during the rainy season,' Ossay said. Unable to go any farther, our outreach team got out of the Rover to stretch our legs.

'They're working hard,' I said.

'No easy to get around the countryside,' Ossay said. It was yet another difficulty in their attempts to fight the Lassa virus.

When the soil-encrusted men finally pushed the stuck vehicle to the side, our driver put our car in low gear and we slithered past, sliding from one edge of the road to the other.

An hour later, we reached our first stop, a small village on the outskirts of Tongo. It was the home of a Lassa patient who had recently received treatment at the ward. The area had been prosperous before the war, but shattered remnants of Western-style buildings were all that remained from that distant era. Only a few rebuilt huts stood among the rubble-filled ruins.

'Now we find the house and warn everyone around about Lassa,' Ossay explained to me. The team's job was to give the people in the former patient's neighborhood a prevention talk, under the premise that they were at a particularly high risk for future Lassa infection. One of the local villagers stopped to stare unashamedly at me with a gaping jaw, and Ossay asked him for directions. The man pointed, his eyes unwavering from my alien features, to a meandering path that led into the village.

Our group hiked through debris to an earthen home, where we found a woman washing clothes with a child strapped to her back. Two more little ones, who froze to gawk at me as we approached, were playing in the surrounding dirt. 'This one,' Ossay said.

Ossay directed the rest of the outreach women to spread out to talk to the neighbors, which they did after rolling their eyes. 'Like we no know,' one of them said. Ossay and I stayed to gather the primary family on their porch. The men were away farming, but two sisters, who shared the poor shelter, were there, along with their six children.

It was not until we sat down that I realized one of the women was the mother of Amber, the girl whose head Amie had shaved into a Mohawk. The child had been one of the first patients I had seen with Dr Conteh upon my arrival at the Lassa ward.

It was only after I had identified her mother that I belatedly recognized Amber within the pack of kids. The girl tilted her head at me in shy recognition while clutching a dirty doll to her chest. Amber's face had healed from its former swelling, and her hair had grown out to form tiny pigtails. She looked like a completely different person. If I had not seen her with my own eyes in the ward, I would never have believed that the child had been deathly ill.

While intermittently translating for me, Ossay questioned the family to determine if Amber had contracted her infection directly from rats or from another person. Since none of the child's close contacts had been sick during the period preceding her illness, it appeared the former was the case.

'I tell them to stay away from the fluids of the sick or dead,' Ossay said, intermittently translating for me during his talk. 'And also, from the rat.'

I could tell that the latter injunction clearly necessitated some serious discussion, with the family talking among themselves and asking Ossay many questions. 'They like the rat,' Ossay said. Rat meat was an important source of protein in their otherwise poor diet, and the group was not fully convinced that it was dangerous to munch on the occasional rodent.

'Some will never stop the eating,' Ossay told me, shaking his head gravely. 'They cannot accept that such a sweet meat can be bad.'

'What do you do then?' I asked him.

'We keep trying,' he said confidently. 'The children be the most easy to change. But the old men, who eat them for life, be very hard.'

I had seen the destructive effects of Lassa firsthand and was surprised that the team's message met with such opposition. Stopping rat consumption seemed like such a simple solution to a clearly devastating problem. But I had encountered enough similar difficulties, when giving smoking-cessation counseling in the States, to recognize resistance to change as a universal human trait.

The lecture continued with a tour of the house, and Ossay pointed out the numerous signs of rat infestation. 'Here,' he said, picking up some pieces of scattered rubbish to reveal black streaks. 'Oil from rat fur, from when they walk by.' A wooden bench also had multiple gnaw marks on its legs – rats have to continuously chew to prevent their constantly elongating teeth from growing into their own brains.

After proving his point that rodents infested the house, Ossay went on to discuss the underlying reasons. A bag of rice with a UN distribution logo occupied one unkempt corner, kernels spilling from a chewed hole. Next to it sat an open bowl containing a half-eaten snack,

'My people do not be good at keeping food,' Ossay told me. West African culture had evolved in an Eden-like land, where fruit and other nourishment grew with easy accessibility. Historically, people simply found their daily meal whenever they were hungry, which made proper storage an unfamiliar concept.

After Ossay gave the family advice on safeguarding their food and rat-proofing the house, we went out back to where they kept their trash heap. With arms waving like a motivational speaker, the outreach worker urged the inhabitants to change their ways and move the pile away from the house.

'Each day we help one more family!' Ossay said to me excitedly, pointing out across the rotting food and brush, as if across his country. 'Until one day there is no more Lassa!' I laughed. After feeling so powerless amid the daily onslaught of patients at the Lassa ward, I found the outreach worker's optimism to be contagious.

By the end of our tour, Amber was running around the house, somehow intuitively aware that we were there because of her. She gave me a high five as we readied to leave, and I tousled her braided hair. It was the first time I had touched one of the Lassa patients as a real person, without an impersonal plastic barrier of PPEs between us.

Our group eventually left the village to follow the empty husks of destroyed buildings into Tongo. The town was in the heart of the diamond-mining area and had been the focus of fighting for over a decade.

We asked those we passed for directions, but even the local populace did not know the locations of the old roads. 'They cannot remember which street is where,' Ossay told me, 'so it can be hard to find the people.' Years of hostilities had shelled the roads into namelessness, a fitting tribute to the unspoken atrocities that had no doubt occurred along their banks.

The team paused at the homes of more former patients, both the deceased and those recovered, to repeat their talk. We were amid the largest Lassa foci in the world, and people greeted the group like old friends. Ossay and his colleagues had visited the area all too frequently.

On the way back out of the town, the driver stopped the car amid the waving prairie grass. 'You want to see the diamond mines, right?' Ossay asked me.

'If we can,' I answered.

While the rest of the team took an afternoon siesta, the two of us made our way up a nearby path. At the top of the ridge, we found rusted equipment scattered haphazardly beneath the overgrowing bush. 'The old mining factory,' Ossay told me. 'They blow it up first, many years ago.'

We continued down a small valley and up the neighboring knoll, while a churning sound grew in the distance. As we crested the hill, verdant green gave way to a pit of churning mocha below us. Several hundred men and boys stood knee-deep in the swirling liquid. They sifted through the murky waters with silver plates while a decrepit motor, at one end of the man-made pond, pumped out the gritty fluid.

Ossay and I stood there silently for some time, gazing out ahead. Silver clouds layered across the horizon, like the soft underbelly of a giant trout, and followed the earth as the terrain transformed from tan chasm back into lush jungle. Much like the gems within it, the land that had caused so much anguish was breathtakingly beautiful.

'These diamonds bring us nothing but pain,' Ossay told me as we turned to leave, for once his enthusiasm having momentarily left him. 'They be the seeds of our suffering.'

33

SOGGY FOOTSTEPS

August 12, 2003

'Like a sacrificial lamb, I give myself for the greater good,' Taylor declared, his charismatic voice ringing in the rising tone of a preacher. In the common room of the guesthouse, Daren and I listened to the day-old sound bites of the dictator, who was humbly comparing his own life to that of Christ. If not for the background commentary, it would have been impossible to know the self-aggrandizing sermon was a farewell speech.

The radio reported that Taylor was allegedly preparing to depart his besieged country, but Daren still maintained his doubts. 'Come on,' I told him. 'Look, he's even getting ready to get on the plane.'

'You wait,' the medical coordinator told me. 'The man is like a championship boxer. He always makes a comeback.' Together, my Nigerian friend and I waited to see if Taylor would land a last-minute punch or if his troubled reign would finally end.

Lila and Mohammad eventually joined us for lunch, along with a Dutch woman who had arrived with Daren the day before. Our new addition was the female physician who was supposed to transition the pediatric ward back to local management. Dr Nassan was at the end of his tour of duty, and the two of us were planning to share a car back to Freetown in a few days.

The five of us aid workers ate lunch while half listening to the radio. The Dutch physician was still getting oriented. 'Can you tell me about this Lassa virus?' she said to me after I told her what I was working on. 'It sounds so horrible.'

'It definitely can be.' I went on to describe the disease symptoms and explain how she could protect herself. 'If you think you have a case, you do have to be very careful,' I told her. 'All it takes is one slip.'

'Have any of you,' the new doctor then inquired with a puckered mouth, trying to recover from an unsuspecting bite of sour potato leaves, 'seen any cases of yellow fever?'

Lila and Mohammad shook their heads.

'Why?' I asked.

'Well, when I was in Freetown,' the Dutch doctor said, 'they told me that the countryside was reporting a new out-break.'

Although no one else in the group had seen any patients who fit the profile, I described the two jaundiced women who had expired so suddenly in the Lassa ward, finally confident I knew the cause of their mysterious deaths. 'I guess the WHO is sending someone to investigate,' the

Dutch woman said. My time almost done, I silently wished that person the best of luck.

A breaking bulletin interrupted our conversation: Taylor had officially left Liberia. 'See? I told you,' I said to Daren. Although waiting for just such a broadcast and despite my comments to Daren, I still found the news hard to believe. In the blink of an eye, the former dictator had taken off, in a private plane, to asylum in Nigeria. Without further incident, one of the main obstacles to peace in West Africa disappeared into the open sky.

As we soaked in the news, our conversation naturally wandered to the rehabilitation of neighboring Liberia and the further movement of Merlin operations across the border. My colleagues knew, from firsthand experience, that reconstruction would be a complicated task. Taylor was leaving a devastated country. Both populace and infrastructure had suffered heavy casualties. I could only wonder what my former refugee patients would find upon return to their homeland.

After lunch, Dr Nassan and I set out from the guesthouse and into the midday rains. 'I'm glad we finally have a chance to do this,' I told Dr Nassan. He agreed. For the duration of my stay, the two of us had been discussing a hike up an adjacent mountain, and we had only a few more days to take advantage of the opportunity. I followed Dr Nassan's retreating multicolored shorts, Hawaiian shirt, and cheetah-patterned umbrella cautiously up the mountainside

My army poncho swished with each booted step as we threaded through the sopping underbrush. When we entered dense jungle, emerald foliage partially protected us with giant leaves that dripped with a soft staccato.

After a particularly steep section, Dr Nassan and I paused to catch our breath under a towering, vine-covered trunk. 'It's ironic it's so rich,' Dr Nassan said, with sadness written across his gentle face.

'What is?' I said.

'The land here.' The professor looked out at the lush land-scape that lay below us. 'We Ethiopians would die for this.'

Capricious Mother Nature sent frequent droughts to Dr. Nassan's eastern homeland. But in West Africa, amid precious gems, ample rain, and fertile soil, the tragedy was mostly man-made. Revolutions and rebellions, names that depend on one's point of view, perpetually plagued the local region. With Dr Nassan's and my respective journeys coming to a close, it was impossible not to speculate on the roots of the suffering.

'You've been here longer,' I said. 'Why do *you* think the fighting never seems to end?'

'It's hard to say,' Dr Nassan answered. 'I'm sure there's more than one factor.'

'Yeah, maybe Collier is right,' I said.

'Maybe.'

Both of us had read the work of the controversial World Bank researcher Paul Collier, who had challenged the notion that rebellion was simply a protest against oppression. The economist had statistically analyzed civil wars over the last decade to find what characteristics they had in common, but he had been unable to objectively link injustice with a risk for fighting.

Financial inequality, political repression, and ethnic/religious divisions within a country had not correlated with an increased chance of civil strife. Instead, two striking economic characteristics, a dependence on primary commodity exports and a low average income, were the most powerful predictors of impending war. These factors were evident in both Sierra Leone and Liberia, lands rich in diamonds and in which more than half of the populace earned under one US dollar a day.

The proposed hypothesis was that this specific economic combination sustained civil conflict. Primary commodity exports, such as diamonds, oil, or illegal drugs, were all 'lootable,' meaning that opposition groups could easily steal such resources to fund their illicit activities as they took over parts of the country. Low average incomes, in turn, decreased the taxable base of a government, thus reducing its ability to raise money and resist rebellion.

'There certainly are enough diamonds here to make you wonder,' Dr Nassan said. In Sierra Leone, the main spoils of war lay just under the topsoil. As the rebels conquered territory, this had allowed them to erect simple slave-labor mining operations to gather up the gems. Ultimately, this led to the insurgents having more income and better weapons than the official government.

'I wonder if they'll ever have lasting peace here?' I said.

'It's hard to tell,' Dr Nassan replied. 'Who knows what makes any country stable?'

'In the States, we always think it's the Constitution,' I said. 'It's what our history books tell us.'

'That didn't help Liberia much.'

'No, it didn't.'

Liberia's national charter was almost identical to that of the United States, fleeing slaves having reproduced it upon their arrival to Africa — our countries shared more than just a similar flag. But the wonderful separation of powers, which I had studied as a child, had failed to stop Charles Taylor and his long reign of oppression.

'I don't think it's the laws that prevent dictators,' Dr Nassan replied. 'The important part is the belief in them.'

'If an American general tried to steal power at home, I think he would find few soldiers to follow him,' I said.

'Yes, but how do you instill that all-important sentiment in a foundering nation?'

'I'm not sure.'

'Neither am I,' the professor said. 'But I'm sure it takes more than a few sheets of paper.'

Dr Nassan and I dropped down out of dense jungle and into a small valley of budding rice shoots and decapitated trees. As we stepped tenderly through the stubble, I thought of the widespread misery and the unyielding joy that I had seen during my stay. They both felt never-ending.

In the middle of the shallow valley, a wisp of smoke curled high into uncertain skies. It circled above a forlorn lean-to of cut underbrush, one triangular side open to the damp air.

Dr Nassan and I passed with soggy footsteps while four pairs of unblinking eyes peered out from the inner darkness. A voiceless family lived on the dirt floor of that rickety wooden shed.

A river rushed alongside the primitive farm and, with careful steps, Dr Nassan and I followed the current up to the base of a waterfall. Crouching on an outcropping of slick rock, we shared an unadorned lunch of dried fish and bread, the cascade spraying all around us. After finishing, we both stared up into the endlessly falling water. The drops dove swiftly down into the awaiting torrent below.

'Sometimes I wonder if my time here has meant anything,' I heard Dr Nassan say, almost to himself.

'What do you mean?' I said.

'I'm just not sure if I've accomplished anything,' the professor said, sadly shaking his head. It was obvious that my gentle friend, spurred by the pain of his divorce, had spent much of his last year in Kenema searching for inner purpose.

'You can't be serious,' I replied.

'No, I am. Think about it . . . Now that I'm leaving, what will really last?'

I knew Dr Nassan had made great efforts to teach the local pediatric staff, so that his improvements would continue after he left. But he and I had already talked about his increasing frustration as the end of his stay approached.

'The CMO again?' I said.

'Yes,' he answered. 'Even today.'

Dr. Nassan's chief medical officer (CMO) was not one of the pediatrician's best students. The professor had just that day intercepted another of the CMO's erroneous treatments. 'I don't know how many times I've told him,' he said, upset about an improper choice of antibiotic.

Disillusionment can be easy to unearth even among the most dedicated of aid workers, with infinite need and finite resources making it difficult to measure individual progress. While looking at my own limited efforts in the Lassa ward, I had experienced similar feelings of despair more than once and had wondered if my own actions were of any lasting significance.

But I was surprised. With the miraculous change Dr Nassan's year had brought to the pediatric ward, I had assumed the gentle pediatrician was impervious to such reservations. I felt distressed to see one of my resident heroes so disheartened. 'Dr Nassan,' I protested, 'you've done so much for so many here.'

'But what will happen when I'm gone?' the professor asked me forlornly, and I saw true concern on my friend's face at the thought of his looming departure.

Dr Nassan's worries were real enough, and for some time I stared out at the falling water, searching for answers. 'How many children does the peds ward see each week?' I finally asked.

'About two hundred,' Dr Nassan answered solemnly.

'And what happened to the death rate while you were here?'

'When I arrived, about a third of kids that came to the peds ward died there. Now it's down to less than five percent,' the professor said, even more dejectedly, still clearly thinking about what would happen when he left. The majority of the improvement had come, not from new drugs or equipment, but simply from his knowledgeable presence. Despite all his efforts at teaching, there was no doubt the ward would sorely miss him.

'Well then,' I finally replied, 'during the last year you have personally saved the lives of around three thousand children.'

Water plummeted over the cliff, its shower intermingling with the falling drizzle. I watched a drop race across my threadbare poncho before it plunged down to melt into the collective stream. 'Even if everything goes back to the way it was, that has to mean something,' I said.

'I just have to believe it does.'

34

PART OF AFRICA

September 3, 2003

'Countries visited?' the customs woman asked me while she typed rapidly on her keyboard. The TV screens behind her head distracted me with frenzied lights. Below them, throngs of vacationers trailed obedient baggage across polished marble.

'Sierra Leone,' I said, belatedly pulling my gaze from the hypnotic commotion.

'Purpose?' she asked. Her eyes focused unwaveringly on her computer.

'Humanitarian aid work,' I answered.

The woman glanced up at me, and I scratched a full beard under her scrutinizing inspection. My combat pants, hiking boots, and tired shirt felt out of place amid the cleanliness of the modern airport. For the first time since my departure, I became acutely aware that I possessed only a single change of clothes.

'Proceed,' the customs woman told me before efficiently

stamping my passport and looking past me for the next traveler. Evidently, I looked the way an aid worker was supposed to look. With a hesitant step across an arbitrary red line, I officially returned to civilization.

Ghost-white faces hurried in every direction, and I became lost among their masses on my way to the subway. After buying a ticket, I stared warily at the change, reflexively suspicious that the bills were potential fakes. It took almost physical restraint to keep from holding each one up to the light to test their authenticity. *We're in a different place now,* I told myself silently.

A surreal glow pulsed with each passing street sign as my train made its way in from the airport. No one spoke. Instead, passengers with vacant expressions focused their attention on the orderly rows of houses outside. As the city approached, our car dove underground and all eyes settled to the floor tiles.

When we arrived at the main station, a jet of pressing bodies ejected me into swirling masses. Marching feet poured through the automatic doors of the station and into a basin formed of colossal London skyscrapers, which glowed with neon light.

Excited but tired, I waded through eddies of intent pedestrians and honking traffic. Finally, I found a familiar apartment complex, which I recognized as if from a past dream. After taking an elevator up several floors, I rang the bell.

A young woman, known for her charm and beauty, opened the front door. She wore an angelic smile, radiant above soft robes.

'Is that you?' she teased, tugging at my beard. 'What's on your face?'

'I missed you,' I said.

'Yes,' she told me hours later. 'You really did.'

The next morning, having showered and shaved, I returned to my former clothes. After ordering two breakfasts at a favorite restaurant, I visited a park and went to a movie. The familiar luxuries of my prior life were ostensibly the same but felt somehow different. Only a slight looseness in my belt reminded me that it was me, not my previous surroundings, that had changed.

I saw other past acquaintances, and they asked cheerfully about my trip. 'It was good,' I found myself answering in conditioned response. 'A little intense,' I sometimes said. But even over a few drinks at the pub, I found my recent travels impossible to convey – the experience was still too raw to bear description.

In a dreamlike state, I worked to finish my paper and swam through charts of ribavirin dosages and side effects. With clinical detachment, I wrote about 'facial swelling' and 'conjunctival hemorrhage.' Away from the faces of helpless children, the symptoms of Lassa infection became only bizarre medical findings. I was paradoxically both too far, and too close, to feel their pain.

But despite the physical distance from my previous surroundings, the past would not let me go. I belatedly remembered that Lassa's incubation period had still not passed. I was paroled, but not yet free. Three weeks had to elapse since my last contact with patients before I could confirm a true escape from infection. I was sure I could feel the virus reaching out across the globe, somehow stubbornly scratching for one final wound.

The days ticked by slowly, each a notch on invisible prison walls. For most of my trip, I had been able to push the risk of infection to the back of my mind. But having reached the luxury of civilization, the wait seemed somehow much worse. I would be contagious only if symptomatic, so no one around me shared my hazard – I was alone with a private peril.

As time passed, I followed the few snippets of African news that made it into the Western media. Just before I left, on August 15, two hundred US marines finally landed in Monrovia to the joy of the starved populace. I heard Mikhail's relieved voice one last time on the radio as he described the influx of needed supplies. That capeless crusader had passed unharmed through one more crisis – he would lay eyes upon his young twins once again.

Life had returned to Liberia as people began the slow trickle back home, the refugees in Sierra Leone to be eventually among them. A week later, the rebels and the vestiges of Taylor's government signed an accord officially ending hostilities. The factions were now developing a power-sharing government with the UN's assistance.

Another African war had ended, a minor blip on the

collective consciousness of those in Western nations. Despite an open mandate for US intervention, which would have required minimal manpower, a summer of suffering had passed before regional forces finally brought peace to the ground.

There was a tragic juxtaposition between the overt in-action of my homeland in its West African dealings and its veiling of ongoing military involvement in the Middle East within a humanitarian cloak – the might and right of the world's sole superpower had proven painfully wanting.

On the final day of my incubation period, I packed my bags and readied for home. A setting sun reflected off glass sky-scrapers to slowly pardon me into the land of the living. Free from my final hurtle, I could think back to Africa without anxiety as I remembered my last farewell at the Lassa ward.

Dr Conteh, Amie, Zuri, Bryan, and I all huddled within the front alcove of the ward, the familiar mixture of bleach and blood hanging in air humid from another torrential downpour. Our small group of workers took a few last pictures, with the weak flash of my camera attempting to illu-minate the Lassa ward's inner walls.

I wore a recent purchase, a hat and shirt made from the colorfully weaved African thread that the staff wore every Friday. The clothes were the only native souvenirs I could find in Kenema. They were one of the few locally made goods, because of the long history of fighting.

'You be looking very nice,' Zuri said to me with a pearly grin.

'Thank you,' I told him. Bryan nodded his head in grudging agreement.

'Yes,' Amie said proudly, 'you finally learn to dress proper.'

Dr Conteh had recovered fully from his journey and was again working steadily at the ward. 'I want to thank you for traveling out here to write about Lassa,' said the elderly physician, who had become a true mentor to me.

'It was my honor,' I said.

'Actually, you do look quite good in that outfit,' Dr Conteh said with a smile. 'Now, part of Africa will stay with you, wherever you go.'

Eloquence having long left me, only simple words remained. 'Always,' I replied. 'I know it will.'

35

HOMECOMING

September 16, 2003

'Point to the fracture and discuss its treatment,' the professor told me, and I stood to read the X-ray. After reconnecting with family in Minnesota, I had driven cross-country to California to begin my final year of medical school with a relatively easy rotation in radiology.

'Umm . . .' I said. The film was of a hand or a leg, but for some reason I couldn't make out the features. The bones merged, overlapping and retracting like a visual accordion. I squinted, but order refused to emerge. 'Sorry,' I said, before sitting down.

'Humph,' the professor grunted, displeased. Another student rose to give the answer, but I did not hear her words. My heart pounded in my ears as if I had just run a marathon. I couldn't figure out why it was so hard to catch my breath.

Illuminated by X-ray screens in an otherworldly glow, the walls suddenly loomed toward me while I struggled with claustrophobic inhalations. When the overhead lights finally came on, everyone filed out. They left me behind, unnoticed.

Eventually, I got up from sitting, both hands grasping my chair to steady myself. I slowly made my way into the hospital hallway, where a harsh fluorescent light bounced off the gleaming linoleum floor to provide a halo around the reflection of my uncertain figure. I reached an outdoor courtyard, where cherry blossom petals littered the cobble-stone square, before slumping onto a cement bench.

Pinks and greens swam in a psychedelic collage while the morning sunlight caressed my inebriated thoughts. I felt like when I was a little boy and came shooting up out of the pool after holding my breath at the bottom. But this time the sensation wouldn't go away.

I think I may die, I sanguinely decided.

Time blurred, but eventually the severe pounding in my ears receded. Afterward, I sat for over an hour, too fatigued to move. Although calm, I remained short of breath. I rubbed my face and pushed on my chest, but the sensation remained.

With improved cognition, I wondered what strange force had overtaken my body; unsuspecting patients chatted quietly in the surrounding courtyard. I had certainly never experienced anything similar. Was it the few celebratory drinks that I had had with a friend upon my return the night before or something I had eaten? But neither explanation, nor any other common reason, seemed to fit my current symptoms. I simply sat there in a daze, trying to figure out what had suddenly happened to me.

After searching all the possibilities medical school had drilled into my brain, I eventually decided that I might have collapsed a lung. It was a rare problem, called spontaneous pneumothorax, that happened sometimes for unknown reasons, most commonly in men of my age. I had seen a guy with it once during medical school, but I had never imagined diagnosing myself with such a malady. However, there I was, suddenly unable to catch my breath for no clear reason. *It's not so bad,* I told myself. *I just need someone to put a tube into my chest to reinflate the lung.*

Having at last decided the answer to my problem, I was able to gather the energy needed to proceed. I rose with a spinning head and started back toward the radiology area. Shuffling slowly, I moved barely faster than a child and reached the empty room to find my classmates gone for the day.

The professor's dim office was nearby, and I knocked on his door before entering. 'Yes,' he said after recognizing me, not hiding his annoyance that I had missed the rest of his lecture.

'Can I,' I said, 'get a . . . chest X-ray?' My professor blinked a few times, as if an underground creature abruptly startled by the midday sun. 'I think,' I explained, 'I collapsed . . . a lung.'

The radiologist paused for a few seconds, deciding if I were joking. 'Let's bring you next door,' he finally said, referring to the nearby emergency room. I just needed an X-ray, I wanted to explain – I didn't want to go through all that trouble. But I followed my instructor's retreating back without enough energy to protest.

The two of us caught the physician in charge of the emergency department in one of the back halls. He had been one of my instructors before I left for my year off. 'Nice to see you,' he said when I greeted him. 'How long have you been back?'

'Just a day,' I replied. 'But there seems,' I continued, 'to be a . . . slight problem.' Steadying myself with a hand on the wall, I described my symptoms and politely asked again for a chest X-ray.

'Why don't you lie down in Bed Eight?' It was a room for critical patients needing close monitoring, the emergency doctor said, with a concerned look on his face. I was going to protest that I just needed a chest X-ray but started to feel like it might be nice to sit down.

I thanked the radiologist for his help and gradually made my way the few feet to the bed. After removing my white coat and dress shirt, I folded them neatly and placed them on a nearby stand before collapsing onto the awaiting gurney.

A nurse efficiently dressed me in a gown and asked me to take off my shoes. But I pretended not to hear her – it took three times before the point was made. I didn't want to remove them. I would be leaving soon enough, I thought. That was one of my first, of many, attempts at trying to control the situation.

ER personnel, most of whom I recognized, quickly placed monitors over my bared body. As bad as I felt, I helped strap on the blood pressure cuff and stick half the electrodes onto my own chest. It was mostly habit – I had done the same thing to others thousands of times before. Then I watched the screen as the machines began to register.

With oddly detached interest, I noted that my heart raced at more than twice its usual rate and that there was an abnormal beat after each normal one. In a matter of minutes various people swiftly inserted an IV, drew a blood sample, and took a chest X-ray. Medical students and doctors walked past as I waited behind a half-drawn curtain. I could hear a friend, a classmate, unknowingly take a medical history from the patient next door.

The tests came back one by one. The emergency doctor showed me the X-ray himself, holding it up to the ceiling lights. Only hours before, I had viewed similar films in the back room, only feet away. But none of those images had been of me. Each shape and shadow took on heightened meaning.

The picture was normal, without the fine half-moon shape that indicated inappropriate air adjacent to the chest wall, the characteristic sign of a pneumothorax. Both of my lungs were fully inflated, and I stared at the film for a few seconds with deepening worry. My simple problem was starting to seem not quite so straightforward.

'A PE?' I finally asked. A pulmonary embolism (PE) occurs when a clot breaks off from a vein in the leg and travels up through the bloodstream to lodge dangerously in the lung. Long airplane or car trips are major risk factors. I had had recent exposure to both.

'It's a definite possibility,' the emergency doctor said, nodding his head in agreement. The chest X-ray did not rule out that serious diagnosis. 'I sent a D-dimer,' he said. It was a blood test to check for clots in the blood vessels. 'So we'll have to wait and see.'

After all the test results finally came back, the emergency doctor returned to my room. He stood at the edge of the bed, and I looked up at him, straining to read his face. 'The D-dimer is negative,' he told me. I sighed with relief that I did not have a PE.

However, I unfortunately still had no reason for my concerning symptoms. Too exhausted even to think of any further possibilities, I looked up at my former instructor.

'What does that leave?' I eventually asked.

'Maybe the heart,' he answered.

36

A FAMILIAR FACE

September 20, 2003

'So, what seems to be the problem?' my new doctor asked me as I sat on the examining table, dressed again in a flimsy hospital gown.

'I have chest pain and feel short of breath,' I told her, the crisp paper sheet always found in such rooms crinkling underneath my shifting weight. 'Every time I exert myself, the pain grips my rib cage and runs down my left arm to a tingling pinkie finger.'

'Hmm,' she said.

The emergency doctor the night before had told me I should probably see a cardiologist the next day. However, little did he know how difficult it would be even to get to such an appointment. After I left the hospital, my alarming feeling of suffocation had steeply worsened. It had become progressively harder to breathe, and I had almost called 911 several times in the middle of the night as I woke up in bed suddenly gasping for air.

By the next morning, I realized that the sensation in my chest had grown heavier, like an elephant slowly settling down on the left side. As if I were in a sadistic Pavlovian experiment, I soon recognized that any increase in my heart rate immediately exacerbated the pain, and I moved as slowly as I could around my friend's apartment, where I had been staying since my return to Los Angeles. Even the slightest exertion, such as walking or even getting upset, clutched me in an agonizing grip. I had to remain calm, focused on peaceful things, not the sudden change my life had taken.

I called the student health center that morning, and they told me I could come for a walk-in appointment if I was willing to wait. Eventually, I forced myself to leave the apartment's questionable sanctuary. I took the elevator downstairs and dragged myself to my nearby car, although even that act fatigued me greatly. I had to sit alone behind the wheel for some time before being able to muster the energy to drive.

Walking to the student health center after parking proved to be more of a trial than I could have imagined. I slowly shuffled down the sidewalk, having to pause every couple of feet as students quickly walked around me. I kept pretending to check my cell phone or to read some random sign, to keep from looking too strange with my time-consuming tread.

A stoplight near the corner of my medical school brought me to an unexpected halt. I stood gazing at the far side of the street as the light went through its familiar pattern of green, yellow, and red. I wasn't sure if I had the energy to surmount this seemingly mundane challenge. Previously, I could run miles and climb mountains, but now crossing a simple street in time to make the light seemed nearly impossible.

After resting for a few cycles, I waited for the signal to change and started to make my way across. However, the white picture of a confidently walking person all too quickly turned to a flashing, then solid, orange hand, while I was barely halfway to the other side.

Stuck slowly shuffling across the middle of the street, I was unable to summon the energy to hop the few extra steps to the far curb. The driver of the first car in line honked angrily and glared at me. But it was all I could do to continue with my painfully slow course – with my crushing chest pain worsening above previous heights, it took all my strength not to pass out.

In the end, I finally made it to my destination: the student health center. As I methodically approached, the clinic loomed before me like a beacon of hope, with the promise of much-needed assistance. I had dutifully followed the instructions given to me by the emergency doctor and had overcome the trials of hostile cars and seemingly endless side-walks. Although I really had no idea what was going on with my body, I told myself I did not have to be my own physician. All I wanted to do was to put myself in the hands of someone who could help.

After checking in and filling out numerous forms at the front desk, I waited in the clinic lobby to be called. Contentedly resting in one of the cushioned chairs, I felt as if I had run back-to-back marathons. Eventually, a nurse showed me to one of the doctors' rooms, and I surveyed all of the familiar equipment while I waited: an ophthalmoscope hung on the wall and tongue blades lay on the counter, with a container of blue throat swabs positioned helpfully close by.

About a half-hour later, the doctor, a woman in her mid-forties, entered my room. She introduced herself quickly before glancing at the clock on the wall. 'So, I hear you're a med student,' she said. I remembered a joke about hypochondriac medical students always self-diagnosing themselves during their first year of schooling. It was not exactly how I wanted to start the interview.

I described to the new doctor my symptoms and noted that they had worsened precipitously over the last twelve hours. I also mentioned that I had had a chest X-ray and labs in the ER and that the emergency physician had recommended seeing a cardiologist.

My new doctor asked if I had any congestion, and I told her that I had noticed my ankles being a touch swollen and my face a little full, especially if I lay flat. I had worried about those symptoms when I noticed them that morning, since they implied that my heart was not beating strongly enough. Fluid was backing up peripherally, my body's circulatory pump showing subtle signs of overload.

'Ah ha!' my new doctor exclaimed.

'Yes?' I said, eager to hear her thoughts. I hoped that she had figured out what was going on and wished that it would be something easily repaired. My doctor stood up, satisfied, ready to move on to the next patient. 'You have a sinus infection,' she said.

'Huh?' I mumbled. It was not quite the answer that I was expecting. In truth, I had no idea what ailed me, but it seemed little like a sinus infection. I lacked a fever or facial pain, and my nose was not even stuffed up. It didn't feel like that kind of congestion, I explained. But no matter how politely I tried to disagree, my new doctor persisted.

'You should have an X-ray of your sinuses and try some saline nose drops,' she insisted.

Quickly, it became clear to me that my new doctor was not taking my symptoms very seriously. 'It's almost impossible to even walk across the street,' I told her. 'I have difficulties even shuffling through your office.' But she just looked at me as if I were going crazy.

Frustrated that I had gone all the way through campus to find such meager help, I started to get angry. But as my heart rate increased, the pain in my chest tightened precipitously. It physically kept me from arguing any further. After taking some sinus X-rays of dubious utility and being given some saltwater to wash out my nose, I was subsequently sent home, too weak to give additional protest.

It went on like that for a couple of days. In retrospect, it seems even crazier when looking back, but at the time I was just so tired. I felt like the ER had already told me that they couldn't help, and my only health insurance was through the student health clinic. I was so used to being able to solve problems on my own – I just couldn't figure out what else to do.

Admittedly, although otherwise healthy twenty-year-olds do occasionally notice chest pain, they do not normally have heart problems. The vast majority of the time, nothing serious is the matter. The patient part of me wanted to yell at my new physician, 'I can't walk! Don't you get it?' But the doctor part of me could almost understand.

I sat on my friend's couch throughout the day and went back intermittently to the student health clinic. Almost constantly exhausted, I spent most of my time searching the Internet for answers. I had no doubt that I had some kind of serious problem, but I just could not clinch the diagnosis. I took naps, hoping my symptoms would somehow dissipate, but always woke to find that they cruelly persisted.

Seeing modern health care from the other side, I can say that it is clearly not set up for the patient. It is frequently a poor arrangement for doctors as well, but that does not mitigate how little the system accounts for the patient's best interest. Just when you are at your weakest and least able to make all the phone calls, traverse the maze of insurance, and plead for health-care referrals is that one time when you have to – your life may depend upon it.

It was several days before my mom got to California. I know I kept the news from her, and others, for too long. But it took some time before I began to understand what was going on, and I hesitated at having to explain that I didn't know what ailed me. I was, after all, supposed to almost be a doctor.

Word got out eventually, however, after I failed to make my own return party. It was fairly uncharacteristic of me to miss such an event, especially since it was thrown in my honor, and my friends soon began to suspect the seriousness of my sudden infirmity. It's hard for me to say for sure, since I wasn't there, but I've heard it was pretty fun.

That next morning I met with the dean of the medical students. The appointment had been set up long before I had come back to California, to discuss my return to school. Used to slowly traversing campus on my visits to the student health center, I methodically made my way to his office. It took me almost an hour to park and walk the short distance across campus, with frequent stops along the way.

I arrived before the dean did and sat down, grateful for a chance to rest. When he arrived, I remained sitting and made it through the first part of the interview without difficulty. I wanted to mention my symptoms but had grown gun-shy from my recent treatment at the student health clinic. I was still hoping to graduate from medical school that year and soon needed to apply to residency programs. The last thing I wanted was for the dean to think that I had become unhinged during my year off.

However, the dean stood up at one point to get a form from the adjacent room, and I had to hold the table in front of me for a few extra moments as I got up to follow him. He looked back at me, and I could see his mind switch from administrator to doctor as he evaluated me through narrowed eyes.

'Are you feeling okay?' he said. I paused for a moment, not knowing if I should try to keep up a façade of good health.

'You know,' I finally said, 'I'm not really feeling all that good.' As I proceeded to explain my symptoms to the dean, concern came over his face.

I told him about going to the ER and of my exploits with student health. The dean, who was also a physician, had known me for the last four years, over which time I had never once called in sick or been known for melodrama. He looked genuinely concerned – it was a response starkly different from those of the doctors at student health.

After we talked for some time, the dean told me that I should return to the ER. Grateful to be taken seriously at last, I agreed to follow his kind advice, lost as I was in trying to heal myself.

I took the elevator one floor down to the ER, to find that they already had a bed waiting. A resident a few years my senior met me when I arrived. He had already received a phone call from the dean. Once again, I lay down on a hospital cot to look up at the face of yet another doctor.

By the time my mother's plane touched down in LA, I had already interacted with countless physicians, many of whom had been former acquaintances and professors of mine. Despite having held numerous medical jobs and having gone through much of the long schooling, being a patient was a side of medicine with which I had little experience. Everything was the reverse of what I was used to. Now I was at the other end of the stethoscope, wearing the chilly gown that was impossible to tie in the back. Now it was my turn to accept what I had already begun to suspect: I was really in control of very little.

One of the nurses relayed the message to me that my mother was on her way, and I wondered what she would be thinking as she fought her way through traffic. Despite being a grown man, I am not ashamed of what a relief it was to know that my mother was near. I had never before suffered from more than the common cold, except for a bout of mononucleosis in college that was cured by ice cream and the hand of time. This, most obviously, was very different.

My mom would rightly want to know what had happened, I thought as I lay there staring off into the ceiling tiles. I had told her so little. I recognized then how much I had kept from her, from the rest of my family, and from my friends. How much I had hidden away – to protect them, I had told myself, but to safeguard me as well, I now realized. But the past can never be changed. I only hoped that I would have enough time, and enough courage, to tell her.

I could hear the nurses quietly talking at the nearby station when my mother approached them to ask for me. They gave her directions, and my mom finally entered my room, her silhouette illuminated against the open door. She took in the dripping fluids and flashing monitors for a few moments before silently coming to my bedside to squeeze my hand.

Gazing down at her eldest son in a sterile hospital bed, my mother wore a look of concern that I had never seen before on her familiar face. But it was an expression that I recognized only too well from distant lands – by then I had seen similar ones, worn by worried parents, more times than I would have wished.

Don't fret, I wanted to tell her. *God will have his way.*

37

TECHNOLOGIC DREAMS

September 21, 2003

Hearts pulsed in three-dimensional synchrony, floating like ghosts above the gurney, while the coffin-like device responsible for their images whirred away at my feet. A bank of screens projected different views of unseen blood pumping to my head, arms, and toes. Lying beneath, with a bare chest covered in sensors, I silently implored the haunting figures not to falter.

Advanced equipment crowded the room, which looked like a futuristic rocket ship. A technician sat at the main console, as if steering us into unknown territory. Still recovering from the test, I watched him spin the pictures around on the monitor, my eyes glued to the beating of an unheard rhythm. 'No focal defects,' the man said, breaking our unnatural silence.

The daunting machine that took up the room around me had just finished with the final study in my cardiac workup. The test checked for blockage in the coronary arteries that fed the heart itself – it demonstrated no signs of isolated obstruction. Thus ruling out the unlikely possibility of a conventional heart attack, the study pointed toward an alternative diagnosis: myocarditis.

An error of recognition, myocarditis occurs when the immune system attacks its own heart tissues. Occasionally arising weeks to months after the successful clearance of an infection, the process begins with an unlucky structural similarity between a foreign pathogen and native heart muscle.

As the immune system clears the frequently benign head cold or stomach flu, it fortifies itself against future attacks from the same disease. However, in myocarditis, the growing defenses mistake their own tissues for part of the previous illness and assail their own body.

I knew my prognosis immediately, both one of the benefits and drawbacks of medical training. Roughly a third of people with the illness recover completely from the process. Another third suffer permanent damage but manage to continue living, although with varying levels of disability. A final third are so injured that their hearts fail completely.

It seemed as if I had led a series of starkly different lives, the last having started with that sudden change in health that so completely sapped my strength. I had been almost another person then, when I took off my white doctor's coat, folding it neatly and placing it on the nearby stand, before collapsing onto the waiting gurney.

Although it is an uncommon problem, I had seen a case of myocarditis during my third year of medical school. I had met the young woman as she recovered from heart transplant surgery. Organs are in short supply, but, if available, such an operation is the last-ditch treatment for those who worsen precipitously. It is a risky procedure – even if successful, rejection is always a possibility, and the patient's fate is far from secure.

When my friends and family learned of my sudden infirmity, they quickly switched from welcoming me home to offering their care and support. Hushed visits followed quiet phone calls. I had interactions with health-care workers that were more meaningful than I would have thought possible, though I doubt they knew how much their kind words meant. Others were on the opposite side of the spectrum. I experienced both the good and the bad of medicine, the two sides of that important coin challenging me to be better at my chosen profession. But I was unsure if I would again get that chance.

In a search for inciting agents, a Lassa antibody test came back negative from the CDC. Despite my time in the Lassa ward, I had not contracted that disease. Another, unknown process was the cause of my symptoms. A battery of studies looking for other exotic infections failed to elucidate an exact source. I was left only to wonder, never knowing exactly what insult had so quickly sapped my strength.

The main treatment for myocarditis is patience, with medication being of limited assistance. To keep from further damaging the heart in its weakened state, I was to avoid exertion for six months. The hope was that the body would heal, of its own accord, that which it had mistakenly damaged.

I was very lucky to have gotten back to the States before the onset of my symptoms and blessed to have caring family and friends. Surrounded by the height of modern technology, I appreciated every extra electrode and transistor. Nonetheless, it all felt unfair.

I had escaped Africa without crashing in a helicopter, driving off a cliff, or contracting Lassa. My life was supposed to be different, I reasoned in dark nights of fitful sleep. But such logic did little to mitigate the ongoing nightmare.

'Why me?' I asked myself, yearning to shed infirmity and rise healed from the constraints of my bed.

But an inner voice answered, 'Why anyone?'

38

LAST RITES

April 11, 2004

Reflected sunlight swims along the wall above the bed, as if undulating under the spell of some hidden current. High above hang six IV bags and masses of clear plastic tubing, which fill the room like tufts of floating seaweed, slowly dripping their infusions into an outstretched arm. In the background I hear the heart monitor tapping a fading SOS.

I can sense, more than see, movement outside the room, barely visible through a window in the door. But inside, it feels surprisingly tranquil. The thermostat is set to a soothing seventy-five degrees. Comforting pastel hues cover the cabinets and walls.

Even in one of America's most luxurious and high-tech hospitals, some infirmities will always defy cure. Medicine, no matter where you are, invariably has limits. In my heart, I know it truly is the end.

It has been almost seven months since the onset of my illness, over half a year since that sudden change in health. The intervening period has been one of quiet struggle as I have tried to regain what I lost and take each day as a newfound reward.

After the first few days, my constant chest pain slowly receded, but did not go far. The sensation rapidly returned whenever I moved or tried to stand, which mitigated any solace my small improvement gave. An assailant locked me in a prison that I could feel but never see. Trapped within invisible bars, I labored to find some hidden key.

Over the next few weeks, I struggled with my previously healthy body, attempting to will it back to its former state. Friends and family provided their care and support, similar to the way it was with my patients in Africa. But that was about the end of the resemblance. As opposed to being in a crumbling ward with pitifully few tests and only, at least for a time, a medical student providing care, everything was on my side. I had fancy studies and countless doctors. The world's best medical resources concentrated upon me, urging my health to return.

Over time, my exertion threshold gradually increased, and I could eventually shuffle around just shy of chest pain. But when I tried to walk just a bit faster, I spent the next day unable to get out of bed. I took a few steps forward, then a few back. Recovery, I realized, despite the overwhelming resources, was going to be neither easy nor guaranteed.

I could ambulate at a slightly faster pace by the end of the third week and was eventually able to make short excursions outside. I was ecstatic and felt like Steven, one of the first patients I had seen with Dr Conteh, when he was told he could finally leave the Lassa ward. To an observer, I began to look again like a regular person, although inside I felt far from normal. Leveraging my improved appearance, I convinced my mother she could return home to Minnesota. I didn't think I would be dying anytime soon, I told her.

Anxious not to defer medical school another year, I resumed my radiology rotation shortly thereafter. There, I again experienced gradual improvement, punctuated by episodes of overexertion and temporary deterioration. Although I was able to walk at a natural pace, a single flight of stairs felt like a marathon. I took the elevator, squeezed between doctors and patients, unsure on which side of that unspoken divide I truly belonged.

After a month in the dark recesses of the film room, I escaped to more active work on the wards. Although warned not to push myself, I wanted so much to return to my former self and felt a continuous urge to climb the stairs between the floors. At first, I could make it up two, maybe three, flights without the onset of pain. After I tried for four, an acquaintance found me panting in the stairwell, and I spent the next day laid up in bed.

Forced inactivity stole most of my hobbies, and I found six months without normal recreation difficult to endure. Unable to do the things I previously enjoyed, I halfheartedly watched TV and rented movies, but quickly grew bored. Struggling to find meaning and mental release, I began to write down the experiences of my last year, which you now read.

★ ★ ★

Without noticeable fanfare, six long months of compulsory inactivity ended in the beginning of March. Even such simple therapy would have been an unthinkable luxury in Sierra Leone. How could anyone there have afforded to be sedentary for so long? Those far-off people dwell precariously on the edge of disaster, while here in the States we live in a cocoon of safety.

I start my new stage of recovery with light calisthenics and am easily fatigued. I walk on the beach, among Americans carefully coated in sunscreen. Burning off excess calories, people do yoga on the sand and stroll on the nearby paths. Children, encased like football players in helmets and protective gear, rollerblade down the strand. We live in a society obsessed with safety. It seems almost 180 degrees different from a walk down those distant Kenema streets.

Eventually, weeks of labored morning workouts transition into a sluggish jog. I stagger past oblivious tourists as if I am barely reaching the end of a marathon. There are no ribbons and no one cheers, but, with that nominal feat, I feel half a year of pent-up tension miraculously dissipate.

That was only one month before I found myself in the cardiac intensive care unit (ICU). For the last two weeks, I have been at one of Los Angeles's most luxurious hospitals, among countless bypass machines and cardiac drips. It is a setting far different from the Lassa ward.

The medical complex employs at least twenty doctors to care for each patient and has roughly as many cardiologists as all of England. In addition to the many specialists, a primary team coordinates the high-tech intensive care. This latter group currently consists of five physicians and me, the medical student. I am no longer the patient. I have returned, once again, to the other side of that divide.

I make no significant decisions on the service but am content to forgo responsibility while finishing my last month of school. It is an easy senior rotation. Today, my only patient is a thirty-year-old male who has been in a coma for the last few weeks.

Our team dutifully makes rounds on the man twice a day. We carefully adjust his multiple machines and medications but have been unable to stop his slow decline. Through the tubes that stick out of almost every body part, we monitor his progressively deteriorating vitals.

Our patient, in essence, has committed suicide. Despite advanced AIDS, he has refused to take his medication for several years. There is a certain irony to his situation that only I feel – we struggle with such massive resources to save the life of someone who does not want to live, while on the other side of the globe caregivers lack the basic supplies to rescue those who do.

Over forty physicians, including an ethics team, a host of specialists, and several department heads, have all agreed that our doomed patient has no chance of meaningful recovery. The man's family has come to terms with withdrawing care – his mother, father, and two sisters are all gathered at the bedside to say farewell.

I follow the senior resident into the patient's room to find the awaiting family. One of the sisters squeezes tightly at her brother's swollen hand, leaving slight indentations in his turbid skin. The resident mutters a few unnecessary words – the relatives know why we are there.

Then the resident switches off the ventilator, leaving a ringing void with the cessation of its rhythmic hum. The two of us proceed to excuse ourselves quietly, to give the family some time alone with their sorrow. We have reached a place I am only too familiar with after work in Africa: there is nothing more to do.

I busy myself in the adjacent nursing bay to pass the empty time. I write a bit in my journal, as has become my custom, then check e-mail, skipping over the junk to come across a note from Daren. He and I have traded occasional messages since my return to the States.

I open his latest correspondence for the most recent update from the field. It reads:

Dear Ross,

I hope this e-mail finds you well. Things here have been very hectic and I will have to keep this short, but I wanted to inform you that Dr. Conteh recently received an accidental needle stick while caring for a pregnant woman with Lassa. As you know, the ward is understaffed and he had been drawing the blood himself.

Despite treatment and our best efforts, Dr. Conteh became severely ill. I am afraid to report that he died of Lassa Fever over the weekend. I think he actually made it through the acute disease, but passed away from renal failure.

I will write more when I get a chance, but just wanted to pass on the sad news.

Sincerely,

Daren

I read the e-mail three times, only to stare blankly at the computer screen while doctors and nurses continue around me, unfazed, with their busy tasks. The abrupt passing of my former mentor, in a distant land, feels so surreal – it takes me several moments to register it.

Suddenly, images of Dr Conteh's grandfatherly face come flooding back to me. In my mind, I can hear frenzied wails of grief rise up high into the African skies. I picture the people of that continent, whom I have known and loved, mourning for their great loss. They cry for the falling of a great cotton tree, whose sheltering branches have protected them in times of painful struggle.

I feel a pang of injustice that my mentor will never enjoy a quiet, refugee-free home or the well-deserved relaxation of retirement. But it is unsurprising. Dr Conteh's whole existence has been one of humble sacrifice. I realize I miss him already.

Conversations with the elderly physician come back to me unbidden, and I remember one of our last. We stood side by side in the Lassa ward courtyard, under a lazy afternoon sun. I was trying to soak up a few last rays of understanding from the wise man, who had seen so much during his career.

Dr Conteh had suffered through poor working conditions, limited resources, and inadequate staff in the Lassa ward, in addition to the ongoing civil unrest and violations of human rights that occurred outside its high walls. But despite offers to work abroad, he had remained in his homeland to tend to those in greatest need of his skills.

'Do you regret any of it?' I had asked the dedicated physician, referring to the trials and tribulations of his eventful life.

'No,' Dr Conteh softly answered. 'I would make the same choices, given the chance to do it again.'

'Even with everything you've been through?'

My mentor nodded. 'If God carried you on his back,' he told me, 'you would never know that the road was long.'

The departure of family members from the ICU room abruptly interrupts my unspoken memories. They bring me back to the sanitary cleanliness of the hospital, so different from that other world an ocean away. I share with the relatives quiet nods of the head, each of us submerged in our own private grief. Then the mourners pass through swinging doors, out to the world at large.

Drawn to quiet sanctuary, I eventually drift into the emptied ICU room. The monitors are silent, their screens dim. I stand alone next to the drawn white sheet, my mind numb with all that I have experienced over the last year. In quiet meditation I rest heavy hands on the motionless bed.

A beam of stray sunlight, piercing closed curtains,

eventually breaks my pensive daze. It highlights the hourglass-like dispensing bubble of the closest IV bag, which hangs high above the bed. Inside the half-filled reservoir, I can see a shimmering bead clinging to an inner silver thread.

I find myself holding my breath as I watch the teardrop desperately struggle to maintain its precious individuality. Silently, I urge it to hold on and arrest the slippage of time, as if freezing this moment will somehow change reality.

Yet I know it cannot be so – some things that are lost can never be regained. At some point, without warning, the lone gem falls. For one last eternal moment, it reflects back the heart of the sun before melting into a welcoming sea.

EPILOGUE

June 4, 2004

Today, almost a full year since descending over choppy waters to a shadowy African coast, I graduated from medical school. With loving smiles, friends and family gathered under a clear azure sky to watch the long-awaited ceremony. My classmates and I passed through their celebratory ranks, with cheerful winks and waves. We dressed in black robes emblazoned with three emerald stripes that symbolize the medicinal herbs of ancient physicians.

In front of those witnesses we held dear, a hundred and some budding doctors swore the time-honored Hippocratic oath. Together we promised to practice our art for the betterment of patients, to visit the sick only to heal, to keep confidences with steadfast honor, and to maintain with humble hands our sacred chain of learning.

Amid air ripe with generations of well-worn wisdom, I felt Dr. Conteh's presence as tangibly as that of my surrounding professors. Our vows, a combination of earnest goals and solemn commandments, urged us not to falter in the colossal footsteps set down by our predecessors. They spoke of courage, justice, and honor – all fitting reminders of my late mentor's noble life.

Now the sun has set on that joyful day. My friends and family are secure in bed. I sit on the peaceful California sands, near my new residence, and watch the night stars flicker like dewdrops above a peaceful ocean. I feel blessed, for my chest pain and infirmity are now only a distant memory.

With a complete return to health, I have experienced anew the joys of jogging on the beach and surfing in the warm summer waves. After months of determined training, I beat my previous ten-kilometer running record a few days ago and, with that, declared an end to a protracted convalescence.

In my lap sits a well-worn notebook, with dog-ears and doodles to attest to the passage of time. The pages are full now and it is time to put the notebook down, yet it is unexpectedly hard to let go. Even pain can be a comfort, when worn for long like a tattered but familiar sweater.

I find it natural to search for some closing meaning to the events of my last year, but have grown skeptical enough to doubt easy answers. Despite pensive days and restless nights, I am unable to reason away the suffering I have witnessed, to easily justify innocent death and avoidable tragedy.

In the end, I have wearied of searching for life's hidden meaning and come to settle for what we can give to it, instead. In this light, I have been pleased to see that Dr. Conteh's death has proved a fitting catalyst for renewed efforts at the Lassa ward – it has spurred the recruitment of a new physician to continue with his important work and encouraged plans for future research.

I, as well, have tried to give purpose to my forced recovery time by tying memories to ink before they escaped recollection. It is my hope that these pages may effect some greater awareness of what occurs outside most of our sights and minds. At the very least, they serve to bear humble witness.

Tragedies, it is unfortunately certain, are interwoven into the human condition – yet, of this, we need not despair. For although these events frequently result from the worst of our nature, at the same time they provide a window into the best of our species. Through them, we have a privileged view of victims, who tenaciously cling to the hope of survival, and caregivers, who nobly devote their lives without thought of selfish return.

On my last night in Kenema, Dr. Conteh joined the Merlin expats for a good-bye dinner at our sole restaurant. We all ordered the same dish with good-natured smiles. An international family surrounded me at the table, diverse accents all mingling together.

Combined, the years devoted to humanitarian work, by

my colleagues in that group, were legion. In comparison, I was a mere visitor passing through. They were the true heroes, those who stayed behind.

'To peace and health,' I toasted them. 'And to you.'

ROSS I. DONALDSON, M.D., M.P.H.
Venice Beach, California

A NOTE FROM THE AUTHOR

The events described in these pages are true, although the names of patients, colleagues, and friends, with the exception of Dr Conteh, have all been changed in the interest of confidentiality. In accordance with my medical oath, I have, in certain instances, further altered the personal characteristics of individuals, in order to assure their privacy.

Although I wrote e-mails and kept a journal at the time of the events described, I was not originally planning on writing a memoir. Thus, much of the work has had to be recollected from memory and, as such, is limited by human fallibility. As I originally wrote down little dialogue, the majority is reproduced from my general recollection.

For the sake of simplifying the narrative a few minor 'characters' have been merged together in the final work. However, if the memoir is culpable for any deviations from strict fact, it is likely in omission, not addition. There are several individuals and events that I would have liked to include, but ultimately did not have space to fit into the finished memoir. Although not mentioned, they are certainly not forgotten.

ACKNOWLEDGMENTS

There are almost as many people who helped me through this chaotic period of life, as there are ways in which they supported me. First and foremost, I would like to thank the people of West Africa, who so generously welcomed me into their land and trusted my novice clinical judgment.

To the aid workers whom I met in Africa, I also extend my thanks. Your remarkable generosity has taught me a lifelong lesson. I would also like to acknowledge those at Merlin, the London School of Hygiene & Tropical Medicine, and UCLA, who helped make the trip possible.

A special debt of gratitude goes to Jon Sandler, who so generously extended his home to me during my period of unexpected illness and convalescence, as well as to my other close friends in Los Angeles (Josh and Alexandra Bratman, Andy Hock, 'Big Al' Husker, Dan Kiger, Tito Olowu, Chris 'Buddy' Robertiello, and Amy Stenson), who supported me during that difficult time. On the medical front, I would also like to thank Drs. Neil Parker, Barbara Natterson, and Claire Panosian, for being exactly what caring doctors should be.

Another thank-you goes to all of the friends, friends of

friends, and people whom I know only through the Internet, who amazingly responded to my initial e-mails from Sierra Leone, as well as the United Nations workers who so kindly let me use their satellite hookup to communicate to the outside world. Without such overwhelming and unexpected interest, I certainly would never have thought to write a memoir about my experiences.

In addition to deep thanks, I would like to ask forgiveness from my mother, father, and brother for causing them some sleepless nights while traveling distant reaches of the globe. I am especially sorry since those nights may not be the last.

I would also like to thank my other relatives – too many, due to good midwestern fecundity, to be able to name here – who passed a tattered first draft of this memoir through countless hands, until the beginning and end pages had to be stuffed somewhere in the middle to keep them from being lost. Your continued encouragement has made all the difference.

I would like to thank Rachel Zoffness for all of her initial edits and unflinching 'suggestions' on the work. Maria Koleilat, thank you for sharing many wonderful parts of the world with me, as well as for your continued friendship.

I would also like to thank Josh Bratman, a great friend and veteran story-crafter, for his numerous notes and encouragement on the project. Thanks also to Shari Smiley, who helped me find my fantastic literary agent, Gillian MacKenzie. Additional thanks go to Michael Flamini, my editor at St. Martin's Press, and his assistant, Vicki Lame, for making the book into all that it could be. And, not least, thanks to Sarah

Emsley and Kate Tolley at Transworld for bringing the memoir to the UK market.

Finally, I would like to thank my teachers, both those in name and spirit, who helped me become a physician. I owe to Dr Conteh, and others like him but unnamed, an undying debt of gratitude. May I live up to even a shadow of what you have taught me.

The Spiders of Allah
Travels of an unbeliever on the frontline of Holy War

By James Hider

'Required reading'
TIME OUT

'A masterpiece . . . a work of great authority written
with wit and wisdom'
TIM BUTCHER, author of BLOOD RIVER

WHETHER IT'S SHIITE death squads roaming the lawless streets of
Iraq in the aftermath of Saddam or hardcore Zionist settlers still
fighting ancient Biblical battles in the hills of the West Bank, the
bloodshed perpetrated in the name of religion in the world is
nowhere more obvious than in the Middle East.

Dodging bullets, dogma and certainty, James Hider travels around
the region witnessing what he calls the 'crack cocaine of fanatical
fundamentalism', From Israel to Gaza, to Iraq and then back
to Jerusalem, his journey takes him to the very heart of today's
holy wars.

There he meets terrorists and their victims, soldiers and clerics,
ordinary people and extraordinary people. And the question at the
back of his mind is: how can people not only believe in all this
madness, but die and kill for it too?

'Hider's voice is incisive and rich in the human detail that
only first-hand experience bestows. An essential work for anyone
wishing to understand the swirling machinations of Iraq,
its people and its war'
ANTONY LOYD, author of MY WAR GONE BY, I MISS IT SO

9780552775496

Far Horizons

By Frank Gardner

LOST ON A remote Sumatran volcano . . . pursued through a Tokyo backstreet by a Japanese gangster . . . picnicking with the French Foreign Legion in the Horn of Africa: Frank Gardner's idea of a holiday is not everyone's. But ever since his student days, the BBC security correspondent has done some epicly hard travelling in a remarkable number of countries. Drawing on the diaries, sketches and photos he kept during his travels, his immaculately observed accounts of these often strange, sometimes daring, adventures in many of the world's most out of the way places form the backbone of his new book.

In June 2004, while reporting on what should have been a routine assignment in Riyadh, his life – never mind his ability to travel the world – was nearly brought to a violent end by Islamist gunmen. Incredibly, Frank not only survived being shot six times at point blank range but also, against all the odds and through force of will, has found himself looking towards those far horizons once more. He's not only been slalom skiing in the Alps, scuba diving in the Red Sea and explored the jungle in northern Thailand. But he is also reporting once more from far flung destinations like Afghanistan and Colombia – and this is a man who no longer has the use of his legs . . .

This is Frank Gardner's compelling, personal yet unsentimental account of the myriad adventures that made him the man he was on that fateful day five years ago – and of the journeys he's made since, and how they've helped him to become the remarkable and inspiring individual he is today.

9780553819311